LESBIAN VOICES
FROM LATIN AMERICA

LATIN AMERICAN STUDIES
VOLUME 7
GARLAND REFERENCE LIBRARY OF SOCIAL SCIENCE
VOLUME 907

LATIN AMERICAN STUDIES

DAVID WILLIAM FOSTER, *Series Editor*

LESBIAN VOICES
FROM LATIN AMERICA
BREAKING GROUND

ELENA M. MARTÍNEZ

GARLAND PUBLISHING, INC.
NEW YORK AND LONDON
1996

Library of Congress Cataloging-in-Publication Data

Martínez, Elena M., 1956–
    Lesbian voices from Latin America : breaking ground / Elena M.
Martínez.
        p.   cm. — (Latin American studies ; v. 7) (Garland reference
library of social science ; v. 907.)
    Includes bibliographical references and index.
    ISBN 0-8153-1349-7 (alk. paper)
    1. Spanish American literature—Women authors—History and
criticism.   2. Lesbians' writings, Spanish American—History and criticism.
3. Spanish American literature—20th century—History and criticism.
I. Title.   II. Series: Garland reference library of social science. Latin American
studies ;   vol. 7.   III. Series: Garland reference library of social
science ;   vol. 907.
PQ7081.M3617   1996
860.9'9287'08664—dc20   95-37411
                                                                                CIP

Cover illustration by Kathy Buist.

Printed on acid-free, 250-year-life paper
Manufactured in the United States of America

For K. B.
with love and appreciation

In memory of
NANCY CÁRDENAS
(1934-1994)

It is our fiction that validates us.
Monique Wittig

CONTENTS

FOREWORD

The idea to write this book began burgeoning in 1988, when upon finishing my doctoral dissertation at New York University on the narrative works of the Uruguayan writer Juan Carlos Onetti, I read enthusiastically *En breve cárcel* (*Certificate of Absence*), the first Spanish American novel with a lesbian theme, written by the Argentinean literary critic Sylvia Molloy. I was so impressed by Molloy's work that I wrote an essay (*"En breve cárcel*: la escritura/lectura del (de lo) otro en los textos de Onetti y Molloy") on the themes of the "other," "otherness" and voyeurism in *En breve cárcel* and in two works by Onetti, "Bienvenido, Bob" and "La novia robada." However, like other critics who have studied Molloy's novel, I did not address its lesbianism in my essay.

In 1989, my attention turned to the works of a Cuban writer living in Sweden, René Vázquez Díaz, who is the author of *La era imaginaria*, *Querido traidor*, *La precocidad de los tiempos*, *Trovador americano*, *Tambor de medianoche* and *Donde se pudre la belleza*. His novel *La era imaginaria* attracted my interest because of its polyphonic texture as well as its articulation of four major discourses: the literary, the feminist, the humorous and the sexual. The articulation of feminist and sexual discourses interested me in particular because of the author's ability to present and develop a wide range of conflicting possibilities and ideas that contest Western cultural traditions. *La era imaginaria* gives voice to a broader representation of women and gay men, thus creating a more inclusive discourse than other Latin American literary works.

My interest in Molloy's *Certificate of Absence* and Vázquez Díaz's *La era imaginaria* stems from my commitment to the study of literature that presents women's issues and homosexual themes. In 1991, after being appointed Assistant Professor at Baruch College (City University of New York), I participated in a series of workshops on "Multiculturalism and Pluralism" organized by Profs. Paula

Berggren and George Otte of the English Department at Baruch. At that time, I was asked to give a talk on Latin American writers whose works present a different perspective from the mainstream Latin American literary canon. As part of those workshops on "Multiculturalism and Pluralism," I included the study of Latin American works that present gay and lesbian themes, such as the works of the Cuban gay writer Reinaldo Arenas and Sylvia Molloy's *Certificate of Absence*. During those workshops in 1991 at Baruch College, I became more aware of the importance of studying lesbian and gay voices in Latin American literature. Hence, this book grew out of a movement toward raising awareness of pluralistic views on literature and diversity in society.

*   *   *

PREFACE

In spite of the attention that Latin American women writers have attracted over the last two decades, a book dedicated exclusively to those writers whose work primarily articulates a lesbian perspective is still missing.

The purpose of *Lesbian Voices from Latin America: Breaking Ground* is to bring attention to and examine the articulation of lesbian themes, motifs and issues in the works of Magaly Alabau, Nancy Cárdenas, Sylvia Molloy, Rosamaría Roffiel and Luz María Umpierre. It aims to study the problems pertaining to the specific literary representations of lesbianism and to examine the dimensions of a lesbian view in the works of these authors. This study underscores my belief that Latin American lesbian writing merits an independent investigation. By undertaking the study of the works of these women writers, this book contributes to the recognition and legitimization of a lesbian literary discourse.

Magaly Alabau (1945-) is a Cuban poet living in New York City who left her country after the outbreak of the Cuban revolution. She has published *Electra/Clitemnestra* (Electra/Clytemnestra; 1986), *La extremaunción diaria* (The Daily Extreme Unction; 1986), *Ras* (Edge; 1987), *Hermana* (Sister; 1989), *Hemos llegado a Ilión* (Ilium; 1991) and *Liebe* (1993). Her poetry has appeared in Spanish in various journals. Nancy Cárdenas (1934-1994), Mexican poet, playwright, and theater director, was, until her death in April 1994, an activist for women's and particularly lesbians' rights. Her book *Cuaderno de amor y desamor* (Book of Love and Absence of Love; forthcoming) and her play *El día que pisamos la luna* (The Day We Arrived in the Moon; forthcoming) articulates an openly lesbian erotic discourse. Sylvia Molloy (1938-), born in Buenos Aires, is a novelist and a literary critic who has lived in the United States for many years. She is the author of *En breve cárcel* (1981; translated as *Certificate of Absence*, 1989) and numerous articles and books of criticism on Latin American literature, among them *Las letras de*

Borges (1979; translated as *Signs of Borges,* 1994) and *At Face Value: Autobiographical Writing in Spanish America* (1991). Rosamaría Roffiel (1945-) is a Mexican writer who has had a significant role in the Mexican feminist movement. She has worked as a journalist for *Excelsior* and the journals *Proceso* and *Fem.* Roffiel has published a collection of poetry, *Corramos libres ahora* (Let's Run Freely Now; 1986: revised edition; 1994), a documentary narrative, ¡*Ay Nicaragua, Nicaraguita!* (Oh, Nicaragua, My Dear Nicaragua!; 1987), and a lesbian novel, *Amora* (Love in Feminine; 1989). Luz María Umpierre (1947-) is a Puerto Rican writer and literary critic. She came to the United States in 1974. Umpierre has published five collections of poems: *Una puertorriqueña en Penna* (*A Puerto Rican in Penna*; 1979), *En el país* (*In the Country*; 1982), *...Y otras desgracias. And Other Misfortunes...* (1985), *The Margarita Poems* (1987), *En el país de las maravillas* (In Wonderland; 1990) and *For Christine: Poems and One Letter* (1995). At present, she is working on a collection of poems dedicated to people who recently died of AIDS.

The works of Magaly Alabau, Nancy Cárdenas, Sylvia Molloy, Rosamaría Roffiel, and Luz María Umpierre present an unconventional sexual orientation. These writers frame their work within a double marginality: as women and as lesbians, they break with the patriarchal view that has insisted upon seeing sexuality as a function of reproduction. Patriarchy, based on a network of sexual and class restrictions, supports the psychological and physical repression of women. Restrictions imposed on women's sexuality are central to the subjection of women's lives and experiences in general, but in the case of lesbians there is a double exclusion, since they break with the discourse of the official (heterosexual) sexuality.

I have been selective in my study of the works of these women writers. Rather than undertaking an exploration of all their works, this book examines particular aspects of the textual representation of lesbianism. This does not mean, however, that I will attempt to reduce the works of these writers to a homogeneous literary body or to limit the possibilities of Latin American lesbian literature to the particularities of the works of these five writers. Instead, I am interested in exploring the similarities and differences of each writer's literary expressions as well as the complexities of the label "Latin American lesbian literature."

This heterogeneous group of writers offers a good sample of the types of lesbian literature being produced by Latin American women living in the United States (Alabau, Molloy, Umpierre) and in Latin America (Cárdenas and Roffiel). My selections do not correspond to any geographical distribution but rather to my personal literary taste and to the availability of works. My study is temporally limited to writers whose work began to appear in the 1970's and who, except for Cárdenas, who passed away in the spring of 1994, are still writing.

The title of this book, *Lesbian Voices from Latin America: Breaking Ground*, echoes previous literary criticism dedicated to the study of the works of Latin American women authors, such as Naomi Lindstrom's *Women's Voice in Latin American Literature* (1989) and Evelyn Picón Garfield's *Women's Voices from Latin America: Interviews with Six Contemporary Authors* (1985). The word "voices" in the title indicates the heterogeneity of the literary manifestations of the group of writers I am studying and my desire to stress the diversity in their literary expressions.

The perspectives of this book reflect my experiences as a Latin American woman who has been in the United States since 1980 and who completed her graduate studies in this country. Whereas I avoid the appropriation of concepts foreign to the conditions of Latin America, the views presented here have been shaped by my cultural and social experiences in the United States.

My work echoes the works of the Chicanas Gloria Anzaldúa and Cherríe Moraga, American critics like Audre Lorde and Adrienne Rich, and the French lesbian feminist Monique Wittig. In addition, this book is preceded by the valuable contributions of David William Foster, Amy K. Kaminsky, and Luz María Umpierre, who have pioneered the study of gay and lesbian Latin American literature. These critics have all presented valuable insights that have helped me develop an approach to defining and conceptualizing the lesbian perspectives of the writers I am studying. However, while the theoretical background for this book is connected to the vein of Chicana, American lesbian, and feminist literary theories, I recognize the dangers in using literary theories that do not necessarily correspond to the social realities and cultural identities of Latin America.

*   *   *

This book is divided into five chapters. The first chapter, "The Poetics of Space and the Politics of Lesbian Exile: Magaly Alabau's

Poetry and Sylvia Molloy's Novel *Certificate of Absence*" studies the representation of space in Magaly Alabau's poetry (*Hermana, Electra/Clitemnestra, La extremaunción diaria* and *Hemos llegado a Ilión*) and Sylvia Molloy's novel *Certificate of Absence*. The representation of interior and exterior spaces in these works articulates the marginal social positioning of lesbian subjects in society. The representation of space in the works of these two writers has a poetic function as well as an ideological and political value for the theme of lesbianism in Latin American literature. While focusing on Magaly Alabau's poetry and Sylvia Molloy's novel, I shall also draw parallels to Nancy Cárdenas' poetry collection *Cuaderno de amor y desamor* (forthcoming), Rosamaría Roffiel's novel *Amora* (1989) and her poetry collection *Corramos libres ahora* (1994).

The second chapter, "Re-reading a Tradition: Lesbian Eroticism in Magaly Alabau's *Electra/Clitemnestra* and *Hermana*," is dedicated to the study of eroticism in Magaly Alabau's two collections of poetry *Electra/Clitemnestra* (1986), and *Hermana* (1989). Here I study the textual representation of sexual love and emotional intimacy in the lesbian relationships presented in these texts.

The third chapter, "Privileging Lesbian Eroticism: The Works of Rosamaría Roffiel and Nancy Cárdenas," examines the representation of love among women in the works of these two Mexican writers and its connection with Audre Lorde's definition of love. For Cárdenas and Roffiel, reclaiming love and lesbian sexuality are political acts that empower women and challenge their traditional positioning in society.

The fourth chapter, "Lesbian Eroticism and the Act of Writing: Sylvia Molloy's *Certificate of Absence*," examines the relationship of lesbian love, violence and writing in Molloy's novel. I explore the interesting connection between lesbian love and sexuality as a source of literary inspiration. The fifth chapter, "Sexual and Political Affirmation in Luz María Umpierre's *The Margarita Poems* and ... *Y otras desgracias. And Other Misfortunes...*" studies the themes of sexuality as a political affirmation bound to the Latina perspective that is presented in the works of the Puerto Rican writer Luz María Umpierre.

*   *   *

ACKNOWLEDGMENTS

This book would not have been possible without colleagues and friends who have given me the help and encouragement to pursue this project.

First, I would like to thank David William Foster for his interest and support of my proposal to write a book on lesbian themes. I would also like to express my gratitude to Phyllis Korper, senior editor at Garland, for her editorial advice.

I thank my colleagues in the Department of Modern Languages and Comparative Literature as well as in other departments at Baruch College (CUNY), particularly Tom Hayes, who has shown a continuous interest in my work, and to Baruch College librarians who worked patiently and diligently to help me to obtain the necessary material for my research. To Louisa Moy and Edward Keller, many thanks.

I have had the good fortune to have a group of friends who have been part of this literary journey through lesbian voices. I would like to express my most sincere gratitude to my dear friends Mark Albano and Francisco Soto, without whom this book would not have been a reality. I am extremely grateful to the two of them because they have read and criticized each chapter of this book, and have offered me valuable editorial advice. My work has been improved by their criticism and recommendations. I am also indebted to them for the inspiration and the expressions of sincere friendship they have offered me during the process of writing this book.

I also want to thank other friends who read partial sections of the manuscript and who made insightful comments. They are Carolina Grymbal, Mercedes Roffé and Joseph Ulitto. I thank Joseph Arsenault for helping me to proofread the manuscript. I am also thankful to James Cascaito, who has been a source of inspiration, and to Adriana Collado for her encouragement.

Ana L. Sierra, Francisco Nájera, Julio Marzán, and Ileana Ordoñez, friends and colleagues of an ongoing study group, have provided me with support and motivation. To them I am thankful.

I am especially grateful to Ana L. Sierra for her sincere friendship since graduate school.

Finally, I want to express my deepest appreciation to Kathy Buist for her patience, affection, and optimism. But above all, I thank Kathy for believing in this project since its early stages. To her, and to the memory of Nancy Cárdenas, pioneer of the Mexican lesbian and women's movements, I dedicate this book.

*   *   *

A NOTE ON TRANSLATIONS

With the exception of some of Luz María Umpierre's poetry, all the texts that I study in this book were written originally in Spanish. I have included quotations in both the original Spanish texts and English versions.

I have used (with permission of Magaly Alabau and her translator Anne Twitty) the unpublished translations of *Electra/Clitemnestra, Hemos llegado a Ilión,* as well as the bilingual edition of *Hermana/Sister,* published by Editorial Betania.

With the assistance of Anne Twitty, I have translated Alabau's *Ras,* and *La extremaunción diaria* as well as those for Rosamaría Roffiel's, Nancy Cárdenas' and Luz María Umpierre's poetry.

All quotes from Sylvia Molloy's novel *En breve cárcel* are from Daniel Balderston's translation into English, *Certificate of Absence.*

*   *   *

Lesbian Voices
from Latin America

INTRODUCTION

[Lesbianism] is a theme which cannot even be described as taboo, for it has no real existence in the history of literature. Male homosexual literature has a past; it has a present. The lesbians, for their part, are silent—just as all women are as women at all levels. When one has read the poems of Sappho, Radclyffe Hall's *The Well of Loneliness*, the poems of Sylvia Plath and Anaïs Nin, *La Bâtarde* by Violette Leduc, one has read everything. Only the women's movement has proved capable of producing lesbian texts in a context of total rupture with masculine culture, texts written by women exclusively for women, careless of male approval.

The Lesbian Body.
Monique Wittig

There exists in Latin America, like everywhere else, a denial of lesbian existence and thus, of the possibilities of a lesbian literature. It is important to contest the assumption of general heterosexuality that prevails in literature and in the institutions of literary criticism and which, as Adrienne Rich has asserted: "afflicts not just feminist scholarship, but every profession, every reference work, every curriculum, every organizing attempt, every relationship or conversation over which it hovers."[1] Therefore, it is necessary to study the particulars and peculiarities of lesbian Latin American voices because they denote not only a sexual orientation but a network of cultural and social relations that requires careful examination.

The term "Latin American lesbian literature" presents many difficulties, among them the notion of definition. Does the term refer to the content of the literature itself or does it refer to the sexual orientation of the writer? I do not agree with those critics in the United States who have tried to clarify the questions concerning the use of the term by restricting their studies to the works of those

3

women who are openly identified as lesbians. I reject this stance for two reasons. First, the biographical approach that tries to prove the sexual orientation of the writer is non-literary. Second, many Latin American writers have not been able to identify themselves as lesbians due to social and cultural restrictions.

Much of the lesbian scholarship produced in the United States focuses on the definition of "lesbian" and "lesbian writing." The critics working on a theoretical lesbian approach have given different definitions to the term "lesbian." In this book, the word "lesbian" is used to refer to the representation of women who have erotic and sexual interest in each other and whose fundamental emotional connections are with other women. My definition coincides with the one proposed by Catherine R. Stimpson and Charlotte Bunch, for whom both the erotic and sexual involvement of women is intrinsic to the definition of lesbianism. In "Zero Degree Deviancy: The Lesbian Novel in English," Stimpson defines the lesbian writer, character, and reader as a woman who finds other women erotically attractive and gratifying.[2] For some critics, "lesbian" is a word strictly used to describe women who are sexually involved with other women, while for others, like Lillian Faderman and Audre Lorde, "lesbian" does not necessarily imply sexual or erotic involvement with other women. For the latter critics, lesbianism describes an emotional bond where sexual contact may be present to a greater or lesser degree, or it may be entirely absent.[3] I disagree with critics who have used the word "lesbian" in a general sense and who have only paid attention to the emotional connection among women while overlooking the sexual aspect. In my view, desexualization of woman to woman relationships is linked to the sexist opinion that women's sexuality does not exist and that women can only relate to other women on emotional terms. While it is true that many lesbians desexualized their relationships in order to establish solidarity with heterosexual women of the women's movement, that time has passed. The gay and lesbian movement in the United States has taught us that lesbians must claim their sexuality. It is precisely the sexual dimension of lesbian relationships that differentiates them from friendship, support, and solidarity.[4]

A radical argument in favor of claiming lesbians' sexuality is made by writer and lesbian activist Pat Califia in her book *Public Sex: The Culture of Radical Sex* (1994). Califia attacks not only heterosexual institutions, but lesbian and gay groups that attempt to "normalize" sex by accommodating it to heterosexual presumptions. In this book she challenges views of lesbian sexuality and emotional bonding as presented in different veins of Feminism. She argues that the women's movement's position concerning sexuality, and specifically pornography, emerges from a moral view. As its title indicates, *Public Sex* is in favor of the public acknowledgement of sex and the need of accepting all manifestations of lesbians' sexuality without patronizing them.[5]

One of the problems encountered by readers and critics interested in Latin American lesbian literature is the unavailability of the texts. Societies in general have used many strategies for silencing women's history, especially lesbian experience, history, and contributions. Lesbian writing has been minimized and undermined by readers and critics through the assumption that its discourse is personal and belongs to a private space.

The literary canon, hiding its political agenda behind a mask of good literary taste, a supposed objectivity, and the pursuit of a non-ideological discourse, has overlooked texts that present a lesbian perspective. The heterosexism and androcentrism that characterize the literary canon has had a powerful effect on lesbian literature as well as on lesbian writers and readers as other critics have already noted. Lesbian writing has not been taken into consideration because of its social implications and because it presents a system in direct opposition to the male tradition. The canon, with its male-oriented view and through a process of silencing "others"—in this case writers who present lesbian issues—has allowed the literary establishment to remain unchallenged.

The attack on and deconstruction of the mechanisms of the literary canon are essential for the vehiculization of a more inclusive and pluralistic view of literature and society. Any attempt to "rescue" a Latin American lesbian literature has to begin by reconceptualizing the way in which lesbian experiences could be included in literary history, tradition, and cultural and social institutions. The inclusion of a lesbian Latin American literary approach is a political act that has to consider the ideological impact upon social institutions which are being redefined and transformed by the study of this type of literature.

Traditional perspectives have viewed desire and sexuality as part of a private space and, thus, have failed to recognize their connections with ideology, ignoring the ways in which expressions of desire and sexuality have created and maintained specific forms of political authority. With the excuse that desire and sexuality are strictly part of the "private" life, literary critics, editors, and social institutions have managed to ignore cultural expressions that are not part of mainstream heterosexual forms of desire and sexuality. However, the feminist movement has taught us about the relationship of the personal and the political. Feminisms—Anglo, African American and Latino—in the United States have emphasized the relationship of the personal and the political. Cheryl Clarke, in her essay "Lesbianism: An Act of Resistance," has stressed the political value of lesbianism. She has argued that no matter how lesbians live their lesbianism, they rebel against the position of dependency to men and proclaim their autonomy.[6]

The works that I study in this book are highly political. They establish a particular relationship with societal power structures and are very critical of existing (heterosexual) institutions. In addition, these works contest the Latin American literary canon, which has, like literary canons everywhere else, undervalued and dismissed literary and cultural manifestations that are not the prescribed ones and traditionally has only accepted heterosexual forms of desire and sexuality. These works address alternatives and other perspectives, thus challenging culturally approved forms of desire. By refusing to submit to the sexual and gender dispositions that characterize heterosexual cultural norms, the lesbian themes and motifs of these works become an ideological threat and a socio-political issue that encourage transformation to take place in culture and society.

By studying lesbian voices as a separate entity and as a literary alternative, this book will offer an opening for lesbian and gay voices as well as for other emergent discourses. I can see, however, the possible danger inherent in the proposal of an exclusive category of "lesbian voices." As in the creation of any category—Indian, black, women's literature—this practice may ghettoize writers who present a lesbian view, pushing their literature further outside the domain of the mainstream literary space. It could also be argued that the inclusion of the works of these women writers under the category of "lesbian voices" may tend to generalize and dismiss the particularity and individuality of their literary discourses, thus denying, oversimplifying and overlooking ideological differences among classes, races, and groups. The tendency to globalize and to find a common ground within emergent literary discourses has served to make invisible the inherent pluralism of the works. However, some kind of group identification, a necessary evil perhaps, is vital to create a discourse that affirms lesbian existence.

*   *   *

The works of the writers studied in this book (Alabau, Cárdenas, Molloy, Roffiel, and Umpierre) fall into four main categories: the erotic, the autobiographical, the self-reflexive, and the socio-political. The classification of texts (either poetry or narrative) under these four categories resists easy identifications because in many of the texts these themes are intertwined.

Two of Magaly Alabau's poetry collections (*Electra/Clitemnestra* and *Hermana*) focus on love, lesbian eroticism, and emotional intimacy among women. Nancy Cárdenas' poetry collection *Cuaderno de amor y desamor* (Book of Love and Absence of Love) is, as the title indicates, centered on lesbian love either linked with a celebratory tone or with the sorrow of unrequited love. Rosamaría Roffiel's novel *Amora* intertwines the erotic, the autobiographical and the social and political commitment to women's causes. Sylvia Molloy's novel *Certificate of Absence* explores a link between eroticism and the act of writing, allowing for the exploration of the autobiographical, and the self-reflexive aspect of the process of writing. The works of Luz María Umpierre, like the works of other Latinas in the United States, concern themselves with social and political preoccupations such that lesbian eroticism and identity are intertwined with political issues.

In Alabau's *Electra/Clitemnestra* passionate lesbian eroticism and desire is central. Here, the author takes the Greek myths of Electra and Clytemnestra and elaborates on them, adapting and transforming the story. Through the process of re-writing the classical myths, Alabau transforms and changes their heterosexual context into lesbian meanings. Rather than adapting the classical anecdotes, she questions their significance. In Alabau's poetry, heroines, who in the classical story act for the sake of the patriarchal family, carry out a personal desire. The traditional interpretation of the myth of Electra and her desire for her father is changed and transformed into a desire for the mother.

Whereas in *Electra/Clitemnestra* women are united by sexual and erotic desire, in *Hermana* and *Hemos llegado a Ilión*, Alabau presents communication and emotional bonding between women while exploring the marginalization imposed by society on women whose sexual orientation is not the one prescribed. *Hermana* explores the fusion and the communion between two sisters: one, who is in exile and returns to her native country in search of herself and her history and the other, who stayed in her country and who has lived most of her life in seclusion. The sisterhood of these women is a metaphor for the emotional and sexual connection between lesbian lovers.

In Nancy Cárdenas' *Cuaderno de amor y desamor* (Book of Love and Absence of Love) there are two moments that are rigorously synthesized through the use of the words "amor/desamor" (love and absence of love). In this book, the poetic voice states clearly, from the first lines, the affective-erotic specificity of this poetic discourse, that is, its lesbian nature. The grammatical markers make clear that the female speaker is invoking a woman lover. The first pages of the book allude to a new genesis, a re-reading of the foundational myth of the Western World. In Cárdenas' re-reading Adam and Eve have been replaced by two women who alone and naked will write their own history ("Solas./Desnudas./Y la Tierra misma/escribe su Historia" (Only the two of us/Naked/and the earth itself/writing its history) (4).

The poems of the first part of the book, dedicated to the joy of erotic and affective relationships between women, are a celebration of the lesbian body. The poetic voice, through an invocatory tone, establishes a private discourse, a dialogue with her ex-lover, and by publishing it becomes an assertion of the legitimacy of lesbian love and lesbian identities.

In Cárdenas' text there is a clear relationship between lesbian love and the poetic discourse. The desire and the need to write emerge from the speaker's encounters with her lover: "tus visitas me hacen mucho bien:/me dejan llena de poemas"(47) (your visits do a lot of good to me:/they leave me/filled with poems). Cárdenas is aware that her poetic lesbian discourse is a political act, and throughout the book there is the desire to proclaim and establish a lesbian poetic space from which the lesbian subject may articulate her discourse.

The cyclical structure of *Cuaderno de amor y desamor*, the articulation of one long poem of various repetitive motifs, gives the idea of a continuum ("todo fluye: nunca nos hemos separado") (43) (everything flows:/we have never separated from each other), and it gives fluidity to the reading. Moreover, it textualizes the non-authoritarian character of this lesbian discourse and the recurrent theme of love in Cárdenas' poetry from 1984 until her death in 1994.

Sylvia Molloy's *En breve cárcel* (1981; translated as *Certificate of Absence*; 1989) tells the story of a woman who writes about her love affair with another woman. The plot of the novel is double, articulating both the story of the love affair as well as the process of writing about it. The narrator articulates not only her love affair with Vera, her ex-lover, but also memories of her childhood, aspects of her relationship with her family, and her dreams.

At the beginning of the novel the protagonist, secluded in an empty room, which was previously the scene of her love affairs, begins writing. This text, born out of an act of separation, is a cathartic exercise written to recover the lost lover through the writing process. Through the process of writing, the protagonist attempts to come to terms with the loss of her female lover. She brings back to her memory the feelings of the affair with the purpose of exorcising herself from them.

The novel elaborates an interesting connection between tradition and singularity, writing and reading. The singularity of Molloy's novel is that it is based on the protagonist's reading of lesbian relationships in contrast to the traditional (heterosexual) literary discourse that reads female experiences only in terms of their relationship to men. The nameless protagonist engages herself in a process of reading her life through the relationship with others, all of them, with the exception of her father, women (her mother, sister, aunt, and lovers). Thus, the novel is a lesbian novel in the sense of the sexual connection and erotic bonding among women as well as in the sense that it privileges the emotional ties among women.

Certificate of Absence is a narcissistic novel in the sense that the woman writer, through the exploration of her relationships with women, begins a process of self-analysis. The novel is also narcissistic in the sense that it reflects upon its own writing. Linda Hutcheon defines narcissism in this way in her book *Narcissistic Narrative: The Metafictional Paradox,* where she establishes a parallel between the act of Narcissus looking at himself in the waters and the process of self-reflection that some literature inscribes in itself.[7]

Rosamaría Roffiel's *Amora* (1989) begins with an epigraph that alerts us to the fact that what we are going to read is an autobiographical account in which the characters and the plot are real. The dedication of the book states clearly the lesbian character of this novel: "para todas las mujeres que se atreven a amar a las mujeres" (to all women who dare to love women).

The plot of the novel is simple and the way that it is told is linear. Moreover, its language lacks both subtlety and ambiguity. However, what is singular in this novel is the representation of lesbian characters and their relationships. The novel, which starts with the meeting of Claudia and Lupe, the narrator, testifies to the development of this relationship, the crisis that Claudia (a woman who is forcing herself to be heterosexual) experiences, the separation of the two women, and their final coming to terms with their sexuality.

Amora tells a love story from a lesbian point of view. The story intertwines a historical feminist discourse and a reflection upon women's position of inequality in Mexican society. The feminist discourse, elaborated through a chorus of female voices, touches upon such issues as the lack of recognition of women, the prohibition of sexual pleasure, and the limitations imposed upon women's sexual behavior and sexual orientation. In addition, the novel proposes that it is not possible to talk about "feminism" in the singular, but rather in the plural, to make it inclusive of lesbians' experiences.

Roffiel's novel, like many contemporary novels written by women, deals with violence (psychological and physical) against women. That undercurrent of violence is transmitted through education, institutions (the family being the most important), and the relationship among people of different sexes. All of this is reinforced through the media. This violence is evident from the sexual harassment that women suffer in the streets, specifically in Hispanic countries in the form of "piropos" (flirtatious remarks). The fact that the characters of the novel work at a rape crisis center allows for the telling of rape stories that highlight the victims' problems. Moreover, the novel includes the rape of one of the women who works at the center, a scene which clearly indicates the vulnerability of anyone to a crime of this nature.

The works of Luz María Umpierre are part of the literary production of Latina lesbians in the United States. Although lesbian motifs begin to appear in her early poetry collections: *Una puertorriqueña en Penna* (A Puerto Rican in Penna; 1979), *En el país* (In Wonderland; 1982), *...Y otras desgracias. And Other Misfortunes...* (1985), it is in *The Margarita Poems* (1987) that the poet clearly articulates both a lesbian erotic discourse and the political consciousness of her situation as a Puerto Rican in the United States. In the introduction to this collection Umpierre asserts the need to break the silence and to speak openly about her sexual orientation:

> First of all, I needed to say, to speak,"lo que nunca
> pasó por mis labios,"that which I had not uttered,
> and which was being used as a tool in my oppression
> by others, murmured behind closed doors, brought
> up as an issue to deny me my rights by those enemies
> who read my poetry too well. What I needed to
> verbalize is the fact that I am, among many other
> things, a Lesbian. Second, I wanted to communicate
> in some viable form with some One who came to
> represent all women to me.[8]

Umpierre's collection *The Margarita Poems*, as is true of the works of other Latinas, is characterized by its bilingualism and biculturalism. The collection offers nine poems, five of which are in English: "Immanence,""No Hatchet Job,""The Statue,""Only the Hand that Stirs Knows What's in the Pot," and "Título: En que trata de lo que es y no hay mah ná'." The other three poems are in Spanish: "Madre,""Ceremonia Secreta," and "Transcendence."The last poem,"The Mar/Garita Poem,"is in both English and Spanish.

The poems are characterized by unity in spite of the fact that they were born from separations with lovers and by the ambivalent feelings of an immigrant who shares two cultures: the one of the country where she was born, Puerto Rico, and the other of the country where she lives, the United States.

*   *   *

An all-inclusive examination of works by Latin American and Latinas is beyond the scope of this book. However, this section presents an overview of some works that contain lesbian perspectives and themes not otherwise considered in this book, such as the works of Sor Juana Inés de la Cruz, Gabriela Mistral, Alejandra Pizarnik, Cristina Peri-Rossi, Diana Bellessi, Nemir Matos, Sabina Berman, Mercedes Roffé, Albalucía Angel, Reina Roffé, Sara Levi Calderón, Cherríe Moraga, and Gloria Anzaldúa who are part of a lesbian Latin American or Latino tradition. With the exception of Sor Juana Inés and Gabriela Mistral, I limit this overview to the literature produced during the decades of the seventies, the eighties, and the nineties because these three decades have been prolific for the development of a literary body, and here I do not refer to single representations or circumstantial lesbian motifs but to a body of texts that privilege a lesbian perspective. Also documented is the status of literary studies that concentrate on lesbian themes and views in order to emphasize the lack of studies in the field and the need to continue the exploration of lesbian issues and themes as a significant component of Latin American literary criticism.

The history of lesbianism has yet to be rescued from a long history of silence, denial, and euphemisms that have managed to hide its meanings or to communicate them in a secretive manner. Lesbian writers have responded to the silencing of lesbianism through the use of codes and a language of reticence. The phenomenon has been examined by Lillian Faderman in the section entitled "In the Closet: The Literature of Lesbian Encoding" of her anthology *Chloe Plus Olivia: An Anthology of Lesbian Literature from the Seventeenth Century to the Present* (1994). Lesbian encoding is thus a synonym of concealment of lesbianism. As Faderman asserts: "The lesbian writer has purposely encoded her lesbian subject matter so that it is veiled to the majority of the population yet often decipherable by the reader who has knowledge of the writer's homosexuality and understands her need to hide her lesbian material."[9] Because of the way those lesbian meanings have been hidden and transformed into socially acceptable forms in the texts, they have been easily overlooked.

In Latin America, however, since the seventeeth century, from Sor Juana Inés' poetry to the works of Gabriela Mistral (Chile, 1889-1957), there has been ground for a tradition of encoding a lesbian sensibility through socially acceptable ways. Sor Juana Inés de la Cruz (1648-1695) was the religious name of the Mexican Juana de Asbaje who entered the Carmelite convent in 1667. Sor Juana Inés is well known for her lyric and philosophical poetry, her essays, and her drama. Her love poetry, her antagonism toward men, and a strong feminist perspective have provoked controversy about Sor Juana's sexual orientation.

In a poem like "Arguye de inconsecuentes el gusto y la censura de los hombres que en las mujeres acusan lo que causan" (Arguing that there are inconsistencies between men's tastes and their censure when they accuse women of what they themselves do cause) Sor Juana's feminism is evident. Her love poetry dedicated to the Countess of Paredes and the Marquise de Laguna has provided basis for lesbian readings of her works and her life. Poems like "En que describe racionalmente los efectos irracionales del amor" (In which she describes rationally the irrational effects of love), "Filis," "Divina Lysi mía" (My Divine Lysi), "Detente, sombra, de mi bien esquivo" (Stop, Shadow of My Disdainful Beloved) and "Envía las Pascuas de Resurrección" (Happy Easter, My Lady) contain a lesbian love discourse. Recently, the Argentinean film director María Luisa Bemberg has presented a lesbian reading in her film *Yo, la peor de todas* (I, the Worst of All) in which an erotic relationship between Sor Juana and the Viceroy's wife is explored.

However, literary critics like the Nobel Prize winner Octavio Paz have gone to great efforts to avoid the possibility of Sor Juana's lesbianism. Curiously, Paz who in his book *Sor Juana Inés de la Cruz o las trampas de la fe* (1982; translated as *Sor Juana; or the Traps of Faith*) insists on silence as a feature of her works and who has examined the employ of a hidden code and the "other voice" of Sor Juana's speaker, has elaborated several arguments to conceal the poet's lesbianism.[10]

A tradition of strategical silence and concealment that has been the norm with the literary criticism of Sor Juana Inés has been utilized regarding another key literary figure in Latin America, the Nobel Prize winner Gabriela Mistral, whose poetry of love, frustration, and loneliness has, under the "heterosexual compulsion" of the literary critics, been explained as generated by the death of a male lover. Her poetry, however, reflects the sensibility of a woman identified at different levels with other women. The centrality of women's friendships in Mistral's life has been overlooked, and the critics have focused on her desolation because of the death of a male lover. It was not until very recently that her poetry has begun to be rescued for the tradition of lesbian Latin American letters. Sylvia Molloy's "Female Textual Identities: The Strategies of Self-Figuration," Claudia Lanzarotti's "Sospechosa para todos"

(Suspicious for All), and Elizabeth Rosa Horán's essay on Gabriela Mistral published in *Latin American Writers on Gay and Lesbian Themes: A Bio-Critical Sourcebook* are contributions to the study of Mistral's poetry as part of a lesbian tradition.[11]

A lesbian sensibility is encoded in Mistral's poetry through the treatment of certain themes as well as in the tendency to avoid the use of grammatical pronouns that mark gender. The themes of frustration, prohibition, absence, and exile in Mistral's poetry may be identified with the marginal position of lesbians in society. In poems such as "País de la ausencia" (Land of Absence), "Dios lo quiere" (It Is God's Will) and "Todas íbamos a ser reinas" (We All Were Going to be Queens), the poetic voice is characterized by a tragic view of love that seems to go against the establishment and against the accepted ways of society. Mistral's poetry presents the sensibility of an outsider who is displaced, as can be seen in her poem "País de la ausencia":

> País de la ausencia,
> extraño país,
> más ligero que ángel
> y seña sutil...
>
> No echa granada
> no cría jazmín,
> y no tiene cielos
> ni mares de añil.
> Nombre suyo, nombre,
> nunca se lo oí.[12]
>
> Land of absence,
> strange land,
> lighter than angel
> or subtle sign...
>
> Bears no pomegranate
> no jasmine breeds,
> and has no bluing
> skies or seas.
> Its name, a name
> unknown to me.

The literature of Alejandra Pizarnik (1936-1972) and Cristina Peri-Rossi (1941-) intertwines an erotic discourse and a self-reflexive tone that investigates the process of writing.

The works of the Argentinean poet Alejandra Pizarnik are characterized by a concern with the process of writing poetry and the influence of Surrealism. Pizarnik is the author of *La tierra más ajena* (The Most Alien Land; 1955), *La última inocencia* (The Last Innocence; 1956), *Las aventuras perdidas* (The Lost Adventures; 1958), *El árbol de Diana* (Diana's Tree; 1962), *Los trabajos y las noches* (Works and Nights; 1965), *El deseo de la palabra* (Desire for Word; 1975), *Extracción de la piedra de locura* (Extraction of the Stone of Madness; 1968), *El infierno musical* (The Musical Hell; 1971) and *La condesa sangrienta* (The Bloody Countess; 1971).

La condesa sangrienta, based on Valentine Penrose's *Erzébet Bathóry: La Comtesse Sanglante* (1963) which recounts the torture and murder of more than six hundred girls by Countess Bathóry, mixes lesbian eroticism with death, power, and torture. In the section "El espejo de la melancolía" (The Mirror of Melancholy) the countess' homosexual tendencies are referred to:

> Speaking of mirrors, no one was ever able to confirm
> the truth of the rumors about the countess's
> homosexuality. We will never know whether she
> ignored the tendency or, on the contrary, admitted it
> as a right she accorded herself along with all the
> other rights. Essentially, she lived submerged in an
> exclusively feminine universe.[13]

The book, a mosaic of eleven prose vignettes, also works as a metaphor for the political situation of Argentina.

In many of her poems Pizarnik has encoded lesbian meanings through her use of female and masculine pronouns. In "Cenizas" (Ashes) of *Las aventuras perdidas* (The Lost Adventures) she employs the masculine pronoun:

> The night splintered into stars
> watching me dazzled
> the air hurls hate
> its face embellished
> with music.

We will go soon

Secret dream
ancestor of my smile
the world is emaciated
and there is a lock but no keys
and there is terror but no tears.

What would I do with myself?

Because to You I owe what I am

But I have no tomorrow

Because to You I...

The night suffers.[14]

The themes of displacement and exile as well as a tragic
perspective of love that permeates Pizarnik's poetry may be read, as
in the case of Gabriela Mistral, as an encoding of the poet's
lesbianism.

Cristina Peri-Rossi, born in Uruguay, is a short story writer,
journalist, poet, and novelist. She is the author of *Viviendo* (Living;
1963), *Los museos abandonados* (The Abandoned Museums; 1969), *El
libro de mis primos* (My Cousin's Book; 1969), *Descripción de un
naufragio* (Description of a Shipwreck; 1975), *Evohé* (1976), *Diáspora*
(1976), *La tarde del dinosaurio* (The Afternoon of the Dinosaur; 1976),
Lingüística general (General Linguistics; 1979), *La rebelión de los niños*
(The Children's Rebellion; 1982), *El museo de los esfuerzos inútiles*
(The Museum of Useless Efforts; 1983), *La mañana después del diluvio*
(The Morning After the Rain; 1984), *Una pasión prohibida* (A
Forbidden Passion; 1986) and *Solitario de amor* (Love Solitaire; 1988).
In 1969, her book, *Los museos abandonados* (1969), received the award
for young writers from Arca Editorial. A few months after receiving
Arca's prize she won Marcha's Prize for her novel *El libro de mis
primos* (1969).

The poetry collection *Evohé* (1976) was a source of great
controversy, since Peri-Rossi assumes a male voice to speak of desire

for the female body. The ineludible identification between the speaker and Peri-Rossi's own voice suggests that it is indeed lesbian poetry. The title of the collection, *Evohé*, referring to the bacchantes of Dionysus, alludes to the centrality of women in Peri-Rossi's poetry, while one of the epigraphs of the collection, a poem by Sappho, is an obvious reference to the theme of lesbianism.

Evohé encodes lesbian eroticism through the use of male and female pronouns. Sometimes the encoding has been such that the text is full of clichés and the relationship between male and female is stereotypical. However, the employment of a male voice in *Evohé* is an attempt to erase and break gender and sexual categories so bound in literature. This gesture of articulating lesbian eroticism through the use of male and female pronouns allows the speaker to discuss lesbian erotic desire in the form of heterosexual desire, thus encoding the poet's desire for another woman. The strategy of transforming and hiding meanings and themes to avoid political censorship has been a common strategy used by writers everywhere but particularly by Peri-Rossi as she has asserted herself:

> Jamás dejaría de abordar un tema porque supiera que está previamente censurado; haría todo lo posible por referirme alegóricamente al mismo, y este juego sería muy fructífero. Los peligros más serios de la censura son para el público, que tiene que descifrar entonces las claves...[15]

> I would never avoid a subject because I knew it had been declared off-limits; instead I would try very hard to refer to it allegorically, and this could become a very productive game. It is the public that runs the most risk in censorship, because readers then have to decipher the clues...

Evohé intertwines lesbian eroticism with a self-reflexive discourse. The speaker establishes a connection between the female body, language and poetry, words and women, the poet and the lover. The collection emerges from the pain of the separation of the lovers, and the male speaker states that he has found refuge in words after disappointments with women. The speaker, who is not willing to be seduced by the charm of words, connects women's seductive powers with those of the words. Throughout the collection, the words "woman" and "language" are interchangeable. The use of typographical innovations contributes to the exploration of multiple linguistic combinations. On some occasions Peri-Rossi allows for the exchanging of the erotic and the poetic by inverting the words in a phrase. This strategy breaks the expectations of the reader: "La mujer pronunciada y la palabra poseida" (*Evohé* 37) (The woman pronounced and the word possessed). On other occasions the speaker establishes a dialogue between a poem and the one that follows: "Las mujeres vienen de lejos,/a consolar a los poetas/de la decepción de las palabras" (Women come from afar/to console male poets/for deceptive words' deception) and in the next poem: "Las palabras vienen desde lejos,/a consolarnos de la decepción de las mujeres" (*Evohé* 19) (Words come from afar/to console us/for women's deception).

In spite of the fact that through the collection women and words are compared and that women are linked with the origins of the poetic discourse, the body of the woman and her sexual attributes prevail over language and poetry:

> Silencio.
> cuando ella abre sus piernas
> que todo el mundo se calle
> Que nadie murmure
> ni me venga
> con cuentos ni poesías
> ni historias de catástrofes
> ni cataclismos
> que no hay enjambre mejor
> que sus cabellos
> ni abertura mayor que la de sus piernas
> ni bóveda que yo avizore con más respeto
> ni selva tan fragante como su pubis
> ni torres y catedrales tan seguras.
> Silencio.
> Orad: ella ha abierto sus piernas.
> Todo el mundo arrodillado. (*Evohé* 62)
>
> Silence.
> When she spreads her legs

let the whole world be still,
let no one mutter
no one tell tales
or poems
or stories of catastrophes or
natural disasters
there is no better cluster
than her hair
no better opening than between her legs
no vault I would observe more humbly
no forest so fragrant as her pubis,
no towers or cathedrals so secure.
Silence
Pray: She has opened her legs.
On your knees, everyone.

In *Lingüística general* (1979) Peri-Rossi investigates, like in *Evohé*, the relationship of language, meanings, grammar, and gender categories. Whereas in *Evohé* Peri-Rossi uses a system of encoding lesbian eroticism and love, the theme of lesbianism is openly addressed in *Lingüística general*. In several poems of this book ("Haendeliana,""Dolce Stil Nuovo,""Dolce Stil Nuovo II,""3ra. Estación: Campo de San Barnaba," and "4ta. Estación: Ca Foscari") the poet explores lesbian love. In "3ra. Estación: Campo de San Barnaba" lesbian meanings are clearly expressed and the female voice proclaims her love for another woman:

Esta noche, entre todos los normales,
te invito a cruzar el puente.
Nos mirarán con curiosidad—estas dos muchachas—
y quizás, si somos lo suficientemente sabias,
discretas y sutiles
perdonen nuestra subversión
sin necesidad de llamar al médico
al comisario político o al cura.

Tonight, among all the normal people,
I invite you to cross the bridge.
They'll be curious about us—these two girls—
and perhaps, if we are wise,

secretive and subtle enough
they will forgive our subversion
without calling in the doctor
the commissar or the priest.

In "4ta. Estación: Ca Foscari" the poet continues to explore the theme of love between women. The speaker emphasizes the sameness and the exchanging of the women's clothes, bodies, and identities:

Te amo como mi semejante
mi igual mi parecida
de esclava a esclava
parejas en subversión
al orden domesticado
Te amo esta y otras noches
con la señas de identidad
cambiadas
como alegremente cambiamos nuestras ropas
y tu vestido es el mío
y mis sandalias son las tuyas
Como mi seno
es tu seno

I love you as my sister
my equal, my double
slave to slave
couple in revolt
against domestic order
I love you tonight and some others
our identifying marks exchanged
the way we joyfully exchange our clothes
and your dress is mine
my sandals yours
my breast
your breast.

In one of the poems of *Diáspora* (1976) the speaker confronts a male-oriented tradition that has objectified women by presenting a woman who makes public her lesbian identity. Here, the objectified woman assumes the role of subject by making a political statement. Curiously, the public announcement of the speaker's lesbianism is in English and in French contrasting with the rest of the poem written in Spanish. She declares her sexual orientation as a way to reaffirm her existence:

> A los poetas que alabaron su desnudez
> les diré
> mucho mejor que ella quitándose el vestido
> es ella desfilándose por las calles de Nueva York
> —Park Avenue—
> con un cartel que dice:
>   Je suis lesbienne. I am beautiful.

> To the poets who have praised her nakedness
> I say
> much better than watching that woman take off her
>   clothes
> is to see her marching through New York
> —Park Avenue—
> with a poster that reads:
>   Je suis lesbienne. I am beautiful.

The decade of the 80's witnessed the emergence of other lesbian poetic voices. Together with the poetic voices of Alejandra Pizarnik and Cristina Peri-Rossi, we find those of the Argentineans Diana Bellessi and Mercedes Roffé, the Puerto Rican Nemir Matos, and the Mexican Sabina Berman. The poetry of Bellessi, Matos, and Berman is characterized by the presence of a lesbian erotic discourse and the enjoyment of lesbian sensual lives.

Diana Bellessi is the author of several collections of poetry: *Destino y propagaciones* (Destiny and Propagations; 1970), *Alacranes* (Scorpions; 1973), *Crucero ecuatorial* (Equatorial Cruise; 1980), *Eroica* (Heroic; 1988), and *El jardín* (The Garden; 1992). Her poems have appeared in *Hanging Loose, Sing Out!, Heresies*, and *Conditions*. She has translated the works of Adrienne Rich, Denise Levertov, June Jordan, Audre Lorde, Diane Di Prima and Muriel Rukeyser into Spanish.

Bellessi's poetry collection, *Eroica* (1988), presents a strong lesbian erotic discourse and a celebratory tone of sexual and emotional relationships among women. It is a writing of passion and desire for the female body. Through the book's eight sections the speaker unites the erotic enjoyment with that of the word. The poems praise different parts of the female body, emphasize the senses, and connect body and text. In "El texto" (The Text), "El Magnificat" (Magnificat), and "Intempesta Nocte" (Stormy Night), the speaker articulates moments of a lesbian sexual encounter until the lovers reach pleasure. In "Dual," one of the most accomplished sections of the book, like in Peri-Rossi's "4ta. Estación: Ca Foscari," the speaker recalls the reciprocity of desire of the two women lovers which is articulated through the unification and the interchangeable positions of the "you" and the "I."

The reciprocity of the lovers' desire is a feature of the lesbian poetry of Nemir Matos, a Puerto Rican poet who resides in New York, who according to Carlos Rodríguez Matos is the "first Puerto Rican poet to textualize lesbianism openly."[16] Matos is the author of three collections of poetry: *Las mujeres no hablan así* (Women Don't Speak like That), *A través del aire y del fuego pero no del cristal* (Through Air and Fire but Not Glass), and *Ars Morendi* (forthcoming). Her poetry, like some of Peri-Rossi's poetry and Bellessi's *Eroica*, centers around lesbian eroticism. In Matos' poetry the speaker pays a great deal of attention to her lover's body as well as to her own and the couple's desires. Her poetry contains strong erotic images and comparisons with elements of nature. In Matos' lesbian discourse, the use of a colloquial language to speak about sex as a way to challenge the poetic language and the oppression of women's sexuality is central. The openness of the poems of *Las mujeres no hablan así* defies social conventions. In her poem "Oleajes" (Ocean swells) from that collection, the speaker describes the sexual act between two women:

El deseo un potro salvaje que recorre la llanura de tu cuerpo/Desnuda pareces un desierto me llevas al vértigo me lanzas al abismo/de tus manos dunas o espejismos istmos o espejos de mi cuerpo tan parecido/ al tuyo/Eres ave o reptil haces vibrar el ritmo de mi pulso cada vez más/excitado por tu contacto de olas y mar alborotado/Salobre salino de algas/en mi boca de río desembocando en un océano no no que no se acabe.

> Desire wild horse that ranges the plain of your
> body/Naked, you look like desert, bear me to
> vertigo, cast me into the abyss/from your hands
> dunes or mirages or isthmus or mirrors of my
> body/so like yours/You are bird or reptile, making
> the rhythm of my pulse race faster and
> faster/aroused by the nearness of swells and the
> tumultuous sea/Salty, salt marsh of algae in my
> mouth/in my river mouth flowing into an ocean
> that no, no, never stops.

The poetry collection *Lunas* (Moons; 1988) by the Mexican poet, playwright, novelist, and actress Sabina Berman (1945-), is an erotic writing of the lesbian body. In this collection, as in Peri-Rossi's *Evohé* and Bellessi's *Eroica*, the eroticism and the poetic discourse are closely related. Berman plays with the conventions of grammatical gender of the Spanish language. Like Rosamaría Roffiel, Berman explores the possibilities of the language to include feminine forms to speak about women's physical and emotional experiences.

A different vein of lesbian poetry than the one of Peri-Rossi, Bellessi, Matos, and Berman is represented in the poetry of Mercedes Roffé (1954-), an Argentinean poet and literary critic living in New York who is the author of three collections of poetry: *Poemas 1973-1975* (1978), *Cámara Baja* (The Lower Bedroom; 1987), and *La noche y las palabras* (translated by Kathryn A. Kopple as Words and Nights; forthcoming). Roffé's lesbian love poetry detaches itself from the celebration of the sensual and the erotic aspect of lesbian relationships and rather articulates the painful experience of the absence of the lover.

In her collection *Cámara baja*, a book published while living in Argentina, the lesbian theme is encoded in the articulation of a tension between the spheres of the female and the male, elaborated in the book through a series of oppositions: mother/father; aunt/uncle; female lover/male lover; a Jewish girl/a boy, and through the continuous presentation of dialogues that reproduce the confrontation between females and male discourses. In two of the poems of this collection, "Entierra, entierra" (Bury It, Bury It) and "Almita mía" (My Beloved), that tension between female and male becomes more clearly associated with the speaker's quest for the definition of her sexual orientation. Significantly, in the last poem of the collection, "Almita mía" (My Beloved), the lesbian desire emerges with a stronger voice which is intertwined with a rebellion against conventionalisms.

Whereas the poems of *Cámara baja* encoded lesbian love, Roffé's latest collection of poetry, *La noche y las palabras* (Words and Nights) written in the United States, presents the theme of the absence of love and its relationship with the process of writing. This collection, like Molloy's *Certificate of Absence* and Cárdenas' *Cuaderno de amor y desamor*, emerges as a cathartic exercise for the loss of the lover. The speaker, using an intimate tone, expresses in a self-contained manner her desolation and her solitude.

The title of the book *La noche y las palabras* refers to the two main motifs of the collection: "la noche" (night) is the space of emotional emptiness, "las palabras" (words) relate to the concern for the act of writing. In this book, both the absence of the female lover and the act of writing are intrinsically intertwined. The lover's abandonment and the speaker's subsequent emotional devastation are necessary conditions for the act of writing. A feature of these poems is the speaker's insistence on her loneliness and the connection between the self, the poetic voice, and pain. Moreover, the painful voice which emerges as a result of the speaker's sorrow is what defines the speaker's self:

> Motivos para escribir. Una música tristísima. Una
> obsesión dulcificada por una pena extrema. La
> repetición. La pena larga que ya ha dejado de doler y
> es casi un peso apenas, la dulce carga de la memoria.
> La pena. La insistencia de una pena sin la cual no hay
> voz, no hay yo. Repetir. Repetirse hasta el murmullo.
> Hasta que la voz no salga. La pena como una música
> ahogada. Tenía miedo. Miedo de la rajadura del alma.
> Pero ya. Ni siquiera una herida. Más bien un mar
> guardado.

> Motives for writing. The saddest music of all. An
> obsession sweetened by an extreme grief. Repetition.
> The extended grief that has stopped hurting and is
> barely a weight, the sweet burden of memory. Grief.
> Insisting on a grief without which there is no voice,
> there is no I. Repeating. Repeating oneself into a

whisper. Until no voice comes out. A grief like a
drowned music. I was afraid. Afraid of the soul's
crack. But it's alright. Not even a wound. Rather, a
sheltered sea.[17]

*   *   *

Lesbian prose writers in Latin America have been less prolific
than poets. Most lesbian narrative falls under the autobiographical
category and the search for a lesbian past. Some of the works of the
Colombian writer Albalucía Angel, author of *Los girasoles en invierno*
(Sunflower in Winter; 1970), *Dos veces Alicia* (Twice Alicia; 1972),
Estaba la pájara pinta sentada en el verde limón (There Was the Bird
Seated in the Green Lemon Tree; 1975), ¡*Oh gloria inmarcesible!* (Oh,
Unfading Glory!; 1979), *Misiá señora* (My Lady; 1982) and *Las
andariegas* (Wandering Women; 1984) present lesbian motifs
encoded in the exploration of female connectedness. Particularly *Las
andariegas*, which can be read as a lesbian text in the sense that it
tells the story of a community of women from which men are
excluded. Albalucía Angel's project, like the French lesbian feminist
Monique Wittig's *Les Guérillères*, stresses the need of women to bond
with other women in order to rescue a history that has been denied
to them. Moreover, the book establishes a textual dialogue of
convergences with *Les Guérillères*, as the author herself has stated in
interview with Magdalena García Pinto:

> I constructed a dialogue between her guerilleras and
> my wanderers, a dialogue that slowly distanced itself
> from its original but didn't cut itself completely off.
> They don't oppose each other; rather, the texts
> crisscross. They echo each other.[18]

Las andariegas breaks with conventional literary genres by
including features of essay, poetry, and novel. It is a collection of
parables, part of a feminist project to rescue women's experiences
and reframe them outside the cultural context that has suppressed
feminine values, as Malva Filer has already noted.[19]

Also under the biographical mode is the novel *Monte de Venus*
(Mount of Venus; 1976) by Reina Roffé (1951-). *Monte de Venus* was
censored by the Argentinean government due to its portrayal of

political problems and lesbianism. The novel has two main plot lines. One, narrated in the third person, relates experiences in a school for adults. It explores the relationships among the students, the amorous intrigues and the atmosphere of the school. Life at the school works as a mirror image of the political situation in Argentina during the 1970's. The second plot revolves around Julia Grande, a lesbian whose life experiences articulate the lesbian's marginality in a homophobic society.

The lesbian discourse of *Monte de Venus*, full of stereotypes, offers a negative and tragic view of lesbianism. The reader is witness to the treatment Julia is subjected to by her family and society due to her sexual orientation. Rejection and lack of understanding of a different sexual orientation prompt Julia's parents to take her to a psychiatrist who treats her with forms of physical torture in order to "cure" her lesbianism.

In the presentation of the lesbian character in this novel, the reader finds all the cultural clichés and myths created around lesbians and their social behavior, such as the strong attachment of the lesbian to the father, who is the main source of affection and nurturance, and the rejecting mother. The view the author presents of lesbianism follows the Freudian perspective of identification with the father and a desire to be male and be seen as a man, which makes the lesbian character dress like a boy and perform activities that society and culture have long associated with males. Julia feels her true identity to be masculine and considers her feminine identity something fake that she assumes while betraying herself.

Monte de Venus does not present a lesbian perspective and is rather a mosaic of stereotypical constructions that reiterate the prejudices of society. Nonetheless, it is interesting for its open portrayal of sexual and erotic encounters between women and its articulation of the lack of understanding and tolerance toward different expressions of sexuality.

In 1990, the Mexican sociologist Sara Levi Calderón (1942-), published an autobiographical novel that caused controversy because of its portrayal of lesbian encounters, *Dos Mujeres* (1990; translated by Gina Kaufer as *The Two Mujeres*; 1991). It is the autobiographical portrait of Valeria, a thirty-nine-year-old Mexican "petit bourgeois" of Jewish heritage and a divorced mother of two children who is beginning to face life on her own after having been accustomed to being supported by her husband and her family. The novel lacks psychological depth; its characters and situations are one dimensional, and the lesbian characters play traditional sex roles. However, the novel is a testimony of lesbian lives and the conditions of dependency and submission under which women live.

* * *

The 1970's and 1980's saw the emergence and expansion of a body of work by Latin American women in the United States (Latinas). The term "Latina" has been used for Latin American women who have been in the United States since an early age or for Latin American women who live in the United States and identify themselves as part of a minority and with the struggle of other marginalized groups. Furthermore, the use of Latina often supposes a commitment to the interest of working classes and an awareness of the discrimination they suffer.[20]

The literary production of Latin American women established in the United States has emerged as a response to the confrontation of aspects of their culture with American culture as well as with their social, political, and economic condition as immigrants. Therefore, the origins of Latina writing are linked to the need to reaffirm cultural and racial identities articulated through personal discourses within the common ground of their community. This type of literature reflects biculturalism, bilingualism, and an awareness of a dual cultural reality.[21] The category of Latina writing, however, like any other blanket generalization, overlooks the differences among women from different cultural, social, and racial Latin American backgrounds. The use of a generic umbrella has dissolved or diluted the diversity of experience of the writers.

In the mid-1980's, Latina writing became more diversified as lesbian issues appeared in the works of some Latina writers. Thus, a body of literature emerged that can be labeled Latina lesbian writing. This particular lesbian literary production reflects the consciousness of a more complex form of marginality within the social preoccupations of Latina writers. In conjunction with their racial, cultural and social status as a minority in the United States, these women explore an awareness of a different sexual orientation that has been traditionally silenced by the Latinos in this country as well as by the Anglo Americans. Thus, it is not surprising that many of the

Latinas whose works present lesbian issues, themes, or a lesbian sensibility have also been involved in political lesbian activism.

The literature of Chicanas has been the best example of a literature that is being defined by the social and political awareness of the writers. Chicanas have always been involved in political activism aimed at their specific situation as working class women of color.[22] The works of the well-known Chicana writers and political activists Cherríe Moraga and Gloria Anzaldúa have opened a space in the United States for the particular category of Latina lesbian writing. In the early 1980's it was through the publication of *This Bridge Called My Back: Radical Writings by Women of Color* (1981) edited by Moraga and Anzaldúa, *Cuentos: Stories by Latinas* (1983) and Cherríe Moraga's *Loving in the War Years: lo que nunca pasó por sus labios* (1983), as well as the publication of an issue of *Frontiers* (1983) devoted entirely to Chicana writing that these Latina writers became publicly identified as lesbians. In the late 1980's and early 1990's, two anthologies of Latina lesbian writing were published: *Compañeras: Latina Lesbians* (1987) edited by Juanita Ramos and *Chicana Lesbians: The Girls Our Mothers Warned Us About* (1991) edited by Carla Trujillo.

*   *   *

The literature produced by lesbian Latinas in the decades of the seventies and the eighties was influenced by the women's as well as the gay and lesbian movements in the United States. The interest in lesbian literature and lesbian literary criticism that burgeoned in North American universities and within the feminist movement in the United States during the 1970's and the 1980's has yet to be paralleled in Latin American countries. In addition, the development of gay and lesbian journals, publishing houses, bookstores, or university centers dedicated to the study of gay and lesbian literature and other cultural manifestations has yet to occur in Latin America. In fact, the lack of serious critical studies on gay and lesbian Latin American literature is alarming. Whereas a body of lesbian and gay literature indeed exists and continues to grow in Latin America, literary studies that focus on this kind of literature are few. Literary criticism of Latin American lesbian works has appeared in the United States and not in Latin America.

In spite of the fact that Alejandra Pizarnik, Cristina Peri-Rossi, Diana Bellessi, Nemir Matos, Sabina Berman, Mercedes Roffé, Albalucía Angel, Reina Roffé, and Sara Levi Calderón, as well as the writers studied in this book (Magaly Alabau, Nancy Cárdenas, Sylvia Molloy, Rosamaría Roffiel, and Luz María Umpierre), are part of a lesbian Latin American literary tradition, there has not been an effort from literary critics to study lesbian issues as a central aspect of the texts. As a valuable body of lesbian literature emerges and develops, there is great resistance from critics to study and recognize these texts as a separate entity, deserving a critical analysis that focuses on their lesbianism. On the contrary, the practice that has prevailed in literary criticism has been to hide those signs of a lesbian sensibility and dismiss them as unimportant.

In the case of the works of Alejandra Pizarnik and Cristina Peri-Rossi, two writers who have received critical attention, an encompassing tradition of silence has been the norm when it comes to their lesbianism. Some critics, like Celia Correas de Zapata and Lygia Johnson, the editors of *Detrás de la reja: Antología crítica de narradoras latinoamericanas del siglo XX* (A Critical Anthology of Twentieth-Century Latin American Women Writers), have used a language of euphemism to refer to the presence of lesbian eroticism in Peri-Rossi's works while the word "lesbian" has remained conspicuously.[23]

However, there have been some attempts to deal specifically with the issues of lesbian themes or sensibility in the works of Pizarnik and Peri-Rossi. Nuria Amat, Amy K. Kaminsky, and Inmaculada Pertusa are some of the critics who have focused their interest on the lesbianism in Pizarnik's and Peri-Rossi's texts, respectively. Nuria Amat's article "La erótica del lenguaje en Alejandra Pizarnik y Monique Wittig" (The Erotics of Language in Alejandra Pizarnik and Monique Wittig) is one of the few studies that addresses lesbian eroticism in Pizarnik's works. Amy K. Kaminsky's article "Cristina Peri-Rossi and the Question of Lesbian Presence" and Inmaculada Pertusa's "Revolución e identidad en los poemas lesbianos de Cristina Peri-Rossi" (Revolution and Identity in Cristina Peri-Rossi's Lesbian Poems) are studies of Peri-Rossi's works as lesbian texts.[24]

David William Foster's books *Gay and Lesbian Themes in Latin American Writing* and *Latin American Writers on Gay and Lesbian Themes: A Bio-Critical Sourcebook* are important contributions to the study of Latin American gay and lesbian literature. Amy K. Kaminsky's enlightening articles "Sylvia Molloy's Lesbian Cartographies: Body, Text and Geography" and "Cristina Peri-Rossi and the Question of Lesbian Presence" are rare examples of critical works that center on lesbian issues.[25] Prior to Foster's and Kaminsky's studies, there were only minor attempts to apprise gay and lesbian themes or motifs in Latin American fiction: a survey by Kessel Schwartz, "Homosexuality as a Theme in Representative Contemporary Spanish American Novels" and Robert Howes'"The Literature of Outsiders: The Literature of the Gay Community in Latin America," published in *Latin American Masses and Minorities: Their Images and Realities.*[26]

In 1995 Duke University Press published *¿Entiendes? Queer Readings, Hispanic Writings* edited by Emilie L. Bergmann and Paul Julian Smith. The book includes five essays on lesbian aspects of works by Latina and Latin American women writers. Among the studies are Sylvia Molloy's essay on Teresa de la Parra, Licia Fiol-Mata's essay on Gabriela Mistral, and Luz María Umpierre's essay on Puerto Rican literature.

Lesbianism in Latin America—and to a lesser extent in the United States—is still the "unspeakable." The absence of literary criticism concentrating on lesbian texts in such important literary journals as *Revista Iberoamericana, Chasqui, Inti. Revista de Literatura Hispánica, Mester, Letras Femeninas* as well as the refusal to articulate the words"lesbian" and "lesbianism" in literary studies has been the norm. In the early 1990's *Chasqui* and *Letras Femeninas* did publish reviews of Rosamaría Roffiel's *Amora* and Sara Levi Calderón's *Dos Mujeres.*[27] In 1993, in an issue dedicated to Puerto Rican literature, *Revista Iberoamericana* published an article by Luz María Umpierre on the Puerto Rican writer Carmen Lugo Filippi's story "Milagros, Calle Mercurio."[28] In this article, entitled "Incitaciones lesbianas en 'Milagros, Calle Mercurio'" (Lesbian Incitations on "Milagros, Calle Mercurio"), Umpierre reads Lugo Filippi's story as an encoding of the theme of lesbianism. She argues that while there are several texts in contemporary Puerto Rican literature written by women that deal with male homosexuality and others that present hints of lesbian sensibility, for the most part there is a lack of lesbian texts in Puerto Rican literature.

A practice of omission of lesbian issues still prevails in journals dedicated to women's studies. Encouragingly, however, in

1993 *Signs: A Journal of Women in Culture and Society* published an entire issue on lesbian literature. In 1989 *Connexions: An International Women's Quarterly* published an issue dedicated to lesbian activism. In that issue there were four short articles focusing on the situation of lesbians in Latin America and interviews with lesbians from Nicaragua, Chile, Peru, and Mexico.[29] In 1991, *Ms. Magazine* published a short article by the Colombian writer and activist tatiana de la tierra on lesbian visibility in Argentina.[30]

It is my hope that this study will urge others to further explore an area of Latin American literature that has received scant critical attention. By undertaking a study of literature that presents a confrontation with tradition (patriarchy and heterosexist values), I do not intend to further marginalize the works of these writers. On the contrary, my intention is to open ways towards acceptance of pluralism and diversity. The essays presented in this book will help to create a framework in which Latin American lesbian literature can be studied. I want to encourage other critics to pay attention to literature that presents lesbian characters, themes and motifs as well as to provoke a dialogue with them, thus breaking ground for further studies in the field of lesbian Latin American literature.

*   *   *

NOTES

1 Adrienne Rich, "Compulsory Heterosexuality and Lesbian Existence," *Blood, Bread and Poetry: Selected Prose. 1979-1985* (New York: W.W. Norton and Company, 1986), p. 63.

2 Catherine R. Stimpson, "Zero Degree Deviancy: The Lesbian Novel in English," *Where the Meanings Are: Feminism and Cultural Spaces* (New York: Methuen, 1988), p. 97.

3 Lillian Faderman, *Surpassing the Love of Men: Romantic Friendship and Love between Women from the Renaissance to the Present* (New York: William Morrow, 1981), p. 157-177; Audre Lorde, *Zami: A New Spelling of My Name* (Freedom, California: The Crossing Press, 1982).

4 Charlotte Bunch, "Lesbians in Revolt," *Lesbianism and the Women's Movement*, Nancy Myron and Charlotte Bunch, eds. (Baltimore: Diana Press, 1975), p. 30.

5 Pat Califia, *Public Sex: The Culture of Radical Sex* (Pittsburgh, Pennsylvania: Cleis Press, 1994).

6 Cheryl Clarke, "Lesbianism: An Act of Resistance," *This Bridge Called My Back: Writings by Radical Women of Color*, eds. Cherríe Moraga and Gloria Anzaldúa (New York: Kitchen Table: Women of Color Press, 1981), p. 128.

7 Linda Hutcheon, *Narcissistic Narrative: The Metafictional Paradox* (New York: Methuen, 1984).

8 Luz María Umpierre, *The Margarita Poems* (Bloomington, Indiana: Third Woman Press, 1987), p. 1.

9 *Chloe Plus Olivia: An Anthology of Lesbian Literature from the Seventeenth Century to the Present*, Lillian Faderman, ed. (New York: Penguin Books, 1994), p. 445.

10 Octavio Paz, *Sor Juana Inés de la Cruz o las trampas de la fe* (Mexico City: Fondo de Cultura Económica, 1982). Translated by Margaret Sayers Peden, *Sor Juana; or the Traps of Faith* (Cambridge, Massachusetts: Harvard University Press, 1988).

11 Sylvia Molloy, "Female Textual Identities: The Strategies of Self-Figuration," *Women's Writing in Latin America: An Anthology*, eds. Sara Castro-Klarén, Sylvia Molloy and Beatriz Sarlo (Boulder, Colorado: Westview, 1991), pp. 107-124. Claudia Lanzarotti, "Sospechosa para todos," *Apsi* 418 (1992): 30-33. Elizabeth Rosa Horán, "Gabriela Mistral," *Latin American Writers on Gay and Lesbian Themes: A Bio-Critical Sourcebook*, ed. David William Foster (Westport, Connecticut: Greenwood Press, 1994), pp. 221-235.

12 Gabriela Mistral, "País de la ausencia," *Poesías de Gabriela Mistral* (Mexico D.F.: Editores Mexicanos Unidos, 1983), p. 167.

13 *Alejandra Pizarnik: A Profile*, edited and with an introduction by Frank Graziano. Translated by Suzanne Jill Levine (Durango, Colorado: Logbridge-Rhodes, 1987), p. 100.

14 *Alejandra Pizarnik: A Profile*, edited and with an introduction by Frank Graziano (Durango, Colorado: Logbridge-Rhodes, 1987), p. 30. Translated by María Rosa Fort and Frank Graziano.

15 John F. Deredita, "Desde la diáspora: entrevista con Cristina Peri-Rossi," *Texto Crítico* 9 (1978): 134.

16 Carlos Rodríguez Matos, "Nemir Matos," *Latin American Writers on Gay and Lesbian Themes: A Bio-Critical Sourcebook*, ed. David William Foster (Westport, Connecticut: Greenwood Press, 1994), p. 216.

17 Translated by Kathryn A. Kopple.

18 Magdalena García Pinto, *Women Writers of Latin America: Intimate Stories*. Translated by Trudy Balch and Magdalena García Pinto (Austin: University of Texas Press, 1991), p. 69.

19 Malva Filer, "Autorrescate e invención en *Las andariegas*, de Albalucía Angel," *Revista Iberoamericana* LI, números 132-133 (julio-diciembre 1985): 649-655.

20 Eliana Rivero, "From Immigrants to Ethnic: Cuban Women Writers in the U.S.," *Breaking Boundaries: Latina Writing and Critical Readings*, Asunción Horno-Delgado et al; eds. (Amherst, Massachusetts: University of Massachusetts Press, 1989), pp. 189-200.

21 Eliana Ortega and Nancy Saporta Sternbach, "At the Threshold of the Unnamed: Latina Literary Discourse in the Eighties," *Breaking Boundaries: Latina Writing and Critical Readings*, Asunción Horno-Delgado et al; eds. (Amherst, Massachusetts: University of Massachusetts Press, 1989), pp. 2-23.

22 Yvonne Yarbro-Bejarano, "Chicana Literature from a Chicana Feminist Perspective," *Chicana Creativity and Criticism: Charting New Frontiers in American Literature*, ed. Helena María Viramontes (Houston, Texas: Arte Público Press, 1988), p. 139.

23 *Detrás de la reja: Antología crítica de narradoras latinoamericanas del siglo XX*, Celia Correas de Zapata and Lygia Johnson, eds. (Caracas: Monte Avila, 1980), p. 15.

24 Amy K. Kaminsky, "Cristina Peri-Rossi and the Question of Lesbian Presence," *Reading the Body Politic: Feminist Criticism and Latin American Women Writers* (Minneapolis: University of Minnesota Press, 1993), pp. 115-134. Inmaculada Pertusa, "Revolución e identidad en los poemas lesbianos de Cristina Peri-Rossi," *Monographic Review: Revista Monográfica* Vol. 7 (1991): 236-250.

25 Amy K. Kaminsky, "Sylvia Molloy's Lesbian Cartographies: Body, Text, and Geography" and "Cristina Peri-Rossi and the Question of Lesbian Presence," *Reading the Body Politic: Feminist Criticism and Latin American Women Writers* (Minnesota: University of Minnesota Press, 1993), pp. 96-114; 115-133.

26 Kessel Schwartz, "Homosexuality as a Theme in Representative Contemporary Spanish American Novels," *Kentucky Romance Quarterly* 22 (1975): 247-257; and Robert Howes, "The Literature of Outsiders: The Literature of the Gay Community in Latin America," *Latin American Masses and Minorities: Their Images and Realities*, ed. Dan C. Hazen (SALALM Secretariat, Memorial Library, University of Wisconsin, 1985) I: 288-304, 580-591.

27 David William Foster, "Review of *Amora*," *Chasqui* Volumen XIX, Número 2 (Noviembre 1990): 119-122. Elena M. Martínez, "Review of *Amora* and *Dos Mujeres*," *Letras Femeninas* XVIII, núms. 1-2 (Primavera/Otoño 1992): 175-179.

28 Luz María Umpierre, "Incitaciones lesbianas en 'Milagros, Calle Mercurio' de Carmen Lugo Filippi," *Revista Iberoamericana* LIX, Números 162-163 (Enero-junio 1993): 309-316.

29 *Connexions: An International Women's Quarterly*. Lesbian Activism. Special Issue 29 (1989): 10; 14; 16; 26.

30 tatiana de la tierra, "Argentina: Lesbian Visibility," *Ms. Magazine* 1 (May-June 1991): 16.

CHAPTER I

THE POETICS OF SPACE AND THE POLITICS OF LESBIAN EXILE: MAGALY ALABAU'S POETRY AND SYLVIA MOLLOY'S NOVEL *CERTIFICATE OF ABSENCE*

When I have said "love you" I have said
Nothing at all to tell you; I cannot find
Any speech in any country of the mind
Which might inform you whither I have fled.
In saying "I love you" I have gone so far
Away from you, into so strange a land;
You may not find me, may not understand
How I am exiled, driven to a star.

Till now deserted. Here I stand about,
Eat, sleep, bewail, feel lonely and explore,
Remember how I loved the world before,
Tremble in case that memory lets me out,
Islanded here, I wait for you to come—
Waiting the day that exiles you to home.

The Nature of the Moment.
Valentine Ackland

In Magaly Alabau's collections of poetry, *La extremaunción diaria* (The Daily Extreme Unction; 1986), *Hermana* (Sister; 1989; *Hermana/Sister* bilingual edition; 1992), and *Hemos llegado a Ilión* (Ilium; 1991), as well as in Sylvia Molloy's novel *Certificate of Absence* (1981; translated into English; 1989), the dialectical representation of interior and exterior spaces is a function of the theme of lesbianism because it articulates the marginal social positioning of the lesbian subjects in society. The representation of space in the works of these writers has a poetic function as well as an ideological and political value for the theme of lesbianism in Latin American literature. In this chapter while focusing on Magaly Alabau's poetry and Sylvia Molloy's novel, I also draw parallels to Nancy Cárdenas' poetry collection *Cuaderno de amor y desamor* (Book of Love and Absence of Love; forthcoming) and Rosamaría Roffiel's novel *Amora* (Love in Feminine; 1989) and poetry collection *Corramos libres ahora* (Let's Run Free Now; 1986; revised edition; 1994).

I am interested in the study of the inside/outside dialectic because it can be interpreted as a textual manifestation of the conventionally opposed binaries heterosexual and homosexual. However, I do not intend to reaffirm the hierarchies that have supported the opposition. Rather, I explore how the binaries are literally and linguistically constructed in terms of the interior and exterior physical spaces in the works of Alabau and Molloy.

The dialectic of inside/outside is complex in the works of Alabau and Molloy since it can have different meanings. To be inside can mean to belong, to be part of society, or it can mean to be in the closet, invisible, to be in the realm of the unspeakable.[1] To be outside can be identified with living in the margins, and it is a synonym of exclusion or displacement. However, to be outside is also to be out of the closet and therefore, to be visible and to be political. In the works of Alabau and Molloy, to be inside is synonymous with being in the closet, but the phrase nonetheless reaffirms the speakers' and characters' lesbianism. The positioning of the speakers and the characters in the interior spaces marks their marginality but paradoxically interior is also a space for the establishment of their lesbian selves.

I connect space and exile because exile in Alabau's works and in Molloy's novel *Certificate of Absence* is used to designate the social positioning of the women. The most common connotation of exile is the geographical removal from homeland, but exile is mainly used here as a metaphor for the exclusion that lesbians experience in their lives. Exile in lesbian literature serves as a metaphor for the disenfranchisement of lesbians, for the experience of outsiders in a society that is hostile to non-conventional forms of love and desire. Thus, exile is a psychological condition as well as a geographical one. However, it can also be seen as a positive space in which lesbians can construct an intermediary space located outside the mainstream, and where they create a place for themselves and for their lovers, as presented metaphorically by the English lesbian poet Valentine Ackland (1906-1968) in a sonnet published in 1935 and reprinted in *The Nature of the Moment*.[2] The lesbian subjects, by living apart under values different from the mainstream, live in exile.

There are different types of space in Alabau's poetry and Molloy's novel: inside, familiar spaces (homes and bedrooms), inside, unfamiliar spaces (hotel rooms and mental institutions), the outside (streets and natural spaces), and intermediary spaces such as windows, staircases, and elevators.

In Alabau's poetry and Molloy's novel, there is an insistence on marginal interior physical spaces while the references to exterior spaces are minimal. It can be argued that Alabau and Molloy, by presenting lesbian characters in marginal spaces, do not make a political statement; but in publishing their works, they nevertheless make public the lesbian discourse and thus their works have a political impact, albeit indirectly. Through the writing process, these two authors create a literary space in memory and forge a place for their lesbian characters and for a lesbian perspective. In contrast, Rosamaría Roffiel's *Amora* and *Corramos libres ahora*, and Nancy Cárdenas' *Cuaderno de amor y desamor*, present a different relationship between space and the lesbian characters from that of Alabau and Molloy. In *Amora*, *Corramos libres ahora*, and *Cuaderno de amor y desamor*, the lesbian characters and speakers appropriate for themselves certain public (rural and urban) spaces. The latter representation is more directly political because it removes lesbians from marginal spaces and reinstates them in visible places. Thus lesbians, traditionally displaced and shut off in the limited space of a "closet," are, in Roffiel's and Cárdenas' works, rescuing for themselves exterior and public spaces that have been heretofore denied them.

Exile has been a significant theme in many kinds of literature and at different times. In Hispanic literature in particular, the theme of exile has occupied a paramount place in the works of nineteenth- and twentieth-century writers. As a result of the social, economic, and political situations in Latin America, exile has been a common experience with large groups having emigrated to Europe and to the United States. In this century, Latin American writers such as Julia de Burgos, Gabriela Mistral, Cristina Peri-Rossi, Luisa Valenzuela, Julio Cortázar, Severo Sarduy, Reinaldo Arenas, José Donoso, Lourdes Casals, Manuel Puig, Magaly Alabau, and Sylvia Molloy have experienced exile and have transformed that experience into a literary motif in their works. However, exile in this chapter is not just a geographical separation from one's land, it rather designates the emotional and psychological attitudes of those who live at the margins of society.

Magaly Alabau left Cuba in 1967 and settled in the United States. As has happened with other exiled writers, the experiences of living in a new country have marked her writing. For Alabau, exile is a constant theme and it occupies a central position in her poetry, which is characterized by the representation of a spatial duality (metaphorically, Cuba versus the United States) as well as by the cultural duality that goes along with the experience of exile. Her poetry shares with the literature of exile the urge to recover or to find memories from the past, a place of origin or a sense of cultural identity that is attached to the past and one's native land. Many Latin American women writers, especially Puerto Ricans and Chicanas who live in the United States, deal with the same type of cultural duality through the use of two languages, Spanish and English. While Alabau's works do not present two linguistic codes, they do reflect the experience of exile as well as the need to recover a lost time and space.

That the desire to recover a time and space has created an ambivalence in those who suffer exile has led critics to define exile as the experience of "someone who inhabits one place and remembers or projects the reality of another place."[3] Some writers elaborate the theme of exile by expressing nostalgic feelings for the past or by attempting to recreate the scenario of the homeland. Argentinean novelist and storyteller Julio Cortázar, for example, categorized the literature of exile in two recurrent forms. One form appears as an almost sick nostalgia for the country that one no longer inhabits or that no longer exists. The other form is a literature that idyllically reconstructs in some nebulous future what has been lost.[4]

In Alabau's works there is neither nostalgia about the past nor an idyllic reconstruction since the female speakers are aware that they are marginalized in both the countries they settled in and their native lands. For Alabau, as for other Latin American women writers, such as Gabriela Mistral and Cristina Peri-Rossi, exile is related to a double sense of displacement.[5] One aspect of exile is the general sense of dislocation that both males and females may experience; the other is related to the marginalized social and cultural position women have traditionally occupied in Latin

America. This sense of alienation and the feelings of being excluded by the host culture have been pointed out by Librada Hernández in referring to the experience of Cuban women writers: "For the women, the pressure to deal with identity and the past becomes even more compelling since when they look back they find themselves left out of the discourse of the past."[6] The double displacement and exile of the female subjects create alienation. Alabau's *Hermana, La extremaunción diaria*, and *Hemos llegado a Ilión* as well as Sylvia Molloy's *Certificate of Absence* are characterized by the recurring representation of an absence which bespeaks the alienation of female speakers and characters.

The theme of exile is central in Alabau's *Hermana, La extremaunción diaria*, and *Hemos llegado a Ilión*. In these texts the female speaker recounts the experience of geographical exile and the psychological and emotional consequences by continuously mentioning two spatial realities (here/there). The constant motif of a journey in Alabau's works bespeaks the theme of exile. In *Hermana*, the speaker goes back to Cuba to rescue her history and her relationship with a twin sister. In *Hemos llegado a Ilión*, the speaker, evoking the myth of Persephone and Demeter, goes back to her homeland after a long absence to discover that she no longer belongs there and after spending a period of time there, a period that is compared with a season in hell, she returns to her exiled homeland. In Molloy's *Certificate of Absence* exile designates the symbolic experience of social detachment. The novel presents the voluntary exile of a lesbian character who isolates and cuts herself off from social and cultural bonds in order to write about her life and her lesbian affairs.

The representation of interior spaces in Alabau's poetry is varied, in *Hermana, La extremaunción diaria*, and *Hemos llegado a Ilión*, these spaces are very significant and are a function of Alabau's poetic universe. Throughout these works, a dialectic of inside and outside, related to the theme of exile and marginalization, is articulated in conjunction with the lesbian motif. There are abundant references in particular to interior spaces in Alabau's poetry: houses, bedrooms, living rooms, hotel rooms, mental institutions, jails, and cages while allusions to exterior spaces remain minimal. The emphasis on interior spaces allows for the exploration of aspects of the female speaker's psychological life and the significance of those aspects in Alabau's poetry.

The speakers in *Hermana* and *Hemos llegado a Ilión*, as well as *Certificate*'s lesbian protagonist in exile, attempt to reconstruct, rescue, or invent their past by bringing back forgotten memories associated with interior spaces. In these books, the reconstruction of a lost space and a lost time occupies a central position and becomes an obsession for Alabau's speakers as well as for the protagonist of Molloy's *Certificate of Absence*.

In the recreation of that past, home has a paramount significance, as Michael Seidel has pointed out: "Home is locus, custom, memory, familiarity, ease, security, sanctuary. And centuries of tradition do not alter the power of home as an image."[7] However, in lesbian texts like *Hermana* and *Certificate of Absence*, the idea of home is necessarily marked by the feelings of rejection that lesbians experience in the family home because of the heterosexual laws attached to it that exclude and deny lesbians' experiences and existence. Gaston Bachelard in *The Poetics of Space* has examined the significance of the house, its unity and its complexity. He argues that the house is one of "the greatest powers of integration for the thoughts, memories and dreams of mankind."[8] However, in these lesbian texts the literary representation of home varies from the traditional one found in texts that present a heterosexual view. Here, the lesbians inside the home are outsiders who need to reinvent their family structure through the process of memory. Through imagination the lesbians change the value of the home to insert themselves and their own history.

In *Hermana*, the speaker stresses the importance of home and reconstructs it through the process of memory in order to create an interior space for an erotic relationship with her twin sister (a metaphor for her lesbian lover) in which the lesbian relationship will fit. There is a consciousness of inventing a space that is more inclusive instead of merely recreating a previous space. In this book the "small invented island" is a metaphor for the house as a symbol of the sisters' sensual, sexual, and emotional connections and their need to create for themselves a place within the larger patriarchal home. Thus, the process of writing is a way to re-inscribe a lesbian perspective that only existed in the sisters' secretive world: "Siento que tenemos que hurgar/como si tuviéramos que escribir una pequeña historia,/hacer una islita en el patio" (14) [as if we had to write a little story,/create a small island in the patio (15)].

In *Hermana*, the exiled speaker elaborates not only a relationship between the house and the sisters' intimacy, but also between the house and the native land (an exterior space). The house, seen as an island ["La casa tiene sus limitaciones. Es una isla" (14) (The house has its limitations./It is an island), stresses the equation home = native Cuba. At the same time, the comparison of the house with an island alludes to the isolation of those "in exile," either in a literal or in a metaphorical sense, which is reinforced by the fact that the house is a fragmented space. The fragmentation of the family house and the fact that each family member is identified with a space within the house (the kitchen is identified with the grandmother; the bathroom with all of the family members; the dining room with the grandfather; the living room with the mother; meanwhile, the bedrooms are identified with the sisters) reinforce the isolation of the lesbian speaker and the underlying irreconcilable differences and separateness among the family members while stressing the sisters' emotional and erotic bond.

In spite of the fact that in *Hermana* and in *Certificate* home is the site of the conflict between patriarchal laws and lesbian desire, the speaker in the former and the protagonist in the latter want to rescue the family home since it is the site of lesbian desires stemming from the speaker's and protagonist's relationships with their sisters. Thus, in *Hermana* the speaker's search for the past takes place in the company of her sister. The book begins with the speaker's invitation to her sister to embark on a journey to forgotten memories of their childhood home. The speaker cannot accomplish her journey back home to her origins by herself and acknowledges that this process of rescuing the lost home has to be a common task of the two sisters, that it depends on the processes of memory:

> Se puede traer el recuerdo, dormirlo
> entre los años, despertarlo
> en un poema, hacerle una visita
> como a un presidiario
> Siento que tenemos que hurgar
> como si en la saleta hubiera un tesoro enterrado,
> como si tuviéramos que escribir una pequeña historia,
> hacer una islita en el patio,
> estirar las ramas y vernos dos plantas
> encaramándose en el aire. (*Hermana* 14)

> Memory can be brought along,
> put to sleep among years
> woken up in a poem, visited
> like an inmate.
> I feel we must dig into this
> as if there were buried treasure in the parlor,
> as if we have to write a little story,
> create a small island in the patio,
> stretch out the branches, and reaching into the air
> reveal ourselves as two plants. (15)

It is clear that the speaker's attachment to the family house is due to feelings of special bonding with her sister and not because of the house itself, as the poetic voice points out: "Hubiéramos salido de la casa en cualquier momento" (14) [We would have left the house at any moment (15)]. Here, the desire for that lost home becomes a substitute for home as well as a symbol of that lost female bonding that existed before and that the speaker wishes to bring back through imagination, evocation, and writing.

In *Hermana* the bedroom is a privileged space. In the bedroom the sisters sleep, dream, and make love. The bedroom is a place of secrecy and the unspoken, while the living room, a place of maximum visibility and exposure, is a place of exclusion for the sisters in which their relationship, symbolically a lesbian one, does not fit. The speaker, later on in the poem, clearly expresses that she was well aware of the exclusion and rejection she suffered. She indicates that rejection by combining verbs of opposite actions "All went away" and "we returned" as well as by the emphasis on going inside and going outside:

> Sé que todos se iban cuando regresábamos.
> Sé que todos cerraban las puertas y nos lanzaban
> como pedradas a la calle que era la sala.
> Pero la calle nos empujaba hacia adentro
> y nos sacaba la lengua,
> hacía muecas, abría el molar. *(Hermana 16)*

> I know they all went away when we returned.
> I know they all closed the doors and hurled us
> like stones into the street that was the living room.

I know the street pushed us back inside,
stuck its tongue out at us,
made faces, opened its jaws. (17)

It is not accidental that *Hermana* begins and ends with bedrooms. Being the site of lesbian passion, the bedroom links memories and provides a space for the sexuality of the sisters and their emotional intimacy. The bedroom is, in this book, also a space of transgression, since lesbian incestuous desire and union take place in them. This space where lesbian passion is explored, although separate and protected from the outside world, is interestingly represented as fragmented and divided within itself; it is a space with limitations and restrictions, and it is protected by a fragile demarcation. In spite of its limitations and lack of visibility, the bedroom assures the privacy of the sisters' lesbian erotic relationship providing the two women with a place in which to feel protected and safe enough to play out their erotic fantasies and to imagine a larger space of their own. The contrast between the sisters' space and the rest of the house is stressed throughout the poem by the rhythmic repetition of the words "outside and inside." The outside is represented as a hostile space while the inside, although uncomfortable and with limitations, is a well-protected area. The inside, the sisters' space, is identified with repetition of the "I" and the "you," as well as with allusions to touching each other and physical closeness, underlining the lesbian erotic quality of this discourse:

> *Proscritas* del mundo de afuera
> el mosquitero nos protege y aunque el aire se agote
> y nos sofoquemos, te cantaré tu canción.
> *Fuera* del mosquitero está el sol,
> la canción dice.
> *Fuera* del mosquitero está el sol
> y el jardín prohibido.
> *Dentro* los monstruos grandes feos
> que la noche y el espacio pequeño precipitan.
> Fuera no nos pertenece.
> Lo que vemos al extender los brazos y suspirar, escapa.
> *Dentro* estamos tú y yo. Podemos tocarnos
> Podemos dormir. Mirar los insectos que atacan.

Palpamos la noche pequeña de un mosquitero endeble.
Fuera el sol escapa,
por más que cantemos, escapa
Hermana, conformémonos esta noche.
Imaginemos un barco en este espacio, el mar.
una isla completa. (36-38)

                    *   *   *

Banned from the *outside* world
we shelter under the mosquito net and despite the
    smothering,
the failing air, I'll sing to you your song.
Outside the mosquito net there is the sun,
says the song.
Outside the mosquito net there is the sun,
and the forbidden garden.
Inside, the large ugly monsters
born of night and the cramped space.
Outside is not ours. What we see
when we stretch out our arms and sigh, runs away.
You and I are inside. We can touch each other.
We can sleep. Watch the insects attack.
We stroke the small night of a flimsy net.
Outside the sun is running away,
no matter how loud we sing, it goes running away.
Sister, let us reconcile this night.
Let us imagine a boat in this space, the sea,
an unbroken island. (37-39) [9]

In addition to symbolizing the sexual attraction between the sisters in *Hermana*, bedrooms are also the site where remembering and writing take place. The poem begins with the bedroom of the speaker's childhood and ends with the bedroom where memories are revived and where writing takes place. This is clearly reiterated in the last pages of *Hermana* in which the sisters, removed from their intimate space, are placed nowhere: "Los árboles de aquel campo en que nos dejaron/repiten en mi cuarto: memoria viva" (66) [The trees from that camp where they left us/recur in my room: living memory (67)]. Thus, the site of lesbian passion is symbolically transformed into the space of writing, as is clearly articulated in *Hemos llegado a Ilión* in which the exiled speaker, in a journey back to her country, returns to visit her childhood bedroom and remembers her nights in this room, her papers, her bed and her orgasms:

> Ya estás en el cuarto, lo has reconocido, tus noches,
> tus papeles echados en la cesta, la imagen diosdada
>   del asfalto
> se interpola en los mosaicos de esta triste casa.
> Están tus puntos, los centauros, las paletas consignas,
> los retratos, están tus camas, tus orgasmos están en
>   las paredes desplegados. (*Hemos llegado a Ilión* 13)

> You are already in your room, you recognize it,
>   your nights,
> your papers thrown into the wastebasket, the
>   godgiven image of asphalt interpolated into the
>   mosaics of this melancholy house.
> There are your periods, the centaurs, the palette
>   slogans,
> the portraits, your bed, your orgasms displayed on
>   the walls.

Hotels are other interior spaces that abound in Alabau's poetry. They are transitory places that allude to lesbians' displacement in society as well as underlining the decenteredness of the lesbian poetic discourse, a discourse which has developed within neither a cultural place nor a literary tradition.

In both *Hermana* and *Hemos llegado a Ilión*, the speaker, in journeying to her country, stays in a hotel during her short visit. In *Hemos llegado a Ilión* the positioning of the exiled speaker in a hotel room accentuates the feelings of decentrality of the one who, in going back to her native land, cannot identify with its new reality. The transitoriness of the woman staying in the hotel is reinforced through her identification with a nomad. Her stay in the hotel and her comparison with a nomad stress the idea of not belonging, of not being able to integrate herself: "Una tormenta crean nuestros padres/en el cuarto del hotel a las doce de la noche/Cómo llegué, cuándo, por qué/No sé. Quieren testigos./La noche entra a la escalera de un hotel./Nómada en un ambiente escupido" (*Hermana*,

30) (Our parents create a storm/in the hotel at midnight./How I arrived, when, why./I don't know. They want witnesses./Night enters the hotel stairway./Nomad in a room full of spit). (*Hermana*, 31).

Although hotels are transitory places in Alabau's poetry, they also function as places where the female speakers can reflect upon their lives. They provide a space free from society's impositions. For example, in one of the poems of Alabau's *La extremaunción diaria*, the speaker finds shelter in a hotel. In this poem, the hotel room provides the speaker with a place of her own in which she can rid herself of emotional shields and reflect upon her existence. She finds herself and removes what is artificial:"Ahí voy/a un hotel de cortinas estampadas/a encerrarme/a quitarme el abrigo/a oírme" (16) (There I go/to a hotel with flowered curtains/to lock myself in/to get rid of my coat/to listen to myself).

*   *   *

In *Certificate of Absence*, as well as in *Hermana*, the family house is a place of exile for the lesbian subject. Home and childhood, identified by the protagonist as an "ill-defined limbo," make her remember that as a young girl she felt the need to create spaces for herself to insure her existence and her privacy:

> La cama era un lugar recluido y propio: un barco en
> la tormenta, en medio del viento, o una cama dentro
> de una casita, dentro del mismo dormitorio
> (Levantaba paredes alrededor de la cama, porque
> pocas eran las veces en que su cama era un barco en
> la tormenta; a las paredes añadía ventanas y una
> puerta, imaginaba un techo. Y entonces a partir de esa
> casita, poblaba el resto del cuarto, que era el resto del
> mundo: con plantas, con pájaros, con un cielo azul,
> todos de acuarela. (18)

> Bed was a secluded, private place, a ship at storm in
> the wind, or better still a bed in a little house inside
> her bedroom. She imagined walls around her bed,
> added windows, a door, and thought up a roof. And
> then, working out of that little house, she filled up
> the rest of the room (which in the fantasy was the

rest of the world) with plants, birds, a blue sky, all in
watercolors.) (7)

On many occasions, the girl felt she did not choose marginal
spaces, where life was uncomfortable and full of needs, rather they
were imposed on her, or she felt it was the price she had to pay to
insure her survival. The spaces created by the young girl, in which
she looks to satisfy her own needs, are detached from the rest of the
house and family members:

> Se imaginaba condenada a vivir para siempre allí,
> preveía maneras de subsistir: la bañadera sería una
> cama, se taparía con toallas, comería jabón, pasta de
> dientes, bebería jarabes. Nadie, pero nadie, la moles-
> taría. (18)

> She imagined herself condemned to live there
> forever, and thought up means of surviving: the
> bathtub would be a bed, she would cover herself with
> towels, would eat soap and toothpaste, would drink
> cough syrups. Nobody would disturb her, absolutely
> nobody. (7)

The limited spaces that Molloy's lesbian protagonist creates
for herself are metaphorical closets. The term "closet" has been used
to designate the social invisibility of gays and lesbians. Closets work
as a way to protect identities and to insure survival in homophobic
societies. One of the most obvious closet metaphors in the novel is
the nook: a remote, sheltered, out of the way place in which the
lesbian protagonist studied and read as a young girl. The nook is
clearly similar to the closet. However, the nook here also symbolizes
the exclusion, not only of lesbians but also of women in general,
from intellectual work, since the young girl in Molloy's novel must
pursue her intellectual interests in a hidden place burdened by
anxiety and guilt. In spite of the fact that the young girl pursues her
interest in the nook with anxiety and guilt, the nook offers her some
protection from family life and the world. In the lesbian protagonist's
life as an adult, the nook will be transformed into the room where
she writes.

Like the speaker in *Hermana*, the lesbian protagonist in *Certificate* creates spaces not only for herself but to share with another woman, also her sister. As a child, Molloy's protagonist fantasized about creating a space for her sister Clara and herself in which they could separate from the rest of the house and be intimate. This space is characterized by the sisters' affective bonding as is seen in chapter VI, the last chapter of the first part of the novel. The emphasis on the sisters' physical closeness is intentional and significant since such intimacy works as a mirror image of the protagonist's lesbian relationships as an adult and traces a past of female bonding. In this fantasy, the protagonist and her sister Clara are secluded in the maid's room, which, in spite of being marked by the social inferiority of the servant, is a space free from patriarchal impositions and the censorship of the protagonist's mother. The figure of the maid as a nurturing woman contrasts with the representation of the protagonist's unloving and childish mother. The narrator's use of adjectives such as "tiny" and "narrow" articulates the limitations of lesbian existence as well as accentuates the physical closeness of the two young girls in a small and closed space with different rules that is separated from the rest of the house:

> Están ella y su hermana Clara en el cuarto minúsculo de la cocinera, acostadas en la cama estrecha. Se abrazan, se tocan, parecen quererse. La cocinera— una criolla enorme y pecherona— les lleva leche desde la cocina, en abierta complicidad, como queriendo protegerlas de la censura materna. El cuarto parece desligado de la casa, afuera se oye el ruido del mar. (80)

> She and her sister Clara are in the tiny maid's room, lying in the narrow bed. They hug one another, touch one another, seem to care for one another. The maid—a huge, buxom half-Indian woman—brings them milk from the kitchen, in an obvious sign of complicity, as if wanting to protect them from their mother's disapproval. The room seems separate from the rest of the house; outside, there is the sound of the sea. (58)

The protagonist's desire as a young girl to detach herself physically from her family home and to find a place of her own is continued in her life as an adult by the act of renting a room in which she pursues her writing and reflects upon her past. *Certificate of Absence* begins when the protagonist, a nameless lesbian writer, arrives in an empty room that was previously rented by a woman with whom she had had an affair. The room in which the lesbian writes is significant for the theme of lesbian love and writing and is indicated in the original Spanish title, *En breve cárcel* (literally, in a small cell). The title of the English version (*Certificate of Absence*) alludes to the theme of absence of love at the time of writing as well as the abandonment of the woman's lover. Both Spanish and English titles refer to two diverse poetic traditions. *En breve cárcel* is taken from the poem "Retrato de Lisi que traía en una sortija" (Lisi's Portrait) written by the Baroque Spanish writer Francisco de Quevedo y Villegas (1580-1645) who like Cervantes, Lope de Vega, and Calderón de la Barca, was an important Golden Age writer.[10] The title, *En breve cárcel*, can be found in a line from one of Quevedo's poems which also serves as one of *En breve cárcel*'s epigraphs. It belongs to a Spanish (heterosexual) poetic tradition and is appropriated in Molloy's novel for a lesbian relationship. The English title *Certificate of Absence*, taken from a poem by Emily Dickinson, emphasizes the theme of the absence of love in the novel:

> We'll pass without the parting
> So to spare
> Certificate of Absence–
> Deeming where
>
> I left Her I could find Her
> If I tried—
> This way I keep from missing
> Those that died.

The room, central to the lesbian theme of the novel, symbolizes two different acts of separation in order to proclaim the protagonist's identity. On the one hand, it symbolizes the lesbian's detachment from traditional literature that privileges and presents heterosexual relationships and desire since the woman is dedicated to writing about her lesbian love affairs, and on the other, it symbolizes the separation of the lesbian lovers in the novel. However, both acts of separation, synonyms of a form of cultural and emotional exile, are necessary to liberate the writer from feelings for her ex-lover and to reaffirm the protagonist's lesbian identity. It is interesting to note that most of the critics who have written about the novel have avoided dealing with its lesbianism and have focused on other aspects. Perhaps this oversight is because in *Certificate of Absence* the lesbian identity of the writer-protagonist and the identities of her lovers are not problematized. Although the space created to allow for lesbian desire seems to be marginal since it is limited to a small rented room, lesbian existence is at the center of the novel. The narrator focuses on the lesbian love affairs and overlooks the conflict and systems of oppositions heterosexist societies have created between heterosexuality and homosexuality. Yet, the room, an empty and transitory place, site of casual encounters, love affairs, and break-ups, works as a metaphor for the lesbian writer's marginality and the exclusion of lesbianism in repressive societies. Thus, the writer faces the problem of many lesbians who write from the space that mainstream (heterosexual) literary tradition has assigned to lesbian literature. It could be argued that Molloy's strategy of focusing the reader's attention on this room without social or cultural ties is apolitical and narcissistic. However, the novel is quite political in stressing lesbians' needs to establish and reaffirm their own space. It is also political because the author forces the reader (both gay and straight) to feel secluded with the woman writer and her lesbian affairs, thus temporarily forgetting heterosexual conventions. By erasing heterosexual references from the text, Molloy forces the reader to forget them. The feelings of entrapment that the protagonist and the reader experience reinforce the idea of lesbianism as a form of exile, exile always being a political act of those who do not conform to the realities of their native land. In spite of the fact that the room makes us think of a rootless place, it provides the lesbian writer with protection. In this room, the writer is aided by the lack of external references and is able to pursue her lesbian desires as well as her passion for writing.

The room is not only empty and rented, it is also a place characterized by deficiencies, since it is not well suited for the writing task that the woman has undertaken. The room does not have lamps or bookshelves, as the woman noticed herself upon arrival:"No hay bibliotecas -dijo—, no hay mesa para escribir y la luz es mala" (13) [There are no bookshelves (she told the landlady), no desk, and the light is bad (3)]. The room without objects related to literary work appears as an ill-defined place and symbolizes women's traditional exclusion from intellectual activity. The fact that Molloy's protagonist does not own the room and needs to rent speaks of the dispossession of women, in particular, that of lesbians in literature since ownership and authorship are concepts that have been traditionally linked to the notion of the father and patriarchy.[11]

The title *Certificate of Absence* alludes to the centrality of the theme of absence of love clearly presented in the physical emptiness of the room. The description of the room emphasizes what is missing, thus, the narrator connects the room and the transitory character of love in the protagonist's life. There is a correspondence between the room and the woman's emotional life. The theme of emptiness due to a lack of love, as well as the geographical and emotional displacement, is reiterated throughout the novel:

> El exagerado cuidado de algunos detalles, la falta de otros, señala que ha sido previsto para otro uso del que pensaba darle; de hecho para el que ocasional-mente le da. *Cuarto y amores de paso.* (13)[12]

> The exaggerated attention to certain details, the lack of others, are signs that it was intended for a purpose other than the one she planned for it: indeed, for the very purpose she occasionally makes of it. *A place of transit for transitory loves.* (3)

The redundancy created by the words "transit" and "transitory" underlines the protagonist's disenfranchisement and the fact that she does not belong; despite that, she tries to appropriate the room for herself, knowing that she will never be able to fully own it: "Sabe con todo que la protegen, como defensas privadas, marcando un espacio que siempre marcó suyo sin hacerse plenamente cargo de él" (13) [She knows, however, that they (the walls) protect her, like defensive weapons, marking off a space that she has always called her own without fully taking possession of it (3)].

The theme of the lack of a female literary tradition and the relationship of the woman writer to the room reminds the reader of Virginia Woolf's foundational essay, "A Room of One's Own" (1929).

By situating a woman writer in a room detached from social and cultural roots, Molloy's novel evokes an indirect dialogue with Woolf's essay and the tradition of female writing. In the novel, however, the woman writer does not deal with the material conditions of the writer like Woolf does in her essay. The lack of a female tradition is presented not only in the novel but also in Molloy's essay "Sentido de ausencias" (A Sense of Absence), an autobiographical essay in which she discusses the lack of a female tradition in her early years. The title of the essay "Sentido de ausencias" alludes to the lack of female literary role models and the fact that the study of the works of women writers was not emphasized or accessible to Molloy in her formative years. In the essay, Molloy recalls an anecdote from her last year of high school during which she won a literary award and the prize was any book she wanted. When Molloy chose Katherine Mansfield's works, she was asked to change her choice for a more mainstream (read, male) writer.[13] In her novel Molloy challenges a patriarchal tradition that has excluded women from intellectual work, by placing a lesbian writer in a room devoted entirely to the acts of reading and writing. By re-appropriating her life for herself the lesbian writer rescues a political history that has been denied to all lesbians.

*   *   *

In addition to bedrooms and hotel rooms, there are other significant interior spaces in Alabau's poetry and in Molloy's novel. In *Electra/Clitemnestra* and *Hermana*, doors, windows, and staircases are intermediary spaces that divide and connect interior and exterior spaces. There is an emotional and affective quality attached to them. These intermediary spaces reflect the emotional ambivalence of the speakers and characters as well as distance and closeness, love and jealousy. In Alabau's first book, *Electra/Clitemnestra*, doors serve to emphasize Electra's exclusion from her mother's affective life. This exclusion is textualized by the physical place Electra occupies; she is relegated to the outside, behind the closed door of her mother's room. Electra is an outsider who observes her mother from the intermediary space of a door, thus indicating her emotional displacement as Clytemnestra herself acknowledges: "Cada vez que te paras en la puerta no te veo" (17) (Every time you step at the door, I fail to see you). In poem IV of *Electra/Clitemnestra*, "Electra at the door" symbolizes not only that she is shut out from Clytemnestra's affective and sexual life but also is a function of the daughter's jealousy and frustration resulting from her mother's rejection and denial of her love. The fact that Electra cannot see her mother and only hears her indicates the distance between and separation of the two of them: "Electra oye a su madre/y empieza a pintar círculos y cráteres/En la puerta/las uñas se comen a los dientes./Electra actúa, Electra muerde" (16) (Electra hears her mother/and begins to paint circles and craters/In the doorway/fingernails are devoured by teeth./Electra acts, Electra bites).

Other instances in which Electra is relegated to the role of spectator and is visualized at the door, indicating the rejection she experiences, appear in poems VII and XIX of *Electra/Clitemnestra*. In poem VII, Clytemnestra and Medusa make love while Electra, who desires her mother, is left out of her mother's erotic union with Medusa. The half-closed door increases Electra's desire to see. The forbidden aspect of this lesbian incestuous desire is shown in the separation of the spaces caused by the door. If in poem VII Electra is left out of her mother's relationship with Medusa, then in poem XIX Electra is excluded from her mother's life involving Clytemnestra's heterosexual union with Aegisthus. In both instances the daughter has been deprived of her mother's love and closeness and that deprivation is presented by the physical position Electra occupies by her mother's door. On some occasions, the adjectives that are used to classify the door serve to specify the emotional attachment or the affective side of the situation and the mixed feelings of the speaker: "La duda,/la puerta tibia entreabierta,/ve a Egisto sin cara en su cama,/ve un bulto de desnudeces cuchicheando./Su madre en piernas colgando/El sacrificio perpetrándose en su lecho" (34) (Doubt/the warm door half-open,/she sees Aegisthus faceless in her bed,/sees a whispering bundle of nakedness./Her mother's legs hanging/Sacrifice perpetrated in her bed).

In *Certificate of Absence*, as in *Electra/Clitemnestra*, the references to doors indicate an affective connection and the relationship of lesbian subjects with one of the parents. Whereas in *Electra/Clitemnestra* doors separate spaces between Electra and her mother Clytemnestra, in Molloy's novel the door indicates the special connection between the lesbian protagonist and her father. In Molloy's novel the protagonist as a child always felt the need to close her door to insure her privacy and detach herself from her father, who insisted on keeping the girl's door open to have access to her bedroom. Here, the lesbian's conflictive relationship of love and competition with her father is presented through the father's insistence on opening the door to her bedroom and the girl's need to detach herself by closing the door.

In *Electra/Clitemnestra, Hermana,* and *Certificate of Absence,* windows frame the difference between the inside and the outside. They denote an intermediary space that symbolize the impossibility of the lesbian subject to identify herself with either the inside or the outside and the impossibility of being fully integrated into an intolerant society. The fact that in *Electra/Clitemnestra* and in *Hermana* windows are generally open helps the reader to visualize the prohibition against trespassing certain spaces and the distance between the inside and the outside. On other occasions (poem VI, "Los despojos" (The Remains) of *Electra/Clitemnestra*), Electra and Orestes appear at the window. Positioning them at a window reinforces their role as mere spectators who see things at a distance without any affective involvement.

Casual encounters between female lovers or women with strong affective bonds are associated in *Electra/Clitemnestra* with staircases, and in *Certificate of Absence* with elevators, representing two directions and feelings of confrontation. In Molloy's novel, the lesbian writer's allusions to the elevator that she hears from inside her room reinforce the ambiguity of her feelings for her ex-lover Vera and her present lover Renata and the two alternatives that the different personalities of the two women offer to the protagonist in her relationships with them. In *Electra/Clitemnestra*, staircases are mentioned several times, and they are the site of Electra and Clytemnestra's casual encounters. Placing female characters on staircases going in different directions emphasizes the tension that prevails between mother and daughter because of the intensity of the erotic desire as seen in poem III:

> No se vieron más.
> Se entrecruzaban en la escalera de piedra,
> dos líneas rojas
> tirando cada una la ira.
> Se escrutan los ojos hinchados.
> Los de Clitemnestra exhalan púrpura
> Electra se aguanta los párpados violetas de los muslos.

Las bocas cosidas
se sofocan.
En la escalera de piedra es donde se conocen. (14)

They never saw each other again.
On the stone stairway, two red lines
crossed
each one tugging rage behind it.
Swollen eyes scrutinize each other.
Clytemnestra's exhale purple
Electra scrunches the violet eyelids of her thighs.
The sewn mouths
suffocate.
On the stone stairway they know each other.

*   *   *

When used, common exterior spaces in Alabau's *La extremaunción diaria* and *Hemos llegado a Ilión* are city landscapes with desolate streets, New York City, or the open sea viewed from a window or a balcony. In most of the poems of *La extremaunción diaria*, New York City is a central theme. The city is the site of the exiled speaker and her desolate feelings of displacement. The streets and the subways are the most commonly represented places in this book in which the speaker experiences the city as a foreigner who identifies with other immigrants, a Jewish woman in "Ya en la balsa nos hemos quedado Dios y yo" (Still on the Raft God and I Remained), or a Palestinian man in the poem entitled "Al." These two poems present extreme images related to the condition of displacement because of geographical exile and indicate the speaker's solitude and desperation.

In *La extremaunción diaria*, New York City streets play a significant role while in *Hemos llegado a Ilión*, it is the streets of Havana that are central to the theme of exile and exclusion. In either place the speaker does not feel comfortable. In the hotel she feels like a prisoner, unfree. However, compared to the streets, the hotel, although transitory, is a more authentic place for her. She finds refuge in it and sees it as a more sincere place than the streets: "es una habitación sin los desdoblamientos de allá fuera" (18) (it is a room without the outside duplicity). For the speaker, the streets of

Havana have a strong emotional connotation as they are a source of anxiety and of discovering that things are not as they were in the past:"La ciudad me recuerda los que faltan./Falta el conocimiento de los nuevos,/el crecimiento de las contradicciones./Faltan más rostros, más risas al paisaje,/falta algo que no sé descifrar, que no conozco" (17) (The city reminds me of the missing./Missing the knowledge of the new,/the growth of contradictions./Missing more faces, more laughter in the landscapes,/missing something I cannot decipher, do not know). The speaker introduces the confrontation between the present and the past and the idea that things have changed:

> Llegamos buscando a tientas por la calles,
> perdíamos las aceras en el trote,
> los paisajes urbanos hervían derramados.
> Aquel. Aquí. Estamos. Este es Carlos III.
> ¿Te acuerdas de Galiano? ¿De la Calle Monte?
> ¿De Corrales? ¿De Gloria? ¿Del Encanto? (17)

> We arrive searching blindly through the streets,
> lost the sidewalks in our hurry,
> urban landscapes were seething and spilling.
> That. Here. We're here. This is Carlos III.
> Do you remember Galiano? From Calle Monte?
> Corrales? Gloria? Do you remember El Encanto?[14]

In addition to the emotional role that Cuban streets and landscapes play in *Hemos llegado a Ilión*, they also have a political value. Through such images, the speaker emphasizes the general alienation of the people and the poverty that characterizes the landscape. All the images of the landscape and streets in *Hemos llegado a Ilión* are ones of poverty, destruction, and solitude: "El Malecón está lleno de botellas vacías" (16) (The Malecón is full of empty bottles). Through the repetition of the metaphor "the prison of my people," the speaker emphasizes that this place is characterized by its lack of freedom, while she attests that those who stayed in the country are there not by choice, but because they do not have the possibility of leaving.

    These references to the Cuban landscape and streets have an existential connotation of desolation as well as an aspect of political criticism in regard to the state of affairs in Cuba after the revolution. Through references to the streets of Havana, the speaker articulates the socio-political transformations and restructuring that Cuban society has undergone after Castro's revolution.

*   *   *

In *Certificate of Absence*, Molloy privileges interior spaces as have other River Plate region writers such as Juan Carlos Onetti and Jorge Luis Borges. There are few geographical references and when they appear they are vague and ambiguous. Maintaining the non-specificity of place is clearly the narrator's intention. From the beginning of the novel, there is a desire to avoid naming places (in chapter one the woman herself asserts her intention of not naming places), and it is only at the end of the novel that names appear:

> Ha tenido que mencionar nombres de ciudades. Esto
> la molesta, pero son parte de sus sueños. Por lo tanto—
> ahora—dirá todos los lugares. La ciudad nevada donde
> conoció a Renata y volvió a ver a Vera es la ciudad de
> Buffalo, en el estado de Nueva York. La ciudad donde
> volvió a encontrar a Renata y a Vera es París. Y la ciudad
> donde creció y—si le dieran la elección— volvería a
> crecer, es la ciudad de Buenos Aires. (147)

> She has had to mention the names of cities. This
> troubles her, but they are after all part of her dreams.
> She now decides to give places—all her places—their
> name. The snowy city where she met Renata and
> spied on Vera again is Buffalo, New York. The city
> where she met up again with Renata and Vera is
> Paris. The city where she grew up—and where she
> would grow up again, given the choice—is the city of
> Buenos Aires. (116)

The strategy of the woman writer, and ultimately Molloy's strategy, of not mentioning places helps to erase the effect of realistic representation and contributes to the plurality of meanings in the novel. This practice of not fixing places and characters recalls a textual strategy that has been used by Borges and, curiously, studied carefully by Molloy in *Signs of Borges*.[15] Molloy insures the ambiguity of the text and reinforces the theme of exile by creating a character who is a traveler and by using demonstrative adjectives to denote the cities. The narrator emphasizes that the protagonist suffers from an inner exile as well as a geographical exile and since the geographical references are characterized by vagueness, the ambiguity of the text prevails. Not only are places not fixed by name, but there is also the desire to erase their representation. By using demonstrative adjectives rather than naming places and cities ("this city"; "that city"), the author avoids specificity: "Ciudad que no nombra por ahora, que acaso no nombre: en cada nueva copia de este texto propone geografías vagas, una latitud frígida aceptable..."(19) [A city she will not name for now, that she will perhaps never name; each new version of this text suggests vague topographies, a suitable bleak latitude... (8)].

The bleakness and coldness of the generic city underlines the emotional desolation of the protagonist, who walks through the streets without interest, totally involved in her memories:

> Afuera las calles estaban blancas, los árboles
> cubiertos de nieve, mientras caminaba hacia su casa
> le pareció que la ciudad se había vaciado de ruidos o
> que ella se había vuelto sorda. Cruzaba las calles
> mecánicamente, pensando sólo en la piel muy blanca
> de Renata a quien dejó de ver durante mucho
> tiempo. (52)

> Outside, the streets were white, the trees covered
> with snow, and as she walked home it seemed to her
> that the city had been emptied of sound or that she
> had gone deaf. She crossed the streets in a
> mechanical way, thinking only of Renata's very white
> skin, Renata whom she then stopped seeing for a
> long time. (35-36)

Molloy's lesbian protagonist is seen as an international traveler who moves through three continents: South America, Europe, and North America. The election of three continents reinforces the triangular dimension of the woman's relationships (first with her parents and then with her lovers Renata and Vera). The triangle avoids the fixity implied in dichotomies and allows for some openness. Moreover, the mention of Buffalo, Paris, and Buenos

Aires introduces an alteration of the traditional Latin American literary topos of Buenos Aires and Paris. If on the one hand, references to Buenos Aires make the reader (familiarized with Molloy's biography) think of a reference to her life, the fact that the lesbian writer is always displaced avoids fixing and closing meanings.

The geographical references in Molloy's novel are of two types. One type is associated with the women in the writer's life: her mother, her sister, her lovers; the other one is associated with the writer's father. The first type of place is real, while the places associated with her father are mythological ones, as Amy K. Kaminsky has already noted.[16] Kaminsky has contrasted the geography that the woman travels with her mother, her sister and her lovers with the father's mythical geography. According to her, the first can potentially be transformed, while the latter, with which her father exhorts her, is rejected because it is static.[17] However, it is important to emphasize that the woman in both geographical spaces (in the dream with the mother and the sister and in the dream with the father) feels like she is not going to be able to find either place and that in both cases the woman appears out of place and suffering from an inner exile. Therefore, what is important is that in both spaces the lesbian protagonist feels lost and disoriented, as if always looking for a place that she cannot find:

> ...en estos sueños que sin cesar la hacen visitar ciudades—Amberes, París, Roma, Buenos Aires— donde con su madre, donde con su hermana, recorre espacios sin saber adónde va. En todas hay un punto secreto y ella no lo encuentra. (147)

> ...dreams that have her continuously leading her mother and sister through cities—Antwerp, Paris, Rome, Buenos Aires—without knowing where she is going. In all of them there is a secret point she never finds. (116)

The geographical references related to the father are marked by the authority that he possesses. In the Ephesus dream, there is an imposition, a command. The woman's father asks her to go to a specific place to see Artemis, the goddess of fertility, but the woman feels that she will not be able to get to that place: "Sabe que al decir Efeso está rompiendo la geografía apenas nombrada de este relato para llamarle la atención a un lugar único al que nunca podrá llegar" (153) [She realizes that, in saying the word Ephesus, her father was altering the almost nameless geography of her story, calling attention to the only place she would never be able to reach (121)]. The dream underlines the daughter's position of inequality and the power that the father enjoys over her. Conversely, in the dream with the mother and the sister, the issue of authority is not presented. The male/female relationships in the novel are ones of inequality since the males prevail. Relationships among females in the novel are characterized by equality.

In *Certificate of Absence*, references to open spaces appear in dreams, fantasies, and memories from the woman's childhood. Natural and open spaces contrast with the entrapment of the room where the woman writes and with the space of the family house that entails the social and cultural exclusion of lesbians.

As a child, the writer dreamt of escaping to the sea where she could be independent and free. This desire to run away to the sea is, in Anglo tradition, a break from parental authority and the road to adventure.[18] The sea provided the protagonist with a space without boundaries, where the waves swelled and crested before collapsing, that is, a space intangible, difficult to apprehend and which always threatened to disappear.

In the woman's life as an adult, fantasies of the sea offer freedom and liberation from herself and from the room she lives in: "Hoy querría estar sola en el mar: cómoda en el agua, dejándose ir, sin que nadie la llame desde la costa, sin salvatajes espectaculares" (65) [Today she would like to be alone in the sea: at ease in the water, letting herself go, without anyone calling her from the shore, without spectacular rescues (46)].

*   *   *

The motif of the journey, so present in Alabau's poetry and Molloy's novel, is a constant and fecund motif of the literature of exile and one of the oldest motifs in literature. However, in these texts the journey has a symbolical rather than a literal value; in addition to alluding to the experience of exile it alludes to the condition of the de-centered lesbian subjects.

The repetitive mentioning of arrivals and departures as well as of such objects as trunks and suitcases and the continuous mentioning of modes of transportation (ships, rafts, airplanes, subways, buses, and cars) help the reader visualize the connection of two different spaces, two countries, and the speaker's emotional ambivalence as a result of the experience of exile.

The speaker and the protagonists of Alabau's narrative poems are usually described and identified as passengers, people who do not stay in one place but rather are commuting, going somewhere. The identification with passengers reaffirms the characters' alienation and the routine character of their lives: "Sentada entre los tranquilos pasajeros que meditan/en un vaivén mortífero de ruedas y de baches/me resigno a verte y a aceptar la condición de pasajero indefenso" (20) [Seated among tranquil passengers who meditate/past a deadly jolting of potholes and tires/I resign myself to seeing you, to being a helpless passenger (*Hermana*, 21)]. In many of the poems of *La extremaunción diaria*, there are references to the experience of riding subways in New York City. These experiences accentuate the feelings of helplessness, solitude, and hopelessness that the speaker feels in a foreign land. In addition, subways are a clear allusion to an underground experience, and the connotation of secretiveness can be interpreted to refer to possessing hidden homosexual feelings in a society that is hostile to lesbians.

The fragmentation of identity as a result of the experience of exile is explored by Alabau as well as by other Latin American women writers, among them the Uruguayan writer Cristina Peri-Rossi in "El exilio son los otros" (Others Are My Exile).[19] In *Hemos llegado a Ilión*, the speaker, in journeying back to her homeland, experiences alienation and has ambiguous feelings that originate in her inability to identify with what she finds in her native land. This is symbolical of a lesbian who, turning back to heterosexual society, cannot find a place for herself. The speaker, while visiting in Cuba, goes through a process of objectification, fragmentation, and transformation.

The speaker identifies herself with objects she sees around her: a refrigerator, a sofa, a window, a bed or with animals: "Soy la ventana que da a un par de gatos salvajes/que yacen en las ramas del patio del vecino. Gatos de esos/que no se ven en las ciudades. Descuidados, rabiosos,/maltratados, sin gentes regalando abundancia./Soy esos dos" (20) ([I am] the window that opens on a couple of wild cats/lying in the branches of the neighbor's patio. Cats like those/you don't find in cities. Neglected, rabid, mistreated, lacking the gifts of abundance./I am those two).

It is interesting to note that in Alabau's poetry the consequences of exile are not only suffered by those who left the country but also by those who stayed behind. *Hemos llegado a Ilión*, a book that emerged after the poet's painful experience of a trip to Cuba, shows how the speaker's mother and her relatives and friends who stayed in the country are also torn apart because of the loss of those who left. In addition, those who stayed have suffered because of the abrupt socio-political transformations in their country and because of the lack of communication with the outside world.

Fragmentation of the body, one of the most prominent features of Alabau's poetry, serves different poetic functions. In *Electra/Clitemnestra* it indicates erotic intensity, while in *La extremaunción diaria* and *Hemos llegado a Ilión* it is a consequence of the experience of exile. In *La extremaunción diaria* and *Hemos llegado a Ilión*, the speaker and the female characters are presented either as physically fragmented or objectified, thus emphasizing their decentrality. This fragmentation is textualized through a lack of agreement between body and mind, since there is no correspondence between physical actions and the intellect. This non-correspondence is commonly presented through the disintegration of body parts, i.e., separation of the head from the rest of the body:"la cabeza sola, sin mí arremete el aire" (*La extremaunción diaria*, 9) (the head by itself strikes the air). On other occasions, the body is not seen as a whole but as fragments:"Brinco, no me falles, pierna/Brazo sé mi amigo" (*La extremaunción diaria*, 10) (I jump, leg don't fail me/Arm be my accomplice). At times, bodies are depicted with missing parts: sin/brazos pero con piernas/sin boca y ojo pero con nariz...(*La extremaunción diaria*, 25) (without/arms but with legs/without mouth or eye but with a nose).

The use of doubles in Alabau's poetry, particularly in *Hermana* in which the speaker has an identical sister, in addition to representing lesbian lovers alludes to the fragmentation of personality. The theme of the divided self and the search for an identity, a common issue in the works of immigrant writers, is at the center of *Hermana* and *Hemos llegado a Ilión*, and it is related to the need to recuperate cultural roots. This motif is a feature that Alabau's poetry shares with the poetry of other women writers, Latin

Americans, and North American poets of the last three decades. *Hemos llegado a Ilión* narrates the experience of a double journey, one physical and spatial, the other internal, a search for a part of the speaker's divided self.

Related to the motif of the divided self and the need to hide is the use of masks in Alabau's poetry and in Molloy's *Certificate of Absence*. The mask, as a device used to cover up an identity, is connected to the motif of the double, the duality of the individual pretending to be someone else, and the absence of a centered self. One of the poems of *Ras* textualizes the relationship between the allusion to mask and the absence of a centered self:

> Vivo con una máscara
> buscando una obsesión
> No la dejo reposar
>
> I live with a mask on
> searching for an obsession
> I won't let it alone

In this same poem the speaker expresses the tension created between the mask she uses and her own face:

> Aspavientos que entre máscara y rostro
> no permiten ni una tranquila hora,
> ni un segundo de paz. (25)
>
> Theatrical gestures between the mask and the face
> that won't let me rest,
> not an hour, not a second of peace.

As such, the mask is clearly related to the theme of lesbianism, and Alabau herself has stated that she has used the mask to protect herself.[20] The mask motif in Alabau's poetry has had a prominent role since her first book, *Electra/Clitemnestra*, and it has appeared in *La extremaunción diaria, Ras,* and *Hemos llegado a Ilión*. Even the cover of *Electra/Clitemnestra*, a painting by the Cuban Gladys Triana of two masks, makes evident the significance of that motif in Alabau's book. In *La extremaunción diaria*, the speaker has a series of rituals to protect herself, to hide the fragmentation and alienation of the self and to face daily routines. Masks and make-up (serving as a mask) are continuously used to hide. One sees clearly that for the speaker it is necessary to cover up who she is and to pretend to be different. In several instances, the speaker is presented as someone involved in a ritual of covering her face with a mask or with make-up: "El maquillaje chorrea como la sangre en el Monte Getsemaní/Para ponerme la máscara indispensable y pugilista/hay que encuadrarse delante del espejo" (11) (Make-up drips like blood on Mount Gethsemane/To put on the required and pugilist mask/I have to face myself in the mirror).

In *Hermana* and *Hemos llegado a Ilión*, the tension between mask and face is expressed by the speaker's antithetical desires to manifest herself and to protect herself with a mask. This contrast appears in *Hemos llegado a Ilión*: "En dos carteras divido la vida. La que guarda/la pluma con punto afilado y con sus gritos./La que guarda la máscara diaria"(10) (I divide life in two portfolios. The one that holds the pen with the sharpened point and their cries. The one that holds the everyday masks). In both collections, as well as in Molloy's novel, the protagonists experience the discomfort of exploring the past and the feelings attached to it. However, they acknowledge that self-reflection is a necessary act that has a cathartic effect and that it would be easier to protect the "I" with a daily mask since the journey back to one's homeland or to the other side of oneself is a painful exercise. As the speaker in *Hemos llegado a Ilión* expresses, self-examination is a necessary challenge that she has imposed on herself:

> Esta es la estadía siniestra del infierno. Este avión, esta
> corazonada, este examen que rasga con papel la tinta.
> Hay que ir al nacimiento de la pena, a la herida mayor
> hay que curarla, hay que sobornar la sangre y entrar en
> cuatro patas a las entrañas de tu propio monstruo. (10)

> This is the sinister stopover in hell. This plane, this blow
> to the heart, this examination that scratches the ink
> with paper. You must go to the birth of grief, cure the
> greatest wound, bribe your blood and crawl on hands
> and knees into the entrails of your own monster.

The reader witnesses the process of transformation of the speaker's self: "Ya está la bayoneta preparada,/ya la barraca donde te ejecutan./Ya la memoria crece con sus crines./Eres otra, eres el difuso correr del arrebato de aquél que se desploma y lo reviven para una vez más reencontrarse con otra sombra y otra" (13) (The bayonet is already fixed,/already the barracks where they will execute you./Already memory sprouts with its mane. You are another, are the mad uncontrollable stagger of one who faints and they revive him to reencounter yet one more shadow and one more). The speaker reaffirms the "I" and the double experience of identification and lack of identification. The repetition of "Yo soy" (I am) gives the impression of creating and establishing a center; however, that affirmation is denied by what follows, a fragmentation of the speaker's identity:

> Yo soy la que no canta la esperanza,
> la que encuentra defecto en cada gesto,
> la que ausculta cada giro de voz,
> soy la ofensa,
> el rencor
> soy el golpe escondido que aprovecha
> el dolor con menosprecio. (25)

> I am the one who does not sing hope,
> who finds a defect in every gesture,
> who auscultates every nuance in the voice
> I am insult
> and rancor
> the hidden blow that disdainfully
> exploits pain.

In one of the poems of *Ras*, Alabau presents an extreme experience of a journey as a metaphor of existential concern. Here, the speaker arrives in a deserted, completely desolated land in the middle of nowhere. The speaker is by herself and, without knowing who she is, tries to understand her situation. The impossibility of finding out who she is persists until the end of the poem where she is seen at a dock, a place of arrivals and departures:

El sueño recurrente.
Llego a la isla.
Un valle de mar rodeado por un muelle
Oscuro el amanecer
Un avión aterriza
y deambulo buscando.
Hay que montarse al avión.
Se va.
Busco a alguien,
no sé a quién
El mar
El avión arranca.
Aterrada lo miro
Sola en la isla, en un muelle.
(*Ras* 34)

The recurrent dream.
I arrive at the island.
A valley of sea surrounded by a dock.
The dawn is dark
An airplane is landing
I stroll around looking
One must board the plane.
It is leaving.
I look for someone,
I don't know who
The sea
The plane is taking off
Terrified I watch it
Alone on the island, on a dock.

*   *   *

    In Molloy's *Certificate of Absence*, like in Alabau's poetry, the motif of journey is accentuated. Whereas in Alabau's poetry the speaker is usually between two spaces (Cuba and the United States), in *Certificate* there are no geographical points of reference as becomes apparent through the vague and diverse allusions to Buffalo, Paris, and Buenos Aires. The lesbian writer is a traveler who does not have a center or a place of reference. Moreover, the motif of the journey appears both at the beginning and at the end of the novel. The novel begins with the woman writer's arrival in the room and at the end the woman, finally liberated from the entrapment of the room, appears at an airport, feeling afraid and with her manuscript as her only comfort. The reference to the airport is not accidental but rather significant since it alludes to a transitory place, a place of arrivals and departures.

In Alabau's *La extremaunción diaria*, it is not only the speaker who experiences exile but also other immigrant women such as the Jewish woman in the bookstore, Aunt Claribel, and the tarot reader. In this book, there is solidarity among women who share the experience of exile in New York City. This solidarity functions as an introduction to the motif of sisterhood, which will be central in *Hermana*. In one of the poems of *La extremaunción diaria*, the speaker transforms one of the ten commandments, "love your neighbor," into a commandment of love among women: "cuando pienso en cristiana/pienso/ama, ama a tu hermana" (19) (When I think as a Christian, I think, love your sister). Here, the foreignness of the speaker is emphasized through her comparison with a Jewish woman, a wandering Jew, the classic outsider. In several interviews, Alabau has compared her own marginalization with that of Jews: "soy una automarginada de por sí, más bien como esos escritores judíos que siguieron escribiendo en ídish y que no aprendieron el proceso de darse a conocer" (I am a self-marginalized writer. I am like those Jewish writers who continued to write in Yiddish and never learned how to promote their own work.)[21] This connection reinforces the idea of displacement since a Jewish woman suffers a double marginality: as a Jew and as a woman. In *La extremaunción diaria*, the speaker's self-comparison to a Jewish woman may allude to the poet's marginality as a Cuban woman and as a lesbian who feels she does not fit the role prescribed for women by the Cuban community in exile: "me sentí la exiliada en el mundo del exilio/me sentí como lo que soy, la judía/me sentí como lo que soy, la escapada/ me sentí como lo que soy, la perdida" (19) (I felt I was the exiled woman in the world of exile/I felt like what I am, the Jewish woman/I felt like what I am, a runaway woman/ I felt just like what I am, the lost woman). The idea of being cut off from society has been reiterated by Alabau herself who lives under conditions she does not accept: "Some poets have seen the world we inhabit as a city of sorrow where they feel cut off. I share the same feelings and write about them. I guess it has to do with not accepting the conditions of life more than not just liking them."[22]

Whereas in *La extremaunción diaria* the speaker identifies with a Jew, in *Hemos llegado a Ilión* the speaker, while in her homeland, identifies herself with a shipwreck survivor. Such identification stresses the feelings of displacement attached to the condition of exile. By alluding to the survivor, the poet creates the notion of a double exile, since there is a strong connotation of decentrality and helplessness; the shipwreck survivor is someone already displaced (on a ship) who then loses that space. The references to Jewish women and shipwreck survivors are related to Alabau's own marginality in the world of exile and as a lesbian, as she has asserted:

> I suffer from different forms of exile, coming from
> another country, and being a woman, and a lesbian.
> I feel the last the most. Because of it I was forced to
> leave Cuba. To hide one's identity in fear of who
> knows what scorn is a punishment. With references
> gone, it becomes a very static way of life; it is
> anonymity, desertion.[23]

In *Hermana* and *Hemos llegado a Ilión*, representatives of legal and bureaucratic systems, policemen, immigration employees, and postal employees emphasize the motif of exile and marginalization of lesbian lives. In *Hemos llegado a Ilión*, the speaker elaborates her encounter with an immigration employee and with a woman who works at the post office. By calling the airport employee a "migratory woman" instead of the woman from Immigration, Alabau transforms a representative of legality and order into an exiled individual: "Me parece tener la compañera dentro, esa mujer migratoria que estampa pasaportes que dice como sabiendo que la lengua se traba, como sintiéndome el calor en las orejas: 'preséntese mañana'" (10) [I feel I have the Companion within, that migratory woman stamping passports who says as if aware that my tongue tangles, as if she feels the heat in my ears: "Come back tomorrow"!]. The certainty of the Immigration woman's discourse contrasts with the name the speaker gives her: "migratory woman." Here, the name the speaker uses to denote the employee suggests a relationship between the exilic condition and an existential concern: a routine job—checking passports—may provoke a condition of alienation like the one suffered by those who have left the country.

The discourse of bureaucracy and legality reminds the speaker of limits and social impositions. In *Hemos llegado a Ilión*, the identification card that the speaker has to carry with her at all times to present to authorities reminds her of the legal aspect of her exile as well as of issues of identity, since she is seen as a foreigner who needs to clarify who she is. There is also the ambience of fear and powerlessness originated in authority figures such as policemen or custom house officials. Aside from the universal elements of fear of discovery and punishment that accompany homosexual life, a distinctively Latin American component exists, a bloody history of dictatorship and repression.

On another level, the dialectic of inside/outside in *Hermana* and in *Certificate of Absence* is a metaphor for the marginality suffered by those who are"in the closet,"that is, those who hide their homosexual orientation to protect themselves in repressive societies. In *Hermana*, exile, criminality, and love affairs are linked, highlighting the secretive and transgressive character that prevails in the book. Both sisters (the one who left the country and the one who stayed behind in a mental institution) are presented as social outcasts. Through the representation of the sisters, Alabau expresses two different forms of marginality: that of those who are inside the closet living an alienated life and that of those who are outside the closet dealing with social criticism. In *Hermana*, the use of numerous verbs that indicate hiding, such as "scuttling away" and "slipping it off," attest to the relationship of lesbianism and marginality. An example of this secretiveness follows in a passage based upon the sexual intimacy of the sisters:

> Ser desertor
> implica que en cualquier ocasión
> cuando se habla de honor o de fidelidad,
> o de amor, o de heroicidad o de qué altura,
> uno se escurre por donde pueda.
> Significa quedarse fuera de las conversaciones
> y si uno se atreve a ponerse una máscara
> luego retirarla con alivio de que no había
> por ahí uno conocedor.
> Es no comer con fruición, no dormir a pierna suelta,

llevar una soga en el bolsillo
y ver, en caso de que el recuerdo volviera,
dónde aguantar la soga del ahorcado.
Es ser Pedro, el gallo y las tres veces,
es saber la sentencia de antemano,
es leer y no identificarse con la protagonista.
Es renunciar a los discursos y a los premios,
a las pequeñas alegrías. (18)

To be a deserter
means at any moment
whenever people talk of honor or fidelity,
or love or heroism or any noble sentiment,
scuttling away through the nearest hole in the wall.
It means being left out of conversations
and if you dare to put on a mask,
slipping it off with relief
when you find that your secret is safe.
It is not eating your fill, or sleeping at ease,
carrying a rope in your pocket
and in case memory returns, looking for a spot
where the gallows rope could be swung.
It is being Peter, the cock and the three times,
knowing the sentence beforehand,
not identifying with the protagonist in the book you
     are reading.
It is giving up speeches and prizes,
and small joys. (19)

These words underline the marginality and tenuousness of lesbian lives in patriarchal societies. Moreover, the two sisters in *Hermana* represent two conflictive sides of the same individual, one that strives towards homosexual identity and the other that reacts homophobically, rejecting the "abnormal" sexual orientation and identifying it with a destruction of the individual core:

Veo tu enfermedad afuera con formas,
esquemas, ruedas, presentándose
alimaña.
Aterida registro el interior

rapado, comiendo el primer hueco
que rastrillo.
La isla es cercenada desde el centro. (36)

I see your sickness emerging, its shapes,
its schemes, its wheels, a
predator.
Stunned, I examine my ravaged
entrails, probing the first hole
like a rake.
The island is being eroded from the center. (37)

Whereas in *Electra/Clitemnestra* madness is a central part of the erotic and the poetic discourse, in *Hermana* the speaker's sister's madness and her seclusion in a mental institution make clear the rejection of lesbianism and the connection that culture has established between lesbianism and madness. Thus, the theme of mental illness attests to the imposition of a pathological character on lesbians during the nineteenth and twentieth centuries.[24] The sister in the mental institution is an outcast living on the margins of society who suffers a form of exile in her own country. However, the motif of the insane sister in *Hermana* brings forth not only the myth of lesbians as madwomen but also the association of women in general with madness. That association has been common in patriarchal societies as documented by Phyllis Chesler, Elaine Showalter, and Jane M. Ussher.[25] Madness in Alabau's poetry also stands for women's anger, and it is a result of repression of female sexuality. The asylum is a territory with self-contained borders, limitations, and impositions in which the speaker's sister is shut away from society's sight and where she is controlled, and feared.[26] The speaker's sister, existing in a "bell jar" (echoing Sylvia Plath) and confined to an asylum for exhibiting antisocial behavior, is someone that society would like to eradicate: "...quisieran deshacerte, pobre huérfana, pobres ojos,/pobre bulto de pruebas y de mutilación" (30) [... they want to get rid of you, poor orphan, poor eyes,/poor bundle of trials and mutilation (31)]. Her madness and confinement are expressions of female powerlessness and function as a mirror image of the destiny imposed on women who do not fit the role of femininity dictated by society. Moreover, the sister's seclusion in Alabau's *Hermana* has an autobiographical and historical value since it alludes in particular to the experience of lesbians in Cuba in the 1960's during the infamous UMAP [Unidades Militares Ayuda en la Producción (Military Units to Enhance Production)] in which gay men were persecuted by the government and put in camps to "re-educate them"(as the revolutionary discourse phrased it) by trying to change their sexual orientation. In the film "Improper Conduct" by Néstor Almendros, another Cuban writer, Ana María Simo, stated that during the period of the UMAP camps lesbians were put in mental asylums and treated with electro-shock to change their sexual orientation.

In sum, the representation of interior and exterior spaces in Alabau's works textualizes the marginalization of female subjects who, from an exiled land, either a country or a room cut off from social and cultural bonds, attempt to go back to the space that they created in their imagination and their memories in order to rescue a history and cultural roots of which they have been deprived because of their lesbianism. In *Hermana* and *Hemos llegado a Ilión*, the speakers discover that there is no place for them either in exile or in their homeland. But at least, as Perla Rozencvaig has asserted in referring to Alabau's work, exile "offers her a space where it is possible to recover, in continuous circular variants, a familiar language, a terrible and marvelous time and, above all, a redeeming essence which allows her to recognize herself in the blurred and alienating mirror of that strange wall."[27] At the end of *Hermana* and Molloy's novel the subjects remain in exile, with language as the only possibility for creating a space in which they can represent themselves. Only through the journey in search of the past can the lesbian lovers create their own space somewhere in between homeland and exile, a horizon, as the speaker in *Hermana* asserts:

> Podemos fabricar en este descanso
> pegando las cabezas,
> juntas,
> un horizonte. (40)

> In this siesta time placing our heads together,
> the two of us
> can create
> horizon. (41)

When the writing process is completed, *Certificate of Absence*'s lesbian writer liberates herself from feelings for her ex-lover, and she is ultimately able to leave the room in which she has written and undergone self-analysis and self-recovery. Thus, the absence of love and the geographical exile have positive consequences in Molloy's novel; the lesbian writer, by completing her book, is able to gain strength:

> Desamparada se aferra a las páginas que ha escrito
> para no perderlas, para poder releerse y vivir en la
> espera de una mujer que quería y que, un día, faltó a
> una cita. Está sola: tiene mucho miedo. (158)

> Unprotected, she clings to the pages she has written
> so as not to lose them, so as to be able to reread
> herself and continue to live, waiting for a woman she
> loved who, one day, broke a date. She is alone: she is
> very frightened. (125)

*   *   *

"No hay cosa más pública que el amor."

There is nothing more public than love.
Lope de Vega

The ideological function of the relationship between inside and outside in Rosamaría Roffiel's *Amora* (1989) and Nancy Cárdenas' *Cuaderno de amor y desamor* (forthcoming) contrasts strongly with that in Magaly Alabau's poetry and Sylvia Molloy's novel *Certificate of Absence*. Although different to that in Alabau's works and Molloy's novel, the representation of interior and exterior spaces is still connected to the theme of lesbianism and love among women. Both in Roffiel's novel *Amora* and in Cárdenas' *Cuaderno de amor y desamor*, the lesbian subjects/speakers occupy a position of visibility that states their need to reappropriate cultural and social spaces which have been denied to them. In Roffiel's and Cárdenas' works, the characters are politically conscious lesbians who struggle to gain their rights. This particular representation in the works of these Mexican writers is due to several reasons, among them the fact that Roffiel and Cárdenas have been activists in both the Mexican Women's Movement and the gay movement and therefore have worked to gain political power for women, and in particular for lesbians. Thus, their texts reflect a didactic intention and articulate a direct political message that is not found in Alabau's works and Molloy's novel. In addition, Roffiel and Cárdenas have not suffered, like Alabau and Molloy, the experience of exile. Rather, they have been integrated into Mexican society.

In all four authors' works, lesbian characters need to detach themselves from the family home to have a space of their own. However, in Roffiel's *Amora* and Cárdenas' *Cuaderno de amor y desamor*, the lesbian characters and speakers live in apartments that they have obtained by themselves and in which there are no limitations or impositions. If in Alabau's poetry and Molloy's novel lesbians are in spaces that they do not own but which are temporary and transitory, then in the works of the Mexican writers there is a celebration of the lesbian subjects' homes and the harmony between the self and the home.

In *Amora*, there are two different types of home: the patriarchal home with heterosexual values, from which the lesbians need to escape since it is a place characterized by the undervaluing of women's lives, and the home that the lesbian characters establish by themselves and share with female lovers or lesbian friends in a lesbian community.

In *Amora*'s chapter I Lupe, the narrator, presents an identification between the discovery of her lesbianism and finding her own physical space:

> Hasta que fue una presencia cada vez más necesaria. Eso me ayudó a sobrevivir las últimas semanas antes de venir al encuentro de mi propio espacio y de mi tiempo en este departamentote, frente al Parque México, en el que vivo ahora con Citlali y Mariana. (13)

> Until it became a more necessary presence. That helped me to survive the last weeks before I came to find my own space and my own time in this huge apartment, in front of Mexico Park, where I now live with Citlali and Mariana.

Whereas in Alabau's poetry and Molloy's *Certificate of Absence*, lesbians occupy marginal or transitory places such as rented rooms characterized by narrowness, a metaphor for the closet, in Roffiel's novel the lesbians' home is characterized by its spaciousness, comfort, and the connection with the characters' affective lives:

> Nuestro departamento es inmenso, o al menos así
> nos lo parece después de meses de peregrinar en
> busca de un sitio decente donde vivir. Es de cuando
> las personas importaban, de esos de techos altos y de
> alma anciana. ¡Y tiene tres récamaras! Y son grandes,
> no de ésas de "compermisito" que construyen ahora,
> donde sólo caben la cama y la depresión que te
> invade por vivir en semejante espacio. (21)

> Our apartment is huge or at least that's how we see it
> after a long search for a decent place to live. It is from
> a time when people really mattered, with high
> ceilings and an ancient soul. And it has three
> bedrooms! They are big, not like the "excuse-me's"
> they build these days where all that will fit is one bed
> and the depression that hits you for living in a place
> like that.

The language that the narrator uses to talk about her house and its different rooms reinforces the feelings attached to it. The repetition of possessive adjectives and the use of the diminutive to talk about the space accentuates an emotional quality: "Mi balconcito, mi cocinita, mi departamentito entero se llenó de colores y de esa sensación tan especial de vida que dan las plantas y las flores" (22) (My dear balcony, my dear little kitchen, my whole darling apartment filled up with colors and with that special sense of life that plants and flowers give).

Amora's three main lesbian characters, Mariana, Citlali, and Lupe, living together and sharing responsibilities and life experiences, articulate the idea of a lesbian community or a new model of family:

> Las tres hemos formado una familia y hemos hecho
> de nuestro espacio un templo. Le hablamos, le

prendemos incienso, le ponemos música, le
compramos flores. Lo llenamos constantemente de
buena energía, de olores, de risas. (24)

The three of us have formed a family and made a
temple out of our home. We speak to our home, light
incense, play music, buy flowers for it. We keep filling
the house with good energy, odors and laughter.

The narrator emphasizes women's gatherings and meals
together, especially at breakfast, a time for the women to socialize
and talk about their dreams and emotions. In this novel, the
lesbians' space is not burdened with domestic tasks as has been the
common experience of women but rather with the enjoyment of
sensual and erotic pleasure as well as deep feelings of spirituality.

In *Cuaderno de amor y desamor*, as well as in *Amora*, the
speaker pays attention to the house and takes good care of it, and
she establishes a connection between her house and her emotional
and spiritual states. Cárdenas' speaker also establishes a relationship
between her house and the memories of her ex-lover. After her lover
abandons her, the speaker needs to re-establish her home and to
remove the memories of her lover from her house. The idea of home
is bound to the speaker's ex-lover:

Como dejaste la casa repleta
de pensamientos inexpresados
quebrantos
inútiles y promesas burladas
borré tus huellas de todas las perillas
quemé—a la vista—lo que me habías regalado
(con los retratos ya rotos)
y saqué cada uno de los clavos que clavaste en mis
    paredes. (*Cuaderno de amor y desamor 30*)

Since you left the house stuffed
with thoughts you never said
useless
sorrows and broken promises
I scrubbed your prints off the doorknobs
burned all your presents

(even torn scraps of your photographs)
and took out every nail you had nailed in my walls.

The speaker's process of rebuilding her home is a way of re-arranging her life and her emotional well-being without her lover:

> Aunque
> trafique todo el santo día con los objetos
> recompongo, uno a uno, los rincones de mi casa
> no se me vaya a poner como dicen que tienes la tuya
> bien entilichada.
> ¿No ves que las moradas son transfiguraciones del
>   alma? *(Cuaderno de amor y desamor 29)*

> Even though
> it means spending the whole day with things
> I move them around in my house, fixing up every
>   corner
> I won't let it look like yours
> a junk shop, they say.
> Don't you know that homes are mirrors of the soul?

Whereas in Alabau's *La extremaunción diaria* and *Hemos llegado a Ilión*, and Molloy's *Certificate of Absence*, interior spaces abound and are related to the characters' exilic condition, in Cárdenas' *Cuaderno de amor y desamor* and Roffiel's *Amora* there are continuous references to exterior spaces in which the lesbian characters are free to act and show their love for other women in public. The lesbian love discourse traditionally marginalized by culture and society becomes public in Roffiel's novel and Cárdenas' poetry. The public aspect of love is clearly expressed in Lope de Vega's verse "No hay cosa más pública que el amor" (There is nothing more public than love) which is one of the epigraphs of Cárdenas' *Cuaderno de amor y desamor*.

Expressions of physical intimacy between women in *Amora* take place in city parks and city streets. In chapter 11 "¡Horror!: El amor sigue su curso" (Love Follows Its Own Course), Claudia and Lupe show their love for each other in public. At the park the women caress and embrace each other sitting close together while children play and the routines of city life take place.

In *Cuaderno de amor y desamor*, there are many references to natural spaces, geographical places, and locations in Mexico City. Cárdenas, by placing lesbian relationships in exterior spaces, either rural or urban, contributes to the re-affirmation of the lesbian existence in either place. The co-existence of references to rural and urban spaces is synthesized in one of the appellatives that the speaker uses to call her ex-lover: "flor silvestre y citadina" (wild and urban flower). The speaker compares her ex-lover with natural elements, like a spring in the middle of a desert:

> Como fuente
> de enriquecidas aguas
> brotas de ti misma
> en la mera mitad del desierto. (12)

> Like a spring
> of nourishing waters
> you are born from yourself
> in the very midst of the desert.

While the first part of this book is a celebration of love with references to natural spaces, the second part—a diatribe against the ex-lover—focuses on urban life in Mexico City and alludes to Los Angeles, London, Acapulco, Jalapa, Guadalajara, and India. Cárdenas presents a contrast between rural and urban life, between the villages and Mexico City.

In addition, the speaker also uses metaphors connected with the city to name her lover. Such is the case of "muñeca del asfalto" (Asphalt Doll):

> Si habitamos el Distrito Federal
> las pueblerinas románticas tenemos que resignarnos:
> la vida no transcurre junto a un estanque
> sino a un costado del periférico.
> Allí, Muñeca del asfalto
> —bajo la lluvia—
> decidiste que esa noche dormirías conmigo. (7)

> If we live in Mexico City
> even we romantic rural types must face it:

life doesn't happen beside a pond
but right next to a highway.
Asphalt Doll, that's where
—one rainy day—
you made up your mind to sleep with me.

Cárdenas and Roffiel appropriate city landscapes by continuous references to highways, streets, cafes, and restaurants. In Roffiel's *Amora* the female lovers are seen in restaurants and cafes. In the streets the lesbian lovers confront men's flirtatious remarks. The lesbian lovers are presented as travelers, but not travelers in exile like Molloy's protagonist or Alabau's speakers. Rather, they are subjects who appropriate for themselves geographical spaces and who may move freely in public.

In summary, the representation of interior and exterior spaces in the works of Alabau, Molloy, Roffiel, and Cárdenas is a function related to the theme of lesbianism in their works. However, the treatment of the space in the works of Alabau and Molloy is different from that of Roffiel and Cárdenas. Whereas the first two authors represent the exclusion of lesbians from public and exterior spaces and the marginalization and repression of lesbians in homophobic societies, Roffiel and Cárdenas place their lesbian characters either in public or in private spaces that they are able to appropriate for themselves, compensating for the exiled positions lesbians traditionally occupy in Latin American societies as well as in other societies.

*   *   *

NOTES

1 Diane Fuss, *Inside/Outside: Lesbian Theories/Gay Theories* (New York and London: Routledge, 1991), p. 1.

2 Gillian Spraggs, "Exiled to Home: The Poetry of Sylvia Townsend Warner and Valentine Ackland," *Lesbian and Gay Writing*, Mark Lilly, ed. (Philadelphia: Temple University Press, 1990), p. 123.

3 Michael Seidel, *Exile and Narrative Imagination* (New Haven and London: Yale University Press, 1986), p. IX.

4 Julio Cortázar, "América Latina: exilio y literatura," *Cuadernos Americanos* no. 6 (November-December 1984): 7.

5 Amy K. Kaminsky, "The Presence in Absence of Exile," *Reading the Body Politic: Feminist Criticism and Latin American Women Writers* (Minneapolis: University of Minnesota Press, 1993), pp. 27-46.

6 Librada Hernández, Prologue to Magaly Alabau, *Hermana/Sister*. Translated by Anne Twitty (Madrid: Editorial Betania, 1992), p. 9.

7 Michael Seidel, Op. Cit., p. 10.

8 Gaston Bachelard, *The Poetics of Space*. Translated by María Jolas (Boston: Beacon Press, 1969), p. 6.

9 Emphasis has been added.

10 Francisco de Quevedo, "Retrato de Lisi que traía en una sortija," *Poems to Lisi*, D. Gareth Walters, ed. (Exeter, England: University of Exeter, 1988), p. 45.

11 Sandra Gilbert and Susan Gubar, *The Madwoman in the Attic: The Woman Writer and the Nineteenth-Century Literary Imagination* (New Haven and London: Yale University Press, 1984), p. 7.

12 Emphasis has been added.

13 Sylvia Molloy, "Sentido de ausencias," *Revista Iberoamericana*, Vol LI, Special number dedicated to Spanish American Women Writers, Numbers 132-133 (July-December 1985): 483-488.

14 I have modified somewhat Anne Twitty's translation.

15 Sylvia Molloy, *Las letras de Borges* (Buenos Aires: Editorial Sudamericana, 1979). Translated by Oscar Montero, *Signs of Borges* (Durham: Duke University Press, 1994).

16 Amy K. Kaminsky, "Sylvia Molloy's Lesbian Cartographies: Body, Text and Geography," *Reading the Body Politic: Feminist Criticism and Latin American Women Writers* (Minneapolis: University of Minnesota Press, 1993), pp. 96-114.

17 Ibid., p. 111.

18 Jorge Luis Borges, "Tom Castro, The Implausible Impostor," *A Universal History of Infamy*. Translated by Norman Thomas di Giovanni (New York: E.P. Dutton and Co., 1972), p. 31.

19 Cristina Peri-Rossi, "El exilio son los otros," *Las voces distantes: antología de los creadores uruguayos de la diáspora*, Alvaro Barros-Lémez, ed. (Montevideo: Monte Sexto, 1985), p. 257.

20 Elena M. Martínez, "El constante vacío de la memoria: Conversación con Magaly Alabau," *Brújula/Compass* 14 (Summer 1992): 6.

21 Ana María Hernández, "Las máscaras en el espejo: Conversación con Magaly Alabau," *Brújula/Compass* 7-8 (Winter 1990): 14-15.

22 "Voices of Three Cuban Women Poets in Exile," *El Gato Tuerto: Gaceta de Arte, Literatura*, Number 12 (Spring 1990): 1-2.

23 Ibid., p. 2.

24 Jane M. Ussher, *Women's Madness: Misogyny or Mental Illness?* (Amherst, Massachusetts: The University of Massachusetts Press, 1991), p. 84.

25 Phyllis Chesler, *Women and Madness* (Garden City, New York: Doubleday, 1972); Elaine
   Showalter, *The Female Malady* (London: Virago, 1987); Jane M. Ussher, *Women's Madness:
   Misogyny or Mental Illness?* (Amherst: The University of Massachusetts Press, 1991).

26 Phyllis Chesler, Op. Cit., p. 26.

27 Perla Rozencvaig, Prologue to *Poetas cubanas en Nueva York: Antología breve/ Cuban Women
   Poets in New York: A Brief Anthology*, ed. Felipe Lázaro (Madrid: Editorial Betania, 1991), p. 14.

CHAPTER II

RE-READING A TRADITION: LESBIAN EROTICISM IN MAGALY ALABAU'S *ELECTRA/CLITEMNESTRA* AND *HERMANA*

In the sea mist, walking blindly,
I, Electra, feel my garments
and the face that in hours became another.

Electra in the Mist.
Gabriela Mistral[1]

The purpose of this chapter is to examine the textual representation of sexual love and emotional intimacy in the lesbian relationships in Magaly Alabau's two collections of poetry, *Electra/Clitemnestra* (1986) and *Hermana* (Sister; 1989 bilingual edition *Hermana/Sister*; 1992).[2]

The first section of this chapter examines the specificity of lesbian eroticism in Alabau's *Electra/Clitemnestra*, its link with violence, competition, and rivalry, and the poetical process through which it is textualized. In the second part of this chapter, I will show how the erotic discourse of *Hermana* differs from that of *Electra/Clitemnestra*, stemming from the fact that *Hermana's* erotic discourse does not include violence or competition among women but rather integrates the physical aspects of women's relationships with the emotional, presenting an erotic discourse that connects love and sensuality.

Alabau's first book, *Electra/Clitemnestra*, presents a vein of lesbian eroticism that continues throughout her work and characterizes her writing. Women's identity, sexuality, and psychology as well as women's bodies are central themes in Alabau's texts. In *Electra/Clitemnestra*, a collection of poetry of great erotic charge, the female body is portrayed as the paramount object of desire. In her second book, *Hermana*, the representation of lesbian eroticism is transformed into an emotional bonding and physical connection as well. In Alabau's other collections, *La extremaunción diaria* (The Daily Extreme Unction; 1986) and *Ras* (Edge; 1987), violence has various manifestations and is not strictly linked to eroticism but rather to the experience of exile or an existential condition.

The erotic discourses in each of these two collections are distinct as they correspond to different definitions of eroticism. Nevertheless, they are both expressions of a lesbian sensibility. *Electra/Clitemnestra* and *Hermana* are lesbian texts because they highlight sexual and intense emotional relationships between women. In *Electra/Clitemnestra*, Alabau explores aspects of rivalry and competition within the context of a mother-daughter relationship whose origin is marked by erotic tension and desire. In *Hermana*, the poet explores the relationship of twin sisters, one who left the country and lives in exile and one who stayed behind and lives in a mental institution, another form of exile. The idea of "twin sisters" recalls one of the expressions used to designate romantic friendships among women in the nineteenth century, "kindred spirits," as Lillian Faderman has pointed out in her book *Surpassing the Love of Men: Romantic Friendship and Love between Women from the Renaissance to the Present*.[3] Following Faderman's hypothesis, my reading of the title of Alabau's book *Hermana* works as a metaphor for a lesbian lover. Very little has been written openly about lesbianism in Latin America due to the repression of women's sexuality in general, what prevails is an encoding (using Lillian Faderman's term) or a system of euphemisms that articulates lesbian and gay experiences.[4]

The title *Hermana* (Sister) is related to two different uses and traditions: one Latin American and the other North American. In some Latin American countries "sister" has been used by lesbians who attempt to protect their lesbian relationships from society's disapproval. Many lesbian lovers who live together claim to be sisters or cousins in order to protect themselves against criticism and rejection. The term "sister" and "sisterhood" within the Anglo and the African American feminist movement refers to the solidarity among women in the struggle for women's rights and it is identified with political power. In either case, Alabau's title *Hermana* (Sister) alludes to the centrality of relationships among women.

*   *   *

Lesbian eroticism in Alabau's *Electra/Clitemnestra* supposes a re-reading of classical Greek myths. The fascination of the Cuban writer with myths is reflected in the paramount function they have in her poetry. Alabau, in her readings of myths, attempts a new recollection that transforms a tradition. Three of Alabau's poetry collections introduce classical Greek myths. In her books, mythological female plots are central. Her books deal with female mythical characters and the readers witness a development in the relationship among the female protagonists from *Electra/Clitemnestra* to *Hemos llegado a Ilión* (Ilium; 1992). *Electra/Clitemnestra*, as its title indicates, focuses on two female mythical characters, exploring the relationship of Electra and her mother Clytemnestra. In *Hermana*, there is a reminiscence of the myth of Orpheus, the return to a past to rescue the speaker's muse, a sister or a lesbian lover, while *Hemos llegado a Ilión* evokes the myth of Demeter and Persephone.

Alabau's interest in mythology is part of a trend among women writers to rewrite the tradition that has silenced women's voices and that has perpetuated myths which stereotype women as passive and submissive. Rosario Castellanos (1925-1974), one of Latin America's most important female writers, and the French writer and thinker Simone de Beauvoir have analyzed the construction of the feminine as a myth. In *Mujer que sabe latín* (Woman Who Knows Latin), Castellanos, after analyzing different physical as well as psychological aspects of the social and cultural construction of the feminine, states that woman is a myth.[5] She points out that the origin of many myths of women is based on a patriarchal desire to paralyze and immobilize women. Simone de Beauvoir, in the section "Dreams, Fears, Idols" of *The Second Sex*, affirms that the construction and the representation of the world has been the work of men, strictly created from a masculine perspective and that it has been confused with absolute truth.[6]

Feminist writers began to appropriate the terrain of mythology, which had traditionally been a male domain, to their writings. The French feminist critic Hélène Cixous and the lesbian literary theorist and writer Monique Wittig have included mythological figures in their writings. In *Souffles* Hélène Cixous insists on the need for women to rewrite mythology and anecdotes from the Bible from their own point of view. Monique Wittig, who has been active in the French women's movement since the 1970's, is the author of several female-centered and lesbian texts:

L'Opoponax (1964), *Les Guérillères* (1968), *Le Corps Lesbien* (*The Lesbian Body*; 1973), *Broiullon pour un dictionnaire des amantes* (1976; translated as *Lesbian Peoples: Material for a Dictionary*; 1979) and *The Straight Mind* (1980). In her groundbreaking lesbian text, *Les Guérillères*, Wittig transforms expectations of male and female mythological characters and attributes female characteristics to male characters such as Dionysus, Prometheus, and Hermes. In *Les Guérillères*, Wittig destroys and recreates a variety of myths, creating her own mythology.[7] The most important myth that Wittig elaborates is the one of the Amazons (whose name derives from a practice attributed to them, the ablation of one of their breasts); women who live outdoors and raise only daughters, killing their male offspring.

In *Fábulas de la garza desangrada* (Fables of the Bled Heron), the Puerto Rican writer Rosario Ferré elaborates the mythological figures Antigone and Ariadne and reads them from a feminist perspective. In this book, which supposes an intertextual reading with *The Iliad* and Sophocles' plays, Ferré incorporates only female characters with the purpose of giving women a different history. The main idea of the book rebels against the way history has been read.

In *Las andariegas* (Wandering Women; 1984) the Colombian writer Albalucía Angel re-reads the myths of the Amazons. This text establishes a dialogue with Monique Wittig's *Les Guérillères* but changes the image of the warrior women. *Las andariegas* is a text that breaks with literary conventions by including forms of essay and poetry into the novelistic form, but it also breaks with the role that women have traditionally played. Albalucía Angel, centering her attention on the Amazon women, rescues feminine experiences and culture that have been in general silenced.[8]

Electra/Clitemnestra, a collection of nineteen poems characterized as myths themselves because of their dramatic, narrative, and circular quality, is marked by the experience of violence. *Electra/Clitemnestra*, like *Les Guérillères*, replaces heroes with heroines or female warriors. The central characters of this collection are Electra and her mother Clytemnestra.

Electra has been the subject of many plays and poems and there are several stories about her. In the twentieth century, the myth of Electra has been the motif of different literary works, among them the trilogy of *Mourning Becomes Electra* (1931) by Nobel Prize winner Eugene O'Neill, and *Antigone* (1944) by the French dramatist Jean

Anouilh. In the Caribbean, some adaptations of the myth have also taken place: *Electra Garrigó* (1941) by the Cuban author Virgilio Piñera and *La pasión según Antígona Pérez* (Passion According to Antigone Pérez; 1968) by the Puerto Rican writer Luis Rafael Sánchez.

Alabau re-elaborates the myth of Electra, daughter of Agamemnon and Clytemnestra, who had two sisters, Iphigenia and Chrysothemis, and a younger brother, Orestes. Her father, Agamemnon, left home, and Clytemnestra had an adulterous relationship with Aegisthus.

In the classical versions, Electra helps her brother Orestes to avenge the murder of their father Agamemnon by killing their mother Clytemnestra and stepfather Aegisthus who are Agamemnon's assassins. Using a different framework, Alabau's Electra kills her mother after she is rejected in favor of Clytemnestra's lover Aegisthus, who is now living in the palace. Unlike the classical myth in which Electra defends the values of the patriarchal family, Electra acts out of her desire for her mother. The classical myth has been read as synonymous with Electra's incestuous desire for her father. In this way Alabau deconstructs the myth of heterosexual love by replacing the Freudian (heterosexual) incestuous desire fantasy with a lesbian union. Here, Alabau re-elaborates the story of Electra and her mother Clytemnestra from the perspective of erotic desire between women.

Alabau's re-writing of this classical and prolific myth in her poetry collection *Electra/Clitemnestra* supposes and underlines the significance of reading and transforming a tradition. The epigraph of the book, taken from *Phaedrus*, connects the lack of correspondence between Alabau's reading and the traditional anecdote: "Falsa es esta historia: nunca anduviste en barco por el mar/ni viste las torres de Troya" (This story is false: you never travelled by ship nor saw Troy's towers). At the same time the reference to *Phaedrus* underlines an important theme of the collection: the theme of love. If *Phaedrus* presents the theme of love as a male phenomenon (since it was just male homosexual love), Alabau's collection will present love from a female perspective, that is, the collection explores the love-hate relationship of Electra and Clytemnestra. Through the process of re-writing the classical myths, Alabau inverts, changes, and challenges the meanings established and reinforced through the various traditional readings. She does not follow the classical interpretation of the anecdote but rather questions it.

In Alabau's poetry, the women, heroines who in the classical story act for the sake of the patriarchal family, are acting to carry out a personal desire for power or the satisfaction of their sexual desire. The women's actions are not prescribed by tradition; they are acting for their own sake, thus breaking the canon of conduct established for women. Their role, traditionally associated with passivity and submission while the man's role has been associated with action, is inverted in this book. Women are presented as ambitious and independent, while men are submissive and passive.

Alabau, in *Electra/Clitemnestra*, explores Electra's feelings of anger and jealousy; as she has killed her mother not to re-establish the order of the patriarchal home but rather as revenge against the woman who did not reciprocate her feelings. Electra acts out of jealousy since Clytemnestra has a male lover. In her revision of the traditional reading of the myth, Alabau rejects the revenge of the father's death as a significant motif in the story. Alabau interprets the killing of the mother as more significant than the killing of the father. She opposes Freud who has described and theorized the murder of the father as the foundation of the primitive horde. In this poetry the matricide takes place because of the intensity of the daughter's desire. With this crime the daughter is validating her lesbian erotic desire and establishing a new order.

The erotic discourse in *Electra/Clitemnestra* articulates diverse views on eroticism and is characterized by two things: the centrality of violence and the superiority of female sexuality. It shares views with those presented by the French writer and literary critic Georges Bataille as well as those of French lesbian writer and critic Monique Wittig. For Alabau as well as for Bataille and Wittig, violence is a key element of eroticism. At the same time, *Electra/Clitemnestra* adopts Luce Irigaray's view that female sexuality is superior to male sexuality since it is more diversified and does not require intermediaries.

Although Bataille's theory of eroticism is highly heterosexual and, moreover, male-centered, there are many similarities between Bataille's theory of the erotic and Alabau's representation of eroticism in her work.[9] The word "erotic," from the Greek "eros," alludes to all forms of love. Bataille recognizes three types of eroticism: physical, emotional, and religious. He defines eroticism as the sexual activity of humans to the extent that it differs from the sexual activity of animals; sexual activity becomes erotic whenever it is not rudimentary and purely animal. For Bataille, the word eroticism applies every time a human being behaves in a way strongly contrasted with everyday standards and behavior: "Eroticism always entails a breaking of established patterns, the patterns, I repeat, of the regulated social order basic to our discontinuous mode of existence as defined and separate individuals."[10] According to Bataille, life is associated with discontinuity while death is associated with continuity, and eroticism opens the road toward death and through death to continuity. It is that tension between consciousness and loss of consciousness that defines eroticism for Bataille. Eroticism replaces human individual feelings of discontinuity through the destruction of self-contained characters, that is, those who participate in erotic activity are imbued with a feeling of continuity and undergo an inner experience.[11]

Bataille also connects eroticism with violence, violation, and the sacred. He sees an undercurrent of violence as an integral part of human life. For him, taboos originated as a way to reduce the violence that prevails in life: the main function of all taboos is to combat violence.[12] For Bataille, eroticism necessarily involves several transgressions of a taboo, that is, the impulse to go beyond the restrictions that humans impose on themselves. In *Erotism: Death and Sensuality*, Bataille studies the incest taboo, the prohibition of sexual relations or marriage within the immediate family, that operates in almost every culture. Both the taboo and the transgression are related to violence since they have to do with the establishment of a law and a violation of that law.

Bataille postulates that there is an anxiety attached to the act of violating a taboo. The inner experience of the individual demands a sensibility to anxiety and links desire, terror, and pleasure with anguish. Eroticism, violating a taboo, is for Bataille intrinsically related to an inner experience of violence.[13] He considers physical eroticism a violation to those who practice it, thereby connecting death, the ultimate expression of violence and sexual arousal, to the desire and need to possess someone.[14] Wittig's erotic discourse, like Alabau's, supposes a different reading than that of Bataille since she explores eroticism and violence from a lesbian perspective. Wittig's *The Lesbian Body* presents rupture and violence at different levels: linguistic and cultural. Wittig innovates with the use of personal pronouns and combines the "I" and the "you." The female body, at the center of the poetic discourse, is presented as fragmented and divided since the speaker considers the body parts by themselves instead of in totality.

In Alabau's first book, lesbian sexual desire originates from an incest taboo and is permeated with violence, fear, and rage. Thus, sexual activity becomes a form of violence. The poetic discourse presents the desire to transgress the taboo that has emerged as a response to the violence of Electra's desire for her mother. Violence as an integral element of lesbian eroticism indicates the intense sexual component of the relationships.

Electra's violence is related to the need of expressing her love for her mother, as well as being an expression of anger, jealousy, and frustration toward someone who does not respond to her feelings. The daughter's exclusion from the mother's affective life is textualized by the position Electra occupies in the house. The mother is always inside the room; the daughter is outside. Electra occupies the place of an outsider as she is separated from her mother by a door. This physical separation is a metaphor for power versus powerlessness, as well as for the emotional distance between the two women.

The erotic discourse of *Electra/Clitemnestra*, filled with incest and images of violence and death, presents a conflict of mind and body; the mind is associated with rationality, the body with mindless impulses and violence. The collection of poetry textualizes the tension between the body and the mind, as the latter tries to control and stop the violence that emerges because of the transgression of a cultural prohibition.

The conflict between body and mind is present in many of the poems of this collection, particularly in poems XV and XVIII. Here, the speaker presents this struggle as the female protagonist wishes to control her desire through her intellect: "Calla pensamiento, atijera el cuerpo" (32) (Quiet thought, slash the body) and "Mis cuchillos son dientes/y sólo me detiene/mi mente"(30) (My knives are teeth/Only my mind/stops me). This struggle is also explored in poem XIII,"Obsession,"in which the head, as symbol of the mind, is central to Electra's guilt stemming from her desire for her mother:

> La cabeza se rellena, se rellena
> La cabeza debió ser corona
> La cabeza se vuelve primitiva

La cabeza camina sola ahora, vuelca el paisaje,
se mastica.
La cabeza es arrepentimiento del deseo entre madre
e hija. (28)

The head fills, is crammed
The head should be a crown
The head turns savage
Now the head walks alone, inverts the landscape,
chewing.
Head streaming repentance for desire between
    mother and daughter. (14)

The motifs of pain, madness, and obsession are clearly related
to violence in this collection. The pained voice of Electra is reiterated
throughout the collection (in particular, poems XI, XII, and XIII
entitled "El dolor" (Pain), "La locura" (Madness), and "La Obsesión"
(Obsession), are at the center of the collection and state the
significance of these three aspects, reaching a climax in poem XIX).
On many occasions the speaker stresses the intensity of her pain:

El dolor es un chorro de espanto.
No basta que se aguante el útero:
se sale por la boca,
borbotea.
Un animal salvaje que revienta con el abdomen hueco.
Electra vomita y se cubre la cara
y el dolor sale por la oreja y el ojo. (12)

Pain is a gush of fear.
Not only the womb must bear it:
it flows out of the mouth,
bubbles
A fierce animal split open its empty belly.
Electra vomits and covers her face and
pain pours from her ear and her eye.

Violence is also present in the representation of the body, an
important part of the erotic discourse in *Electra/Clitemnestra* as well as
in Wittig's *The Lesbian Body*. In Alabau's book, like in Wittig's, the

lesbian body is a fragmented whole and becomes the site of violence or is capable of inflicting violence upon someone else. Alabau's and Wittig's speakers pay significant attention to the face, eyes, ear, neck, head, hands, breasts, mouth, fingernails, teeth, pupils, and orifices as well as to saliva. Breast, milk, and blood are mentioned continuously. The fragmentation of bodies is a result of others' violent actions or violence directed toward oneself. The emphasis on the protagonists' pain in *Electra/Clitemnestra* indicates a relationship between violence and eroticism, with particular emphasis on the representation of the female body. The fragmentation of the body bespeaks the intensity of the erotic discourse. Symbolically, the eyes and the skin are emphasized. The former appears in shreds, splintered, while the skin, like in *The Lesbian Body*, is stripped: "...descuartizos de ojos/hacia fuera,/lanzas embarradas de carne, ropa tiznada de excrementos" (24) (...quartered eyes cut out,/lances smeared with flesh, clothes blackened with excrement).

In the representation of the body, images or metaphors associated with liquids play a central part as they reiterate the eroticism of the text. The mention of blood, sweat, wine, milk, saliva, and tears becomes part of the erotic discourse. These liquids are an important element of both lesbian and heterosexual erotic encounters in the text: "mi cara cadáver/surcos morados en el cuello/mancha en el cuello,/inmundicia/ hemorragia en el cuello" (30) (my face is the face of a corpse/hemorrhage on the neck/purple blotches Clytemnestra's neck/stain on her neck/filth). In poem XIII we read: "Su sangre es sudores negros./No hay quien la ayude./Grita y grita./El cielo se recoge ante su agonía/La agonía, la agonía./Le salen surcos en la piel" (28) (Her blood is black sweat./No one to help her./She cries and cries./The sky shrinks from her agony./Agony, agony./Furrows open in her skin). Moreover, by mentioning liquids like blood and sweat or even by comparing sweat with blood, the violence present in the poem is stressed.

Alabau connects parts of the body which are central to erotic pleasure with violent actions or violent objects. In poem XIX, Electra's hands express violence against her mother and frustration because of her unrequited love. With her own hands, Electra kills Clytemnestra ("La hija, como trofeo, arrancó con la mano el útero/ a la madre/lo lavó,/lo comió, devorando el primer recuerdo de su vida" (35) (The daughter for trophy ripped out her mother's womb/washed it,/ate it, devouring her first memory of life). Some images of bodies compare them to objects, while other images make references to them as the bodies of animals. In poem IV a spider seizes Electra's face and is compared to a hook in the ear gnawing at her head. The hand is compared to a sharp knife. Tadpoles are suckling shame from Clytemnestra's mouth. As Alabau associates the word"breast"with pointed objects such as a knife, axe, or a great mast, the relationship between violence and eroticism is vividly brought forth. On other occasions, the erotic discourse of *Electra/Clitemnestra* highlights the transformations of parts of the body under the effect of violent actions, in particular violent sexual encounters. In poem XIX Clytemnestra's body changes through Electra's aggression. Mother and daughter are disfigured and transformed in the violent act:

> hasta que su cara se hizo arena y llena de contorsiones
> el cuello se volvió raíces y una y otra vez
> los dientes agrietaron el rostro de la madre.
> La cara se volvió una pulpa roja, los tendones,
> alambres deshechos por la ira. (35)

> until her face turned to sand and contorted
> the neck became roots and once again
> her teeth raked her mother's face.
> The face a red pulp, the tendons,
> wires shredded by fury.

Alabau's treatment of lesbian relationships contrasts with her treatment of heterosexual relationships. Men are largely excluded from *Electra/Clitemnestra* as well as from Alabau's other work. Poem IX textualizes men's exclusion and celebrates women's actions and lives under the rule of Clytemnestra, a period which is characterized by its perfection, thus privileging life under a female government. It is a time of harmony with nature, non-coercion, and non-violence; wholeness is valued and the sense of connection between people prevails: "El sol es grande, y Micenas vive" (23) (The sun is great, and Mycenae lives). Clytemnestra here is used to represent a societal organization that is different from one powered by men. This is a period of peace and harmony in which there is time for enjoyment and recreation: "Hay paseos a Corinto, hay juegos" (23) (There are trips to Corinth, games). At the same time this harmony is highly ironic since men are fighting in the Trojan War. This poem provides a relief for the reader from the tension of the collection, and it is a prelude to three poems of rage and madness (Poems XI "El dolor" (Pain), XII "La locura" (Madness), and XIII "La obsesión" (Obsession).

In addition to the lesbian sexual encounters which are privileged in this text, such as Medusa and Clytemnestra's in poem VII, there are sexual relationships between women and men. The representation of both heterosexual and lesbian unions are marked by violence. In the case of heterosexual unions, women assume a physically passive role while demanding violence from men; they offer themselves without participating. However, heterosexual sex is presented as passionless, and it is associated with unpleasant bodily functions. In poem XIX the speaker identifies Clytemnestra and Aegisthus' sexual involvement with vomiting, thus underlining the idea that in this collection, sexual acts between men and women are not linked to pleasure.

The discourse of the body, always a cultural construction, is interesting in *Electra/Clitemnestra* because Alabau transforms culturally and socially constructed images of femininity and masculinity. Thus, she facilitates for the reader a possible reframing of the traditional discourse that has assigned diametrically opposed roles to people of different sexes. Alabau accomplishes this subversion by assigning women characteristics that have long been associated with men. Through a process of "masculinization," the female characters acquire physical strength and carry out violent actions. In poem XVII, Electra's muscular and physical vitality is emphasized ("Electra tiene dos manos fuertes/ejercitadas en su propio cuerpo" (23) (Electra has two strong hands/trained on her own body); while in poem XIX Electra is identified with a male warrior during a moment of rage. The masculinization that Electra undergoes in these poems prepares the reader for her final action as she kills Clytemnestra. Electra's desire to kill her mother emerges in poem XVIII, a poem of jealousy, in which Electra imagines her mother with a man. The use of three different verbs all in the future tense adds determination to the poetic discourse while reinforcing the violent desire to kill Clytemnestra: "Caminaré, simularé/Te sorprenderé" (33) (I will go walking, dissimulate,/ambush you). It is Electra, not Orestes as in the Classical myth, who enraged at her mother's rejection of her and at her own identification with Clytemnestra, performs the act of violence.

In other poems, such as poem IV, the speaker states that Electra is becoming a man. This transformation of the female into the male occurs in parts of the body that are identified as the most feminine (e.g., the breasts). The speaker transposes masculine symbols like knives or axes into female breasts:

> Electra es hombre.
> Sus senos tienen lenguas en el centro:
> un cuchillo, un hacha, un gran mástil.
>
> Electra actúa, Electra muerde.
> Se convierte en el padre,
> tiembla, cae delante de la puerta. (15-16)

> Electra is male.
> In the center of her breast are tongues:
> a knife, an axe, a great mast.
>
> Electra acts, Electra bites.
> She becomes her father,
> trembles, falls in front of the door.

Just as female characters are masculinized, so are male characters feminized. Thus, men are represented with the characteristics that patriarchal tradition has assigned to women. They are physically weak, suffer from the actions of others, and remain submissive. The process of masculinization of female characters and feminization of male characters is clearly seen in the representation of Electra and her brother Orestes. Electra's masculine characteristics presented throughout the collection contrast with her brother Orestes' feminine qualities. If in poem IV Electra becomes a man, in poem VIII, a poem that suggests an incestuous relationship between Orestes and Clytemnestra, Orestes is called "a girl of Micenas." All the adjectives used to describe Orestes highlight his innocence and softness: "limpio, lánguido"; "ojos serenos, sonrisa" (22) (clean and languid child; tranquil eyes and a smile). Similar contrasts appear in poem I "Electra," in which Agamemnon is portrayed as a wailing ewe, while Clytemnestra is compared to a bull. Agamemnon suffers from Clytemnestra's betrayal but cannot do anything about it. Alabau, by inverting expected sexual roles, challenges cultural constructions of the feminine and the masculine.

Throughout the collection, the representation of female bodies is transformed by the intensity of the erotic discourse. As part of the violence of this discourse, we see the animalization of the human body as humans act animalistically. In poem VII Clytemnestra barks and Medusa has hooves instead of nails and is a shameless panther with a crest. Electra's eyes become red hyenas and Electra howls. This transformational quality is underlined further as the body defies the reader's expectations and rejects the tasks traditionally assigned to its parts. In poem XIV, both mother and daughter are compared to animals in their sexual encounter: "La hija en turno aniquila a la madre/y cohabitan/como animales comién-dose"(29) (Daughter in turn annihilates mother/and they cohabit/ like animals eating each other).

Alabau, through the use of metaphors, metonymy, and zeugmas, reinforces the erotic quality of the poetic discourse. In the representation of the body, there are many metaphors in which a breaking with the expectations of the reader is produced through the inversion of elements. In some poems, the poet ascribes actions to certain parts of the body that in reality correspond to other parts. For example, in poem VII, instead of saying that tongues lick, the speaker says that faces lick. Through the use of metonymy, the expectations of the reader are challenged while the poetic discourse is strengthened. Sometimes the poet inverts the order of the metaphor: "Mis cuchillos son dientes" instead of "mis dientes son cuchillos"(30) (My knives are teeth; instead of my teeth are knives).

In other moments, a word signifying a body part is repeated, but in the repetition an adjective is added to qualify it. The repetition of nouns strengthens the body discourse and the correspondence of actions because it creates a more powerful impact on the reader. This repetition also joins the body of one character with the actions or the body of another character: "Si la mente no fuera recuerdo/si el recuerdo no fuera sentido/si la boca no supiera de la dulce boca"(31) (If mind were not memory/if memory did not live in the senses/if mouth knew nothing of the sweet mouth).

Given the erotic aura present in *Electra/Clitemnestra*, it is not surprising that the senses play an important role. The gaze, and the ability to see or observe, are especially relevant in Alabau's work.

This is interesting since the representation of the gaze has been traditionally heterosexual, and the power to look has been traditionally associated with men. There are many heterosexual narratives that privilege the male gaze. The classic French novel *The Princesse of Clèves* is a good example and, within the space of Latin American literature, the works of Juan Carlos Onetti provide other examples of female characters who are observed by male characters and narrators. In *Electra/Clitemnestra* the gaze is ascribed to female characters, and it is transformed into a key element of lesbian eroticism. We are thus presented with many references to the act of "seeing" and "being seen" by another woman. The speaker asserts being able to see and not to see, as well as mentioning the eyes. References to or descriptions of eyes abound in the collection.

The act of seeing is central to poems VI and VII. In poem VI, the speaker emphasizes the impossibility of seeing:"Los ojos no ven, no gimen, no encuentran./Los ojos son dos paños/ojos de efigie" (18) (eyes do not see, do not wail, do not meet./Eyes are two cloths/ effigy eyes). In the last line of poem VII, Electra appears in the position of an observer. She has seen the sexual encounter of her mother and Medusa:"En medio de la perfección vuelve la cabeza a dar el/último beso de la noche/y ve a Electra" (21) (In the midst of perfection she turns her head to give the final/kiss/of the night/and sees Electra). The end of the poem allows for two readings: Electra witnesses her mother's lesbian encounter with Medusa, or Electra, transformed into Medusa has made love to her mother. The last line of the poem maintains the ambiguity of whether Electra or Medusa was the one who made love to Clytemnestra.

The act of spying often occurs in these poems and is an essential element of Clytemnestra and Electra's erotic relationship. The secretive aspect of spying bespeaks the marginality as well as the private and forbidden aspect of an incestuous lesbian desire. In poem V, Clytemnestra asks Electra not to spy on her, demanding that the daughter control and transform her desire for her mother:"No me espíes/esconde la cara./Vuelca tus ojos de niña a mi vientre"(17) (Don't spy on me,/hide your face./Empty your child eyes into my womb).

Alabau takes the mythical character of Medusa, which is related to punishment, pride, and female competition, and transforms her into Clytemnestra's lover. It is interesting that in *Electra/Clitemnestra* Medusa, in conjunction with Electra and Clytemnestra, is part of a lesbian triangle that allows for the unification of motherhood and sexuality. There are different versions of Medusa. In some versions she is portrayed as the female serpent of the Amazons and her name means "Female wisdom."[15] In other versions she is the Ferocious Queen of the Gorgon Amazons who lives in Libya during the Bronze Age. In this version Medusa has an abundant and curly head of hair into which she intermingles black snakes. When she gallops, the snakes move around her neck. But when she joins in battle on her mare, all the snakes rise at once, hissing, furious, agitated with movement, sowing panic among her enemies. According to Wittig and Zeig, Medusa could petrify all those who rose up against her by the look in her eyes.[16] Medusa, who took advantage of the terror she inspired in mortals with her serpent hair and a stare which turned to stone all those upon whom it fell, has often been used by feminists like Hélène Cixous as a symbol of pride and strength.[17]

In poem VII the lesbian love-making of Clytemnestra and Medusa is highlighted by violence. All images in this poem used to present the lesbian sexual encounter denote great passion mixed with rage, jealousy, and fury:

> Medusa la restriega y la desnuda,
> la latiga, la sacude y la alza. Se le monta en el cuello,
> le embarra la cara.
> Lengua con lengua,
> espuma roja, espesa. (20)

> Medusa scrubs her and strips her,
> lashes her, shakes her, and holds her up.
> She mounts on her neck,
> muddies her face.
> Tongue with tongue
> red, thick foam.

Through the use of powerful, vivid language, Alabau imbues Medusa with an erotic lesbian strength. In this poem Medusa is the one who looks for Clytemnestra and finds her seated in her room. The space of Clytemnestra's house is transformed into the site of lesbian sexual encounters. Medusa approaches Clytemnestra and they make love:

Se tiran en una cama larga
Medusa monta un caballo largo
el techo las aplasta
y se unen
y se unen
y se aman
y se cortan de dientes
Medusa le entra por la boca,
por la espalda, y grita. (20)

[they] throw themselves into a long bed
Medusa mounts a long horse
the roof crushes them
and they unite
and they unite
and they love
and they use their teeth, cutting each other
Medusa enters her mouth, her back, and cries out.

The lesbian lovers' actions are reciprocal as is indicated in the repetition of the words "y se unen" (and they unite) y "se aman" (and they love), showing the equality of the lovers.

In this poem the speaker focuses on the power of the sexual encounter. Traditional phallic symbols such as serpents, trunks, and horns are included in the context of a lesbian relationship. The sexual act between the female protagonists is viewed first as a struggle and then as a moment of perfection. It is linked to a new beginning or the rebirth of Micenas: "Dos mujeres vibran, se amoldan/mueren abrazadas/y ya no hay heridas ni cráteres./Micenas renace" (20) (Two women vibrate, mold to each other/die in an embrace/and there are no more wounds, no craters/Mycenae is reborn).

If in poem VII Electra witnesses her mother and Medusa's sexual encounter, in poem XIX Electra witnesses the union of her mother and Aegisthus. Two love triangles emerge in the book, one of three women (Medusa, Electra, and Clytemnestra) and the other of two women and one man (Aegisthus, Clytemnestra, and Electra). Lesbian unions in *Electra/Clitemnestra* confront the predominance of binary combinations or a system of dichotomies, the heterosexual content of the Freudian Oedipus and the traditional stereotyping of lesbians into playing active and passive roles. By challenging the theory of a "heterosexual matrix" of love and desire as it has been accepted, poem VII transforms the Freudian notion of "primal scene." The reader discovers at the end of the poem that Electra has been observing Medusa and Clytemnestra. With the gesture of presenting Electra's love and sexual desire for her mother, Alabau replaces the Freudian incestuous desire fantasy with a lesbian union. Moreover, Alabau confronts the predominance of "binary combinations" since there is a triangle of women in the poem.

In her 1990 book, *Gender Trouble: Feminism and the Subversion of Identity*, Judith Butler discusses the inconsistencies of "binary opposition" theory (that is, a system of asymmetrical oppositions that divides masculine and feminine; culture and nature, etc.) and the assumption of a "heterosexual matrix" of love and desire.[18] Contrary to expectations the transformation of gender roles continues as Alabau's women assume and exchange aggressive and passive roles while giving and receiving sexual pleasure: "La leche de las dos se junta en una sola/y baja hacia el mar" (20) (The milk of the two becomes one/and flows down to the sea). At the end of the poem Clytemnestra and Medusa are united: "Clitemnestra ha dado sus senos duros/Clitemnestra ha recibido manos y manos y carne" (21) (Clytemnestra has given her hard breasts/Clytemnestra has received hands and hands and flesh). After the physical struggle of Clytemnestra and Medusa and their sexual union, the two women reach perfection: "*En medio de la perfección* vuelve la cabeza a dar el/último beso de la noche/y ve a Electra" (21) (*In the midst of perfection* she turns her head to give the final/kiss/of the night/and sees Electra).[19]

In the last poem of the collection, Electra kills her mother. She does not act to restore the patriarchal order but rather out of jealousy. There is a reversal of Electra and Clytemnestra's relationship as Clytemnestra, devoured by her daughter, is inside her. Electra bites and eats her mother's uterus and neck: "La hija, como trofeo, arrancó con la mano el útero/a la madre/lo lavó/lo comió, devorando el primer recuerdo de su vida" (35) (The daughter for a trophy ripped out her mother's womb/washed it,/ate it, devouring her first memory of life). The exchange of roles of mother and daughter reiterates their basic and primal connection. Through this act, Electra shows the desire to possess her mother by annihilating and devouring her. Death is at the beginning and at the end of Alabau's collection. Alabau connects being born and dying, showing the symmetry of both acts. Killing the mother is an expression of violence and the transgression of a taboo as well as an expression of eroticism. As the mother is devoured by her daughter, Alabau suggests a process of identification and appropriation of the mother. Thus, this aggression is a clear displacement of Electra's desire to possess her mother. Ironically, the killing of the mother is not only the realization of Electra's desire to possess her but also an act that makes impossible the realization of that desire.

The violence of the lesbian erotic theme is emphasized in this collection through Alabau's great synthesis and stylistic economy; all words and images produce a dramatic effect that evokes violence. In Poem II, the use of the imperative form emphasizes that violence. Eight of the twelve lines of the poem begin with a verb in the imperative:

> *Clávate* en mis piernas
> *Corrompe* mi vientre
> *Sácame* la noche
> *Entiérrame* la furia
> *Golpea* en un galope
> *Destiérrame*
> *Sacude* la capitulación del hombre y la mujer
> *Espanta*, ejecuta. (13)

> Aegisthus, *nail yourself* into my legs
> *Corrupt* my womb
> *Rip* the night away
> *Sink* fury deep in me
> *Strike* at a gallop
> *Exile* me
> *Jolt* the pact between man and woman
> *Sow* terror, execute.

We also see the use of the imperative in poem V: "No me espíes,/ esconde la cara./Vuelca tus ojos de niña a mi vientre/Nada, húndete en la almohada" (17) (Don't spy on me/hide your face./ Empty your child eyes into my womb./Swim, sink into the pillow). The poem ends with a clear resolution and a command: "Apártate, óyeme: vete" (17) (Leave, listen to me: get out).

Alabau creates an effect of violence not only by an extensive use of commands but also by repeating verbs that suppose aggression, thus increasing the intensity of the erotic discourse. That is the case of poem VII, in which the verbs that allude to sexual encounters are preceded or followed by the repetition of verbs that denote aggression and violence: "y se unen"/"y se unen"/"y se aman"/"y se cortan de dientes" (20) (and they unite/and they unite/and they love/and they use their teeth, cutting each other). Violence also appears in the epigraph of *Electra/Clitemnestra* that reads: "Falsa es esta historia nunca anduviste en barco..." (This story is false: you never travelled by ship...) taken from Plato's *Phaedrus*. The idea that the story is false as well as Alabau's rhetorical manipulation lends a new turn to the myths of Electra and Clytemnestra and suggests a different reading. This reading implies an act of violence because the meanings have been changed and challenged. Thus, the erotic discourse of *Electra/Clitemnestra* is not only founded on violent physical actions but on verbal violence as well. In this way eroticism becomes connected with a return to primitive freedom and with a mythological time. Furthermore, the relationship of Electra and Clytemnestra is conditioned by feelings of anger and rivalry. In poem III we read:

> No se vieron más.
> Se entrecruzaban en la escalera de piedra,
> dos líneas rojas
> tirando cada una la ira.
> Se escrutan los ojos hinchados.
> Los de Clitemnestra exhalan púrpura
> Electra se aguanta los párpados violetas de los
>   muslos. (14)

> They never saw each other again.
> On the stone stairway,
> two red lines
> crossed
> each one tugging rage behind it.
> Swollen eyes scrutinize each other.
> Clytemnestra's exhale purple
> Electra scrunches the violet eyelids of her
>   thighs.

The question of identity and selfhood is at the center of the mother-daughter dyad. In *Electra/Clitemnestra* Electra's selfhood has been defined negatively as separateness from her mother.[20] Competition between the mother and the daughter prevails, but it is interesting to note that sexual desire is presented: "Pero son dos mujeres encerradas en una historia de/espasmos/odios del útero/ entre fauces y cuernos,/hambre de tocarse./Sólo hay llanto/ y amargas luchas por quién es quién" (29) (But two women are imprisoned in a history of spasms/Uterine hatreds/Between jaws and horns/hungry to touch./There is only weeping/ and bitter battles for who is who). In this poem the rivalry between the two women is presented through the juxtaposition of two lines: "La destrucción de una/traería la redención de la otra/La magnitud de una reside en el aborto de la hija/La madre traga a la hija/La hija en turno aniquila a la madre" (29) (Destruction of one/would be the other's redemption./ Grandeur of one demands death for the daughter/Mother swallows the daughter/Daughter in turn annihilates mother). Thus, in *Electra/ Clitemnestra* the representation of the mother-daughter relationship follows the Freudian paradigm in which the selfhood of the daughter depends upon separation from the mother, while both struggle for power and the reaffirmation of self-identity. However, Alabau's reading detaches itself from traditional interpretation as mother and daughter are united by sexual desire. Here, the representation of the sexual desire between mother and daughter occurs through violent actions. The killing of the mother is an act of vengeance by a daughter deprived of love and nurturance. Throughout the collection the daughter symbolically reclaims nurturance and support, but Clytemnestra does not respond to her daughter's needs. In poem XI, "El dolor," Electra says: "Clytemnestra, me muero./Ven, ahuyenta el miedo" (25) (Clytemnestra, I am dying./Come, chase away fear). And at the end: "En su cuarto la madre escucha/muda está/no se acerca" (25) (In her room the mother hears, is mute,/does not come near her).

Culture and tradition have assigned women diametrically opposed identities of being either a bad woman or a good woman.[21] The first has been represented as a temptress and a ruthless destroyer such as Medusa; the second as the mother, the source of life. Alabau subverts this view by presenting Clytemnestra not as a nurturing figure but as an unaffectionate mother, a woman interested in sexual satisfaction. Through the representation of

Clytemnestra, Alabau confronts the masculine construction of the Great Mother archetype that reinforces and justifies women's exclusion from culture. Rosario Castellanos, Simone de Beauvoir, and Adrienne Rich have pointed out that maternity itself, as a natural phenomenon, confers no power on women. In spite of the fact that the mother is respected in her role, she is also subjugated through the institution of motherhood. In the archetype construct, the mother serves the husband in exchange for protection and support within three institutions: virginity, marriage, and the family. These institutions deny women access to sexual pleasure while objectifying them.

In *Electra/Clitemnestra*, the mother-daughter relationship, central to the notion of female as well as lesbian identity, is emphasized. This examination of the mother-daughter relationship has long been neglected in literature, art, and psychoanalysis. As Adrienne Rich stated in her 1976 book *Of Woman Born: Motherhood as Experience and Institution*, patriarchal relationships based on the notion of compulsory heterosexuality have favored the examination of mother-son as well as father-daughter relationships.[22] Rich, like Nancy Friday, the author of *My Mother/My Self: The Daughter's Search for Identity* (1977), is one of the North American writers who turned her attention to the mother-daughter dyad.[23] Rich has examined motherhood as an institution defined by male expectations and the patriarchal system. In the previously mentioned book, she delivers an interesting and well-documented account of relationships between mothers and daughters. She attacks the polarity of mother versus childless woman, insisting that it is false and has been created and reinforced by the institutions of motherhood and heterosexuality.

Most recently, and from a different framework, Teresa de Lauretis in her book, *The Practice of Love: Lesbian Sexuality and Perverse Desire* (1994), examines the mother-daughter relationship by challenging heterosexist presumptions. The role that the mother-daughter relationship plays in the construction of lesbian desire and sexual fantasies is analyzed in de Lauretis' book. In essence, de Lauretis, contrary to the view which sees lesbian desire as a return to a pre-Oedipal mother, sees lesbian desire as the daughter's return to an eroticized mother.

In Alabau's book *Hemos llegado a Ilión*, the mother-daughter relationship is evoked through the re-elaboration of the myth of

Demeter and Persephone. The myth of Demeter-Persephone is at the center of the work of feminist writers who value the Jungian archetype of the Great Goddess and the role of the mother.[24] This is a woman-centered myth. It is a story of separation and love that reinforces the idea of female connection. Demeter searches for her daughter and effects her return through her own divine power. In *Hemos llegado a Ilión* the speaker travels back to her native land to see her mother. The journey back to the speaker's country is a journey to Averno, associated with the underworld and with Persephone, since Persephone was the goddess of death and the underworld.

In *Electra/Clitemnestra, Hermana,* and *Hemos llegado a Ilión,* Alabau reclaims relationships among women: mothers and daughters, sisters, and friends. In her poetry, the mother-daughter, sister-sister relationships are metaphors for the relationships of female lovers. Alabau's treatment of the mother-daughter relationship shares views with the Freudian, neo-Freudian, and Jungian psychoanalytic schools, as well as with French feminism and American women poets such as Anne Sexton and Susan Griffin. Alabau's *Electra/Clitemnestra* follows the Freudian view, since the rivalry between mother and daughter prevails. In the Freudian approach, daughters feel ambivalent toward their mothers, who are seen both as rivals and as objects of desire. The powerful presentation of rivalry and desire among women, as well as the overt exploration of lesbian sexuality, remains Alabau's most radical thematic innovation.

Alabau presents an unusual connection between motherhood and desire. Allusions to milk (traditionally associated with either motherhood or as a metaphor for semen), are used in *Electra/Clitemnestra* in a strictly lesbian erotic context. In Poem VII, nipples, traditionally associated with motherhood, are seen here in a context of sexual pleasure. In addition, breasts and nipples are strongly eroticized and praised: "Sus pezones se hacen fuentes./El placer entra" (20) (Her nipples become fountains./Pleasure enters). Thus, Alabau portrays the body of the mother as the locus of pleasure not of nurturance. The Cuban writer's female protagonists challenge the representation of traditional views that have excluded women from the enjoyment of sexuality, while her poetry reaffirms women's access to sexual pleasure. In *Electra/Clitemnestra,* there is an interesting representation of the body of the mother, traditionally desexualized by men's need of controlling it. Here, Clytemnestra becomes Electra's, Medusa's and Aegisthus' object of desire. If traditional views have denied women access to pleasure, the rationale being the absence of a penis, in this collection, the poet privileges the clitoris as the most significant female sexual organ: "tantas serpientes en un clítoris tanta blandura fuerte, sedienta" (20) (So many serpents in a clitoris/such strong, thirsty softness). In *Electra/Clitemnestra* the presentation of the clitoris as the female erotic zone confronts and subverts the penis-centered psycho-analytic notion of sexuality which has long excluded women from access to sexual pleasure. Freed from the patriarchal discourse which has ignored the realm of women's sexuality, Alabau's women experience a spectrum of sexual pleasure.

*   *   *

Hermana: sisterhood = sameness = mutuality

Maybe all that my verses have expressed
is simply what was never allowed to be;
only what was hidden and suppressed
from woman to woman, from family to family.

"It May Be." *Alfonsina Storni.*[25]

Relationships between women, generally overlooked by society, including those of sisters, mothers, daughters, and female friends, are at the center of Alabau's collection *Hermana*. In this book, the author explores the bonds between two women: twin sisters separated by the circumstances of their lives. Thus, the speaker returns to her country in a poetic journey to reclaim memories of her life and her relationship with her sister. Places and objects that are described evoke childhood. The poetic voice recalls the other woman (the sister, a female lover, or a part of herself) as she reclaims a lost time and space. The speaker searches for her other identity and her connection with the other woman.

In *Hermana*, Alabau re-elaborates the myth of Orpheus which is different from other Greek myths. This male hero's fame was not related to his abilities as a warrior but rather to his skill as a singer and lyre player; he was praised for the power of his voice and the harmony of his lyre. Alabau presents the myth of Orpheus and Eurydice from a woman's perspective. Orpheus, who descended into the world to rescue his wife, Eurydice, is transformed into a female poet who descends to rescue her sister. Thus, a new mythology of the descent into hell is created. In this book, Alabau, like Wittig in *L'Opoponax* (1964), recreates the myth of Orpheus but replaces the heterosexual couple with a union of women. Like in *L'Opoponax*, Alabau's poem begins with the speaker's invitation to another woman to dream and love together. The journey is not the journey of the male poet in search of the woman who is his muse but rather the journey of two women as the speaker invites the other woman, her sister, to make the journey together.

The experiences of the twin sisters in Alabau's poetry are symbols of common experiences of women's lives. The sister who left the country may be interpreted as the woman who detached herself from the path established for her by society and her family. The one who stayed stands for the woman that accepts and succumbs to what has been set for her. Still, she remains an outsider. Through the poem, sisterhood can be read as a biological relationship or as the liaison of two women who do not have biological, but rather emotional, ties. The emotional bonding of the twin sisters challenges the traditional position that women have occupied in society, where they have been denied the opportunity to bond with other women and establish solidarity and support among themselves. However, it could be understood that the celebration of the "other woman" is a celebration of the speaker's "other-self." Thus, the speaker cannot escape the haunting presence of her sister, her other self being a lesbian lover or a representation of a part of herself which works as a portrait, a mirror image, or the threatening reminder of what could have happened to her.

The motif of twin sisters and the theme of sameness evoke the theme of the double. In Hispanic literature there is a rich tradition of doubles, from Don Quixote and Sancho, to the many doubles in the works of Cortázar and Borges, and to the use of female doubles in Rosario Ferré's stories.[26] The double traditionally allows for philosophical, psychological, or social dualisms. In Alabau's book it articulates a lesbian sensibility and it is a function of lesbian connectedness. The double in *Hermana* presents the idea of the opposing self, the "normal" self vs. the insane, but antagonism remains absent. Rather, closeness, empathy, and complementarity prevail. The fusion of the two sisters challenges the notion of normality and insanity as extreme poles. Instead, the speaker presents the contiguity and continuity of both aspects in someone's personality. In *Hermana*, the double also stands for the underlying opposition of psychic forces and the intertwining of normality and insanity.

In *Hermana*, as in *Electra/Clitemnestra*, the reader witnesses different veins of lesbian eroticism. The violent sexual and erotic relationships of the female characters of *Electra/Clitemnestra* disappear in *Hermana* and are redefined through the emotional attachment of the two sisters. The female bonding that defines the erotic discourse of *Hermana* is expressed in its title, "Sister." Contrary to what happened in *Electra/Clitemnestra*, where rivalry was a central aspect of the women's lives, in *Hermana* Alabau exalts sameness. In this book Alabau follows Adrienne Rich's theory which rejects the idea of rivalry among women; she sees rivalry among women as something created by society that does not emerge from a natural instinct. For Rich sameness allows for communication:

> This cathexis between mother and daughter—
> essential, distorted, misused—is the great unwritten
> story. Probably there is nothing in human nature
> more resonant with charges than the flow of energy
> between two biologically alike bodies, one of which
> has lain in amniotic bliss inside the other, one of
> which has labored to give birth to the other.[27]

This affective connection bespeaks a kind of knowledge shared by women, what Adrienne Rich has called a pre-verbal knowledge that flows between two bodies that are alike. Alabau seems to share with Rich the idea that sameness in physical characteristics enhances communication. Thus, lesbian eroticism is elaborated in *Hermana* on the premise that sisterhood = sameness = mutuality. While competition and rivalry define the erotic discourse of *Electra/Clitemnestra*, *Hermana* explores female bonding, tenderness, empathy, and the notions of security and trust:

> Tu mano agarrada a mí en confianza,
> tirando de una tela tan rota como tú, más gris,
> acostémonos en la hierba, suspiremos el momento,

prometámonos ser una, que una muera y que la otra
no quede sin mitad. Prometámonos sacar raíces
   en la otra,
que del abismo una semilla escape y en la lengua
crezca mezclándose con tierra. (26)

Your hand holding me confidingly
pulling at a piece of cloth as ragged as you, only gray,
let's lie down on the grass, breathe in the moment;
let's promise to be one, to let one die and the other
   not linger,
half-missing. Let us promise to root in each other,
so a seed may escape from the chasm, and mingling
   with earth
start to grow on the tongue. (27)

Hermana presents the connectedness of the two women as it
explores the possibilities of exchange between the subject and the
object, that is, the one who writes and the other who is the subject
of that writing. Duality and doubleness are motifs in both *Hermana*
and *Hemos llegado a Ilión* where there is a double search: for the
other woman and for time lost. This idea is expressed in the first
lines of *Hermana*:

Vamos a recorrer los cuartos en que anduvimos
juntas
las casas,
las sombras,
la noche, el mosquitero,
los zumbidos. También la madrugada
y los patios. (12)

Let us travel the rooms where we were
together
the houses
the shadows,
night, the mosquito net,
buzzing. Dawn too
and the patios. (13)

Duality and doubleness in *Hermana* reiterate that the construction of the speaker's identity is not independent from her sister's. The motif of the divided self reiterates the interdependability of lesbian identity as well as the broader meaning of the words sister and sisterhood and the communion of women. The duality stresses the character of the erotic discourse, that is, its lesbianism. Duality, reciprocity, and sameness of the female characters are expressed by the mention of mirrors that appear from the beginning: "tú y yo somos los espejos" (you and I are the mirrors). The allusion to mirrors, and later in the poem, to a carnival, reiterates the idea of a duality and doubleness which is constant in *Hermana*. Mirrors express the motif of the relationship of two of the same sex and the identification with someone else with whom one is in total or partial communion. In *Hermana*, references to mirrors, carnivals, and masquerade suppose the interchangeability of the sisters' identities. The mirror presents the notion that another woman facilitates the reflection of the speaker's self, and vice versa. This idea rejects the traditional presentation of women as reflections of men's lives or as mirrors in which men can see themselves. Furthermore, the poem may allude to lesbians' need to hide their identity as a strategy of survival in a heterosexist society.

The lesbian theme is textualized through the possibility of exchanging the "I" and the "you" as well as in the insistence on the first person plural "we" as the result of the unification of the "I" with the "you." Alabau, in the tradition of Monique Wittig's *The Lesbian Body*, has explored the use of the two pronouns in her work, articulating the communion of the lesbian identities through the fusion of the pronouns "Yo/tú" (I/you): "Dos horas tranquilas en un viaje que podría suscitar alegría/pero encontrarme contigo es como ahora tuyotuyotuyo" (*Hermana*, 20) (Two peaceful hours of a journey that might have been happy/but meeting you is like *Iyou, Iyou, Iyou*).

Hermana is a celebration and an exploration of the fusion and communion of the two women. The deep communication between the women is established at the beginning of the book through an epigraph from Soren Kierkegaard, that reads:

Así, cuando aprieto mis labios contra este papel no es mi sello lo que pongo sino el tuyo. Es tuyo pero yo lo guardo. Sabes también que en los anillos del sello las letras están invertidas: por eso la palabra "tuyo" con

que tú autentificas y validas la posesión, vista desde
mi lado se lee"mía."

So, when I press my lips against this paper it is not
my seal that I place there, but yours. It is yours but I
keep it. You know that in seal rings the letters are
inverted. Therefore, the word"yours"that you use to
authenticate and legitimize possession, from my
stand-point reads"mine."

The sisters' emotional intimacy is textualized through the
physical closeness and parallelism of their bodies:

Pero estamos acostadas en mi cama
gemelas, uniformes, confesándonos,
en un frío, y sin colchas
frente a un poderoso ojo
que me mira insolente
mientras dices: Ya pasó. (*Hermana* 16)

But we are lying in my bed,
twin, just alike, confessing each other,
in the cold, and uncovered
facing a powerful eye
that watches me insolently
while you say: It's over. (*Hermana* 17)

In some instances the sisters' closeness is presented through the
interconnection of their bodies. They are seen as part of one body,
and not as two separate entities: "No puedes extender los brazos/
porque los tienes registrando dentro/de mi espina dorsal" (36) [You
cannot stretch out your arms/because you left them searching/inside
my spine (37)]. The word "inside" denotes physical as well as
emotional ties and recalls the particular closeness of the women.

The erogenous zones of the twin sisters comprise the whole
body, and they are responsive to emotional intimacy. Their sensuality
is not direct and immediate as the speaker emphasizes an
atmosphere of intimacy and tenderness that does not appear in
Electra/Clitemnestra. The sexual climax, the height of excitation, is
seen as the moment of perfection. The orgasm produces a feeling of

pleasure and a fusion of the lovers while blocking the orgasm produces a feeling of anxiety and separation from the love object. In this book of poems the two women are visualized in front of a precipice symbolizing the tension, relaxation as well as the risk implied in the sexual act.

In *Hermana*, body parts are a function of the special connection of the two women as presented through the emotional charge of the sisters' closeness. Verbs such as "to touch," "to embrace," "to be bound together" abound throughout the book: "No nos sentaremos en el sillón/abrazadas, amarradas, donde a toda costa/respiraría en tus orejas música/para quitar el azoro que te circunda" (26) (We will not sit on the sofa/embraced, bound together, where from every side/music would breathe in your ears/to dispel the confusion around you.) Repetition of words such as "eyes" and "orgasm" help to establish the erotic quality that defines the book: "Tú y yo/mirando el techo, con ganas de orinar./Tú, tocándome los ojos./El orgasmo y tu llanto" (32) [You and I/looking at the ceiling/wanting to make water/You, touching my eyes/ Orgasm and your weeping (33)]. The connectedness of the sisters is reiterated through the idea that the speaker is eager to give her sister her own body:

> Abrazada a ella que está a punto de tirarse,
> que quiere llevarme al abismo
> (por la noche la música es dulce)
> una ciudad de sanatorios y uniformes blancos
> entra en mi cuerpo.
> Entregada a la violencia
> me rindo a tus caricias. (*Hermana* 48)

> Embracing her at the edge,
> embracing her who would drag me into the abyss
> (at night there is sweet music)
> a city of sanatoriums and white uniforms
> enters my body.
> Yielding to violence
> I surrender to your caresses. (*Hermana* 49)

Women writers, and especially lesbian writers due to society's impositions and restrictions, have encountered difficulties dealing with aspects of female sexual and sensual life. They have been discouraged from disclosing their own sensual nature. The reception of texts that present explicit lesbian sensual and sexual aspects of a female character has been traditionally negative. Such was the case of Radclyffe Hall when she published *The Well of Loneliness* (1928), Violette Leduc when she published *La Bâtarde* (1964), and Argentinean writer Reina Roffé when she published *Monte de Venus* (1976). Lesbian eroticism in *Hermana* is very subtle, as if Alabau were yielding to some external pressure. The erotic bonding is characterized by the communion of the women and the intimacy they share in bed or dancing together as "sisters":

> Bailamos y sabes
> que te daré mis ojos
> mientras esta canción
> fluya. (48)

> We are dancing and you know
> that I give you my eyes
> as long as this song
> is flowing. (49)

To conclude, the poetry of Magaly Alabau goes through a process of transformation from *Electra/Clitemnestra* to *Hermana* in which the representation of female relationships change from being violent, ambitious, self-oriented, and destructive to being more positive and female centered. This allows for the celebration of closeness and connectedness between women while reconciling their erotic and emotional lives.

*   *   *

NOTES

1 Gabriela Mistral, "Electra in the Mist," Translated by Sylvia Molloy. *Women's Writing in Latin America: An Anthology*, Sara Castro-Klarén, Sylvia Molloy, and Beatriz Sarlo, eds. (Boulder, Colorado: Westview, 1991), p. 133.

2 All references to *Hermana* are from the bilingual edition *Hermana/Sister* (Madrid: Betania, 1992).

3 Lillian Faderman, *Surpassing the Love of Men: Romantic Friendship and Love between Women from the Renaissance to the Present* (New York: William Morrow, 1981), pp. 157-177.

4 *Chloe Plus Olivia: An Anthology of Lesbian Literature from the Seventeenth Century to the Present*, ed. Lillian Faderman (New York: Penguin Books, 1994), pp. 441-445.

5 Rosario Castellanos, *Mujer que sabe latín* (México: Fondo de Cultura Económica, 1984; first edition, 1973).

6 Simone de Beauvoir, *The Second Sex*. Translated and edited by H.M. Parshley (New York: Alfred A. Knopf, 1953), p. 143.

7 Erika Ostrovsky, *A Constant Journey: The Fiction of Monique Wittig* (Carbondale: Southern Illinois University Press, 1991), p. 52.

8 Malva Filer, "Autorrescate e invención en *Las andariegas*, de Albalucía Angel," *Revista Iberoamericana* LI (1985): 649-655.

9 Georges Bataille, *Erotism: Death and Sensuality*. Translated by Mary Dalwood (San Francisco: City Lights Books, 1986).

10 Ibid., p. 18.

11 Ibid., p. 29.

12 Ibid., p. 41.

13 Ibid., p. 29.

14 Ibid., p. 28.

15 *The Woman's Encyclopedia of Myths and Secrets*, ed. Barbara G. Walker (New York: Harper and Row Publishers, 1983), p. 629.

16 Monique Wittig and Sande Zeig, *Brouillon pour un dictionnaire des amantes* (Paris: Grasset, 1976). Translated as *Lesbian Peoples: Material for A Dictionary* (New York: Avon Books, 1979).

17 Hélène Cixous, "The Laugh of the Medusa," *Signs: A Journal of Women in Culture and Society* 1.4 (Summer 1976): 875-893.

18 Judith Butler, *Gender Trouble: Feminism and the Subversion of Identity* (New York: Routledge, 1990), pp. 1-34.

19 Emphasis has been added.

20 See Jessica Benjamin, "The Bonds of Love: Rational Violence and Erotic Domination," *Feminist Studies* 6, no. 1 (Spring 1980): 148.

21 Robert Rogers, "Fair Maid and Femme Fatale," *A Psychoanalytic Study of the Double in Literature* (Detroit: Wayne State University Press, 1970), pp. 126-137.

22 Adrienne Rich, *Of Woman Born: Motherhood as Experience and Institution* (New York: W.W. Norton and Company, 1976).

23 Nancy Friday, *My Mother/My Self: The Daughter's Search for Identity* (New York: Delacorte Press, 1977).

24 Diane Purkiss, "Women's Rewriting of Myths," *The Feminist Companion to Mythology*, ed. Carolyne Larrington (New York: Harper and Collins, 1992), p. 451.

25 Alfonsina Storni, "It May Be," *The Other Voice: Twentieth Century Women's Poetry in Translation*, Joanna Bankier et al; eds. (New York: Norton, 1976), p. 20.

26 Rosario Ferré, "When Women Love Men," *The Youngest Doll* (Lincoln, Nebraska: University of Nebraska Press, 1991), pp. 147-153.

27 Adrienne Rich, *Of Woman Born: Motherhood as Experience and Institution* (New York: W.W. Norton and Company, 1976), pp. 225-226.

CHAPTER III

PRIVILEGING LESBIAN EROTICISM:
THE WORKS OF ROSAMARÍA ROFFIEL AND NANCY CÁRDENAS

The dichotomy between the spiritual and the political
is also false, resulting from an incomplete attention to
our erotic knowledge. For the bridge that connects
them is formed by the erotic–the sensual–those
physical, emotional, and psychic expressions of what
is deepest and strongest and richest within each of
us, being shared: the passions of love, in its deepest
meanings.

Uses of the Erotic: The Erotic as Power.
Audre Lorde

The works of the Mexican writers Rosamaría Roffiel and
Nancy Cárdenas share many of the same views on lesbian eroticism
as the poet and essayist Audre Lorde. Roffiel's novel *Amora* (Love in
Feminine; 1989), her poetry collection *Corramos libres ahora* (Let's
Run Free Now; 1994) and Cárdenas' poetry collection *Cuaderno de
amor y desamor* (Book of Love and Absence of Love; forthcoming)
propose a connection between eroticism, creativity, and self-
expression where, in the tradition of Lorde, eroticism is seen as
positive energy within women, part of their creative force, as well as
part of the social and political discourse for women's equality.

The early 1980's saw a proliferation of texts that reflected the
lesbian experience of African Americans. Audre Lorde's *Zami: A New
Spelling of My Name* (1982), as well as Ntozake Shange's *Sassafrass,
Cypress and Indigo* (1982), Alice Walker's *The Color Purple* (1982;
Pulitzer Prize winner), and Gloria Naylor's *The Women of Brewster
Place* (1982; American Book Award winner), are some of the works

by African-American women writers that were published post-1980 and present lesbian characters or communities formed by women.[1] These women writers are pioneers in breaking the silence surrounding African-American lesbian issues and themes in the United States and they have been supported by publishers like Kitchen Table: Women of Color Press and Naiad Press dedicated to publishing works by women of color and lesbian literature.

Lorde, in her essay "Uses of the Erotic: The Erotic as Power" (1978), defines eroticism as a source of power for women in connection with other spheres of life. She insists on the need for re-examining the significance of the erotic in women's lives and in appreciating the erotic as life-asserting for women:

> The very word "erotic" comes from the Greek word
> *eros*, the personification of love in all its aspects—
> born of Chaos, and personifying creative power and
> harmony. When I speak of the erotic, then, I speak of
> it as an assertion of the life-force of women; of that
> creative energy empowered, the knowledge and use
> of which we are now reclaiming in our language, our
> history, our dancing, our loving, our work, our lives.[2]

For Lorde, the erotic is connected to a sense of self and to an internal sense of satisfaction, and it is an integral aspect of emotional bonding among women. The erotic force in women's lives is also examined in another book, *Zami: A New Spelling of My Name* (1982), a lesbian text that focuses on relationships among women, considered by Lorde a "biomythography," a synthesis of history, biography, and mythology.

In *Zami*, Lorde presents a broad definition of lesbianism. From the beginning, the book explores the physical and emotional issues that arise from the protagonist's relationships with other women, and the protagonist assesses the significance of these relationships in her life as an artist. While using the word lesbian to describe women who have sexual relations with other women, Lorde expands its scope to include women whose emotional connectedness is centered around women regardless of sexual intimacy. Lorde's position of identifying any kind of female emotional attachment as lesbian, though politically convenient for raising cooperation and solidarity among women across sexualities, is also dangerous since it may overlook the sexual component of lesbians' relationships. Emotional bonding between women is at the center of *Zami* and sexuality, usually separated from women's selfhood and presented through the rupture with the emotional life, is presented here as an integral part of the black woman poet's experience and her creative work. Thus, the text raises the possibility of integrating both aspects of the life experience: emotional and sexual. In very political texts such as "Apartheid U.S.A" and "I Am Your Sister," Lorde stresses the need for women to organize across sexualities and examines the way that black lesbians are stereotyped by whites as well as blacks, by men and women.[3]

Lorde's *Zami* has had a definite impact on Rosamaría Roffiel's novel *Amora*, an autobiographical account of self-discovery through a woman's involvement with the Mexican feminist movement. Lorde's impact on *Amora* is evident in one of the epigraphs of the novel, a quote from *Zami*:

> My father leaves his psychic print upon me, silent,
> intense, and unforgiving. But his is a distant
> lightning. Images of women flaming like torches
> adorn and define the borders of my journey, stand
> like dykes between me and the chaos. It is the images
> of women, kind and cruel, that lead me home.

In an interview I had with Rosamaría Roffiel she commented on the influence of Audre Lorde on her work:

> I regret to say that her work has not been translated
> into Spanish. I have only read *Zami: A New Spelling of
> My Name* and her journal. I admire and respect her
> deeply.[4]

Whereas Lorde intertwines the narrator's lesbian love story with a testimony of the life of black women, particularly lesbians, in contemporary New York City, in *Amora* Roffiel intertwines a lesbian love story with reflections of women's experiences in contemporary Mexico City.

Amora bespeaks the centrality of love and eroticism in women's lives. Moreover, the title articulates the desire to tell a love story from a female point of view and to redefine the concept of love since the word "amor" (love), a masculine noun in Spanish, is transformed into a feminine one, thus allowing and reaffirming the novel's lesbian perspective. The transformation of "amor" into "amora" exemplifies the tendency among some women writers to invent a language through which they can articulate a female discourse that reflects their lives, sexuality, and bodies. *Amora's* concept of love is more inclusive than the traditional heterosexual form, and it is subversive because it points to lesbians' demands for visibility in a society in which lesbianism is not accepted.

The notion of love presented in *Amora* stresses emotional intimacy and solidarity among women. The emphasis on emotions and the significance of building a lesbian community are elements that the novel shares with Lorde's works. The narrator integrates a chorus of women's voices that speak of their interdependence. In this text we find great solidarity among women along with a sense of lesbian community and collectivity which provide the women with a sense of identity. The lesbian characters, Mariana, Citlali, and Lupe, live together as a family. Their relationship is based on equality, which contrasts with the inequality that prevails in the male/female relationships in the novel. These women represent a community of women committed to working together against sexist forms of socialization. They work on aspects of the feminist agenda: educating other women, working against violence to end women's sexual oppression.

In *Amora*, there are two chapters that are essential to the discourse of love and sensuality: "Somos mujeres, y nos gusta serlo" (We Are Women and We Love Being Women) and "El amor es una cosa esplendorosa" (Love Is a Splendorous Thing). In these two chapters, the dialogues between Lupe and Claudia allow for a discussion on issues of women's love and the need to redefine love and sexuality from a lesbian perspective. This perspective detaches itself from both the stereotypical constructions that identified lesbian love as unfulfilling and tragic as well as from a conception of love and sexuality that excludes emotional attachment:

> ...amemos diferente, sin cortarnos las venas, sin
> amenazar con tirarnos desde un puente en el
> periférico, terminar vomitando en Garibaldi o
> bajándole la novia a la amiga nada más para que
> vean qué chingona vengo este año, es decir, no

amemos así como dicen que amamos las lesbianas,
como si fuéramos la versión femenina del Charro
Negro. (*Amora* 33-34)

...let's love differently, without slashing our veins,
without threatening to jump off an overpass, or end
up vomiting in Garibaldi Square or laying a friend's
lover just to prove how tough we are; that is, let's not
love following a lesbian stereotype like a female
version of the Charro Negro Cowboy.

In Roffiel's *Amora*, like in *Zami*, there appears a strong claim
for discovering a lesbian form of sexuality that integrates sexual
pleasure with the celebration of other aspects of life such as feelings
and spirituality. The importance of feelings in *Amora* is manifested in
the abundance of romantic scenes in which the lovers share
confessions, listen to music, have long conversations, and enjoy the
atmosphere of romance and intimacy. Love-making takes place in
an idealized space where a celebration of the bodies and the senses
prevails. Intimate moments are romantically described: "Agua de
luna, fresca, con puntos de plata. Sábana de encaje. Sudario de luz.
Lecho de nácar. Dos mujeres. Dos. Cara a cara en este juego
irrepetible que es el amor" (71-2) (Moon water, cool, tipped with
silver. Embroidered sheets. Shroud of light. Nacre bed. Two women.
Two. Facing each other in this unique game that is love).

The concept of love and lesbianism in *Amora* claims women's
need of solidarity with other women; solidarity with mothers,
grandmothers, friends, or even unknown women offers a way of
expanding women's emotional as well as their political power. The
narrator recognizes the importance of women in her life, not only
lesbian women or lovers but women in general:

Y todas aquellas mujeres a quienes he amado,
aquellas a quienes me inventé que amaba, aquellas
que no pudieron amarme. A ellas debo mi fuerza. Por
ellas conocí mi capacidad de amar, y de llorar.
Aprendí la delicadeza de la pasión. Su presencia me
acompaña siempre, porque son parte de mi historia.
(*Amora* 36)

And all those women I have loved, those I thought
I loved, those who were not able to love me. I owe
them my strength. Through them I learned my
capacity to love, and to cry, I learned the refinements
of passion. Their presence is always with me, because
they are part of my history.

Amora's discourse on love and sexuality, as well as the
discourse of *Cuaderno de amor y desamor* by Cárdenas, is connected
to the views on female sexuality, bodies, and language presented by
French feminist critics Luce Irigaray, Hélène Cixous, and Monique
Wittig. These French critics' ideas on sexuality have had an impact on
the views presented by Roffiel in *Amora* and Cárdenas' *Cuaderno de
amor y desamor*.

Irigaray, Cixous, and Wittig have questioned the positions of
traditional psychoanalytic schools in undervaluing women's
sexuality by conceptualizing it in masculine parameters. They have
celebrated female sexuality by seeing it as superior to that of men.
Irigaray, in her book *Speculum de l'autre femme* (1974), attacks Freud's
theories on female sexuality and his Aristotelian concept of woman
as a castrated male, which he presents in his essay "Female
Sexuality." According to Irigaray, Freud's theory on sexuality is
related to the notion of specularization, a central idea in her work
that she discusses in *This Sex Which is Not One* (1984). Here, Irigaray
asserts that societies require that the female body submit itself to a
specularization that transforms it into:

> a value-bearing object, a standardized sign, an
> exchangeable signifier, a "likeness" with reference to an
> authoritative model. A commodity—a woman—is
> divided into two irreconcilable "bodies": her "natural
> body" and her socially valued, exchangeable body, which
> is a particular mimetic expression of masculine values.[5]

In that same book, by asserting that women's sexual pleasure arises
from the two lips of women's genitals touching, without the need of
any intermediary to obtain pleasure, Irigaray argues that female
sexuality is superior to male sexuality.[6]

The phrase "writing the body," coined by Cixous and Irigaray,
is often heard in regard to women's writing. Writing the body,

according to Cixous, refers to the need of women to inscribe their biological differences in their literature through the language they use and through the representation in their literature of body parts which are strictly female, such as breasts and vaginas. Cixous insists on the importance for women to include in their writing their own sexuality and the language that is connected to sexual differences. According to Cixous, writing is related to bodily functions and women, by writing, will return to their body. In her essay "The Laugh of the Medusa" (1975), which has become an essential document of feminist criticism and a manifesto of "écriture féminine," Cixous links sexual differences, language, and body. She insists on the differences in the psychosexual life of women as compared to that of men. Cixous emphasizes the use of language that values the irrational and verbal fluidity. She argues that the use of metaphors breaks with the hierarchy of reason which insists on the old dychotomy men-reason; women-imagination.[7] If the traditional psychoanalytic school has seen male sexuality as superior, centering it in the penis while undervaluing female sexuality, Cixous argues that female sexuality is superior because of its diversified character:

> Though masculine sexuality gravitates around the penis, engendering that centralized body (in political anatomy) under the dictatorship of its parts, woman does not bring about the same regionalization which serves the couple head/genitals and which is inscribed only within boundaries. Her libido is cosmic, just as her unconscious is worldwide.[8]

However, Cixous' analysis of female sexuality seems to be arbitrary. The postulates of Cixous' theories are highly controversial since they denote an inherent essentialism and biologism that help to perpetuate the stereotypes of women, reducing them to the sensual and biological sphere.[9] Roffiel's and Cárdenas' lesbian love and erotic discourses share with Cixous' writings the emphasis on a female language that is close to the body. However, they follow Wittig's lesbian perspective, emphasizing erotic relationships among women as seen, for example, in *The Lesbian Body* and the strength derived from a woman-centered culture as it appears in the Amazon society in Wittig's *Les Guérillères*.

In Roffiel's and Cárdenas' works the treatment of women's bodies and sexuality is central to the discourse of love, a discourse which is subversive since traditionally cultural discourses have either ignored women's bodies or have objectified them. Thus, the representation of the female body in Latin American literature, like everywhere else, has been neglected or used for sexist purposes. Sexuality within the Mexican tradition, beginning with the myth of La Malinche, the young Indian woman whom Cortés used as an interpreter and who became his mistress during the first years of the conquest of Mexico, has been associated with punishment and shame.[10] However, contemporary Latin American women writers, as part of the women's liberation movements and French psycho-analytic thought, are (re)discovering the female body and portraying it in a favorable light. Nancy Cárdenas, in a personal interview, stated the importance for women of valuing their bodies:

> Nuestro cuerpo es sagrado.... Tenemos que aprender
> a respetarlo y parte de ese respeto es identificarnos a
> nosotros mismos. Hasta el siglo XXI tal vez no esté
> más generalizada la idea del derecho que tenemos
> sobre nuestro cuerpo.

> Our bodies are sacred.... We have to learn to respect
> the body and part of that respect is to identify
> ourselves as who we are. It probably won't be, until
> the twenty-first century, that the idea of having the
> right to our own bodies finds widespread acceptance.

In Roffiel's novel and in Cárdenas' *Cuaderno de amor y desamor*, the representation of lesbian erotic encounters proclaims women's independence from men in many spheres of life: economic, social, and sexual. The liberation of women's sexuality from demands made by men allows women to reappropriate their bodies. In some of Latin American literature written by women (for example, the works of María Luisa Bombal, Teresa de la Parra, and Norah Lange), the female characters avoid erotic engagement with men to protect their freedom or to negotiate their freedom or their status.[11] Roffiel and Cárdenas, as well as Alabau, Molloy, and Umpierre, go a step beyond other Latin American women writers as they have created characters or poetic voices whose sexual identification and involvement with other women reaffirm a desire to break with a male-dominated culture.

Roffiel contributes to the creation of a feminist Latin American perspective by exposing readers to life-styles that are in opposition to tradition and that have not been openly presented before in other literary works.[12] Lesbianism breaks with the cultural construction of femininity and motherhood which has been at the core of women's subjection to men and to the private space of the house. By celebrating women's bodies as loci of pleasure, Roffiel helps to liberate the representation of women's bodies from male dominated views. Erotic and sexual scenes among women work as political statements and as claims for women's rights to a sexual life. Presenting relations among women in this way is a political act since it subverts the traditional idea that women are not entitled to enjoy their sexuality.

In *Amora*, as well as in Roffiel's poetry collection *Corramos libres ahora* (1994), a book of seventy-six poems, love and erotic relationships among women are central. The concept of love and eroticism is presented in *Amora* not only through the characters' long discourses but also through the physical and psychological representation of lesbians. Lupe, Mariana, and Citlali, well-centered women in the novel, challenge the stereotype of the lesbian as a tragic character. These characters defy the heterosexual values that insist on seeing lesbians as sick and dysfunctional people. This is clearly presented in the chapter entitled "Oye tía, ¿y cómo son las lesbianas?" (Hey, Aunt, What Are Lesbians Like?), in which Lupe's niece asks her about the behavior of lesbians while another girl defends the stereotypes. In this chapter, while exposing and confronting prejudices against lesbians, Lupe, echoing the discourse of Rita Mae Brown's *Rubyfruit Jungle* (1973), a classic in lesbian literature in the United States, asserts: "Mi querida Verito, las lesbianas son mujeres comunes y silvestres, de todos los colores, edades, nacionalidades y profesiones que simplemente aman a otras mujeres en lugar de amar a los hombres" (101) (My dear Verito, lesbians are ordinary normal women. They come in all colors, ages, nationalities, and professions and simply love women instead of men).[13] In "¡Hay qué susto!" (Oh, How Scary!), one of the poems of *Corramos libres ahora*, the speaker articulates society's fears and prejudices against lesbians while deconstructing the negative view of lesbians and showing the diversity of lesbian lives.

In *Amora* and *Corramos libres ahora*, although Roffiel's layered exploration of lesbian love is similar to Lorde's treatment of love, it does not limit itself to the lesbian option. While privileging lesbianism, Roffiel does not reject the possibility of other forms of love. This gesture allows for some openness in the lesbian erotic discourse since it does not overlook heterosexuality. Heterosexual women are among *Amora*'s characters, and the narrator herself points out that she does not reject the possibility of a relationship with a man even when she prefers relationships with women. She does feel, however, that it is more satisfying emotionally and psychologically for her to be with a woman.

The central theme of the poems *Corramos libres ahora* is love. In these poems Roffiel speaks about love, the female body, and sexuality, such is the case of "Gioconda," "Reencuentro," "Paisajes," "Danzón dedicado," and "Destino mayor." It is interesting to note that in the translation of "Gioconda," appearing in the anthology *Pleasure in the Word: Erotic Writing by Latin American Women*, the translator did not include the dedication, "a las mujeres" (to women) that appears in the poem in Spanish.[14] The inclusion of "a las mujeres" emphasizes the lesbian perspective which may be lost without the dedication. The poem supposes a rupture with the phallocentric views of our culture, in which women are objects for men. It is not accidental that the title evokes one of the best-known symbols of heterosexuality in the Western world, Gioconda or Mona Lisa. This subject of inspiration for Leonardo Da Vinci and symbol of femininity from an androcentric view in the Western world is removed from its heterosexual context and transformed in the context of a collection of lesbian poetry, into a lesbian symbol:

> "Gioconda"
> A las mujeres
>
> Mi vulva es una flor
> es una concha
> un higo
> un terciopelo
> está llena de aromas sabores y rincones
> es color de rosa
> suave íntima carnosa

A mis doce años le brotó pelusa
una nube de algodón entre mis muslos
siente vibra sangra se enoja se moja palpita
me habla

Guarda celosa entre sus pliegues
el centro exacto de mi cosmos
luna diminuta que se inflama
ola que conduce a otro universo

Cada veinticinco días se torna roja
estalla
grita
entonces la aprieto con mis manos
le digo palabras de amor en voz muy baja

Es mi segunda boca
mis cuatro labios
es traviesa
retoza
chorrea
me empapa

Le gustan las lenguas que se creen mariposas
los penes solidarios
la pulpa de ciruela femenina
o simplemente las caricias venidas de mi misma

Es pantera
gacela
conejo
se ofrece coqueta si la miman
se cierra violenta si la ofenden
es mi cómplice
es mi amiga
una eterna sonrisa de mujer complacida.
(*Corramos libres ahora* 7-8)

"Gioconda"
To women

My vulva is a flower
is a shell
a fig
a piece of velvet
full of aromas, flavors, and corners
is rose-colored
soft
intimate
fleshy

When I turned twelve it sprouted down
a cloud of cotton between my thighs
It feels, vibrates, bleeds, gets angry, wet, throbs
talks to me

Jealously between her folds
It guards the exact center of my cosmos
a tiny moon that inflames
a wave that leads to another universe

Every twenty-five days it turns red
explodes
screams
then I squeeze her with my hands
and whisper words of love

It is my second mouth
my four lips
It is naughty
It frolics
drips
drenches me

It likes tongues that are butterflies
supportive penises
the pulp of woman's plum
or simply

my own caresses

It is a panther
a gazelle
a rabbit
openly flirtatious if you pet her
snapping shut if you offend her
It is my accomplice
my friend
the eternal smile of a satisfied woman.

In this poem, the female sexual organ is the prominent motif. The vagina, presented through the metaphor of Gioconda's lips, appears at the center of the poem and is in close relation to the speaker's cosmos: "Guarda celosa entre sus pliegues/el centro exacto de mi cosmos" (it guards the exact center of my cosmos). The verses describe the vagina by using metaphors like flower, shells, fruits and velvet: "Mi vulva es una flor/es una concha/un higo/un terciopelo/está llena de aromas y sabores y rincones/es color de rosa/suave íntima carnosa" (My vulva is a flower/a shell/a fig/a piece of velvet/full of aromas, flavors, and corners/is rose-colored/soft/intimate/fleshy). The personification of the vagina in "Gioconda," as it smiles, speaks, and responds, adds to the supremacy and significance of female organs and female sexuality. The speaker sees her vagina as an "other," but an "other" with whom she has a very close relationship and whom she personifies by calling her: "mi amiga" (my friend) "mi cómplice" (my accomplice). In Roffiel's poems, female bodily processes, especially menstruation, are presented as integral components of women's lives. The poet is not only breaking with the traditional discourse that has undervalued women's experiences and women's physiology but also with the canonical literary discourse that has avoided the representation of bodily processes. Their literary representations reclaim women's bodies from cultural and social constrictions and liberate them from taboos, imposed by male-dominated views. Women's bodies, usually confined and subjected to their capacity to reproduce, are re-examined in these poems. In "Gioconda" and in "Historia," another poem of *Corramos libres ahora*, Roffiel detaches the female body from myths that have surrounded women and that are related to misogyny and to a generalized tendency to objectify women.[15]

In "Gioconda," Roffiel challenges the menstrual taboo, one of the most acute in many cultures, and which has served to exclude women from society and the workplace, since menstruating women are seen as contaminated and dangerous, or as paying the price for an essentially evil spirit that was part of their nature.[16] In this poem, menstruation is seen as a natural part of women's lives and it is transformed into a poetic source: "Cada veinticinco días se torna roja/estalla/grita" (Every twenty-five days it turns red/explodes/screams). These verses bespeak an understanding of the female body as well as an appreciation of its physiology. In this poem, the speaker, by talking about the vagina in a tender and caring way, establishes an intimate relationship with her own body as well as with another woman's body. This relationship is textualized through the insistence on the use of possessive adjectives that reveal the closeness between the speaker and her body. While accentuating the intimate tone of the erotic discourse, the use of possessive adjectives emphasizes closeness to the speaker's own body, since it is not common in Spanish to use possessive adjectives with body parts: "mis muslos/mis manos/mi segunda boca/mis cuatro labios" (my thighs/my hands/my other mouth/my four lips). After this long enumeration of body parts that are related to her own self, the speaker emphasizes a broader conception of herself "mi cosmos"/ "de mi misma" (my cosmos/my own self). The last line of the poem "una eterna sonrisa de mujer complacida" (the eternal smile of a satisfied woman) underlines and synthesizes the correlation between Gioconda's smile and the autoerotic pleasure of the lips that the poem articulates. Gioconda's smile, with its mysterious quality, seems to reaffirm the enjoyment of autoerotic activity and the celebration of female sexual and sensual pleasure.

*   *   *

In Cárdenas' *Cuaderno de amor y desamor,* the poetic voice clearly states the affective-erotic specificity of its discourse, a lesbian discourse in which the female speaker is invoking a woman lover. There are poems—or several moments of the long poem, since the entire book can be considered one poem—that are rigorously synthesized through the use of the words "amor/ desamor" (love and absence of love) taken from the title of the book. The poems of the first part of the book, in the tradition of Monique Wittig's *The Lesbian*

Body, are dedicated to the joy of erotic and affective relationships between women. They are a celebration of the lesbian body, praising the physical as well as the intellectual and emotional characteristics of the female lover.

Cárdenas' text presents a clear relationship between lesbian eroticism and the poetic discourse. The desire and the need to write emerge from encounters with the speaker's lover: "tus visitas me hacen mucho bien:/me dejan llena de poemas" (47) (your visits do me a lot of good/they leave me filled with poems). Cárdenas is aware that the expression of lesbian love is a political act, and throughout the book we find the desire to proclaim and establish a lesbian poetic space from which the lesbian subject may articulate her life and her experiences.

In this collection of poetry, the speaker elaborates an image of herself and an image of the beloved that are contrasted in the first, second, and third parts of the book (the book is not actually divided into three parts but, given its content, I consider the first "part" to end at page 14, the second "part" to be from page 15 to 40 and the third "part" to run from pages 40 to 51). In the last part the speaker overcomes feelings of resentment against her previous lover and begins to feel love for another woman. The discourse of love includes the addressing or the portraying of the lover. In the first part of the book, the image of the female lover is innocent and sensual at the same time, while the speaker contrasts childish and asexual characteristics with erotically-charged metaphors: "Te desnudas como niña/te restriegas como gata" (7) (You undress like a little girl/you writhe like a cat).

The speaker highlights the physical attributes of the lover by the use of rhetorical questions, which abound in the collection. Entire stanzas in the form of questions directed to the lover appear throughout the book. However, the nature of the rhetorical questions of the first part of the book is different from the nature of those of the second part where rhetorical questions are used to attack the lover. These questions create the effect of a dialogue between the speaker and the lover, adding a feeling of directness and communication between the two women:

> ¿Por qué a mi
> criatura de otras edades culturales
> entregarme la firmeza de ese músculo angelical,

las texturas diversas de tu intimidad
bañadas al instante por las aguas sagradas del amor,
el primer estremecimiento de tu entraña profunda? (9)

Why, you
creature from other ages
do you give me the firmness of that angelic muscle
the diverse textures of your intimacy
bathed by the sacred waters of love
the first quiver of your deep belly?

The use of a series of appellatives that name animals or elements of nature to address the lover characterizes Cárdenas' erotic discourse: "Potra/leona/flor/gacela/fiera" (3) (Filly/lioness/ flower/gazelle/wild animal). The use of a series without linking words creates the effect of synthesis and directness in the poetic discourse. On the other hand, since two of these appellatives are names of ferocious animals, they add intensity to the representation of the lesbian lover by stressing the primacy of the sensual and sexual in the women's relationship. In addition to the use of appellatives of ferocious animals to address the lover, the speaker represents herself performing animalistic actions: "ladraría al verte/ronrronearía después del éxtasis/aullaría cuando te vas/ relincharía al asomo de tu recuerdo,/balaría cuando te retrasas" (13) (I would bark at the sight of you/purr after ecstasy/howl when you leave me/whinny in amazement at your memory/would bleat when you are late).

The poet's exaltation of the beauty of the beloved includes the comparison of the lover's traits with elements of nature (fruits, shells, spring, honey, sand). By inverting the elements of the comparison and comparing nature to the paradigm of beauty established by the beloved, Cárdenas ascribes to the lover a beauty that surpasses nature: "Trigales y mieles, flores/tiene tu color/Arenas y conchas/frutas/tiene tu sabor" (5) (Wheat fields and honey/is the color of your skin/sand and shells/fruits have your flavor). Many of the comparisons found in Cárdenas' poetry are clichés in heterosexual poetry. If it could be argued that the poet reproduces poetic values of a heterosexual and male-centered tradition, it is also true that by using them in the context of lesbian love, the poet enriches the scope of Mexican literary tradition.

In Cárdenas' erotic discourse, the elements of a tropical geography are predominant. In her poetry, the use of appellatives of natural life and the representation of exuberant nature abound, and they reinforce the sensual aspect of the poet's discourse and the strength of lesbian eroticism. These images counteract the negative cultural values that have dismissed lesbians' experiences or stereotyped representations of lesbianism. Thus, Cárdenas returns the lesbian form of love to a natural space of freedom that breaks with well-established preconceptions:

> La piel húmeda y ojos fulgurantes
> dos cachorras
> juegan
> un juego sorprendente.
> Suspiros
> frenesí, locura emocionada:
> el orden se trastoca en concierto feroz.
> Delirios animales,
> ríos interiores desbordados
> confundidos.
> Nuestros cuerpos navegan a plenitud. (4)

> Skin damp, eyes flashing
> two pups
> play a surprising game.
> Sighs
> frenzy, wild emotions;
> order deranged in savage complicity.
> Animal deliriums,
> interior rivers in flood
> intertwined.
> Our bodies sailing in plenitude.

Cárdenas' eroticism is characterized by the speaker's desire to give herself to her lover without reservation as well as by a concern for equality in the enjoyment and pleasure of her lover and herself: "Toma,/de esto que soy/lo que desees/como primer regalo/como amoroso gesto que recibo/toma lo que soy" (6) (Take from what I am/whatever you want/as a first gift/as a loving gesture that I receive/take what I am). The lovers' correspondence is asserted through metaphors that articulate the same actions for the two lovers (pájaras hambrientas/íntimas/de vuelo acordado y terso) (7) (hungry female birds/intimate/their flight taut and harmonious). Moreover, the speaker stresses that in the sexual encounters both lovers obtain pleasure: "Algún/ruido imprevisto te arrancó del sueño/gozamos en un mismo gozo/la tibia humedad, los sonidos,/el espanto nocturno: éxtasis simultáneo/que llega por todos los sentidos" (6) (Some unexpected noise woke you/we shared the same pleasure/warm moisture/noises/nocturnal fear/simultaneous ecstasy/arriving through each of the senses). The equality and reciprocity of feelings and actions of the lovers is manifested in the use of a verb in the second person singular (you) and the use of the same verb in the first person singular (I) and then a sort of synthesis in the first person plural (we). The use of the plural "sabemos" (we know) reiterates the understanding, agreement, fusion and equality that prevails between the lovers: "Hablas/yo hablo: viejas historias./"Sabemos que la dicha ha comenzado" (6) (I tell you/you tell me/old stories/We know that joy has begun). In this way, Cárdenas' discourse includes and gives voice not only to the speaker's discourse but also to that of the other woman, her voice as well as her perspective.

Like Roffiel's "Gioconda," Cárdenas' *Cuaderno de amor y desamor*, speaks of women's life cycles (puberty, maturation, menopause) and the physiological and psychological changes these cycles engender. By presenting bodily functions and cycles in such a positive manner, and by integrating a physiological vocabulary (for example, adrenaline, hormones, and hemoglobin) into the poetic discourse, one usually alien to discourses of pleasure and sensuality, Cárdenas supposes a more comprehensive view of the body.

In this collection of poetry, pleasure of the body is attached to forms of enjoyment that are not only physical but also intellectual and emotional. This connection of different aspects of someone's life is presented through the verbal constructions linking a part of the body with a psychological or emotional effect: "Tu cuerpo/me gusta sin reservas:/cintura breve que afina las ideas/cadera liviana: aligera congojas/músculos firmes que mantienen la emoción" (7) (Your body/I like your body without reservations/thin waist to sharpen ideas/light hips to lighten up sorrows/firm muscles that uphold emotions). Cárdenas adds to the physical attributes of the lesbian lover the capacity to produce an emotional benefit by putting together: "waist and ideas," "hips and sorrows, muscles and emotions." This verbal construction (zeugmas) is innovative because the female lover appeals not only to sexuality but also to the intellect and to the soul of the other woman. Cárdenas breaks with the male tradition that has objectified women's bodies and centered appreciation of women in physical attributes rather than in their intellectual qualities as well as with the postulates of "writing the body" of the French feminists.

In both "Gioconda" and *Cuaderno de amor y desamor,* sexuality appears at the center of the text in conjunction with other aspects of women's lives. For Roffiel and Cárdenas, as for Lorde, female sexuality is attached to the emotional life of women. This is evident in the statement of Cárdenas' speaker that she exists only in the emotions that she produces. There seems to be a transformation of Descartes' axiom "I think, therefore I am," into "I feel, therefore I am": "Sé/que soy un recipiente de piel viva/casi repleto de materia palpitante/que existo sólo en las emociones que produzco" (10) (I know that I am a recipient of vibrant skin/filled with palpitating matter/I know that I exist only in the emotions I produce). While this book celebrates the emotional life of lesbians, it also recognizes how emotions can interfere with intellectual and rational capacities.

The lesbians of Roffiel's and Cárdenas' texts are characterized by a well-balanced life that challenges the stereotype of the dysfunctional lesbian, that is, a character that exhibits destructive behavior as is seen, for example, in Henry James' *The Bostonians* (1886), in Radclyffe Hall's classic lesbian novel, *The Well of Loneliness* (1928) and in Reina Roffé's *Monte de Venus* (1976). If traditional discourse has denied women access to sexual pleasure and a sexual life, the lesbian discourse of these writers celebrates women's sexuality by bringing it into other facets of their personalities.

In *Cuaderno de amor y desamor,* there is also a need to bring together women's sexuality, spirituality, and their everyday reality as an important part of the political struggle for women's rights. Cárdenas' discourse seems to evoke Lorde's assertion in "Uses of the Erotic: The Erotic as Power" that there is no dichotomy between the spiritual and the political and that the bridge that connects both of them is precisely the erotic:

> The dichotomy between the spiritual and the political
> is also false, resulting from an incomplete attention to

our erotic knowledge. For the bridge that connects
them is formed by the erotic—the sensual—those
physical, emotional, and psychic expressions of what
is deepest and strongest and richest within each of
us, being shared: the passions of love, in its deepest
meanings.[17]

In *Cuaderno de amor y desamor*, there is a spirituality based on
a trust in the human being, not on a god or an exterior force.
Spirituality in these texts is not related to any form of traditional
religion but rather to an experience of discovering the power of the
erotic. Religious faith and spirituality linked to religion are criticized
in *Cuaderno de amor y desamor*: "Te pavoneas como si las que creen
en algún dios/fueran más perceptivas, más espirituales, superiores
/Y yo pensando que más inseguras, más acomodaticias/más incultas,
más azotadas o todo eso a la vez" (25) (You strut yourself as if those
who believe in a god/were more perceptive, more spiritual,
superior./And I think to myself, more insecure, more opportunistic/
more ignorant, more troubled or all that at once). In Cárdenas'
poetry internal spiritual force is gained through meditation, diet, and
physical exercise. The speaker privileges the mind and the
possibilities of healing through mental and physical activities:

Como el cuerpo y el alma
son una y la misma cosa,
si te atrevieras
a mirarte al espejo
desnuda
te encontrarías con una mujer
rotunda y muy hermosa
a la que sólo le falta
una hora de yoga
diaria
para ser perfecta. (23)

Since body and mind
are one and the same,
If you dare to look at yourself naked
in the mirror
You will find a round, beautiful woman

> who needs nothing but an hour a day
> of yoga
> to reach perfection.

This connection between body and mind becomes more explicit later in the collection:

> el tiempo muerto del conflicto interior
> se transforma, oh dulce misterio de la disciplina muscular
> en energía erótica, armonía sustancial, capacidad
> de amar. (30)

> the lost time of inner conflict
> is transformed,
> oh sweet mystery of physical
> discipline
> into erotic energy, solid harmony, the ability to love.

What I have considered the second part of *Cuaderno de amor y desamor* allows for a broader perspective of love and eroticism, since it also expresses the transformation of happiness and good feelings of a relationship into sadness and vengeful attitudes. Thus, the lesbian eroticism presented by Cárdenas in *Cuaderno de amor y desamor* includes pain and sorrow as well as happiness. Opening the discourse to include the darker side of love helps to destroy the idealized image of the lover created in the first part of the book. The erotic discourse of this part of Cárdenas' book is centered on the speaker's pain: "No quiero hablar de este dolor./Es un invierno demasiado largo,/un árbol roto/ (Sólo puedo hablar de este dolor") (15) [I don't want to talk about this pain/It is too long a winter/ a broken tree/(I can't talk of anything except this pain)]. Here, the speaker's invocations of the lover are changed into angry commands demanding that the ex-lover forget her and not contact her again. The speaker creates a vengeful image of herself and a negative image of the ex-lover, and even uses resentful language with her ex-lover: "Bórrame de tu libreta/No vuelvas a marcar/ninguno de mis teléfonos" (15) (Erase my name from your address book/Don't ever dial/my number again).

This part of the collection is more political than the first part since it articulates, through remarks directed against the abuse of power of the speaker's ex-lover, the abuse of power of social and political institutions: "Soy peligrosa,/es cierto: siempre busco vengarme/de los dueños del capital, los burócratas/los curas y las mujeres que abusaron de mi cariño" (33) (I am a dangerous woman/it's true/ always out for revenge/on capitalists/bureaucrats/ priests and women who took advantage of my tenderness).

The speaker re-examines different aspects of the notion of love presented in the first part of the book by questioning her ex-lover's feelings for her and by attacking her inconsistencies. Thus, the speaker articulates another perspective of the erotic discourse, a discourse on the absence of love: "Me regalaste/sedas, lanas y algodones./No sé si tenerlos junto a mí/¿En el instante en que me los diste/ah, margarita/ me amabas o no me amabas?" (30) (You gave me gifts, silk/wool and cotton/I don't know whether to keep them or not/When you gave those to me/oh, margarita/did you love me or not?). The speaker reproaches the lover for not being able to love her: "¿Ni siquiera en los primeros días me amaste/como sabías que me hubiera gustado que me amaras?/¿Siempre compartí tus labios con extrañas alcoholizadas,/amantes ocasionales, amores pendientes?/¿Siempre, siempre?" (37) (Not even in those first days did you love me/did you know how much I would have liked to be loved? Did I always share you with alcoholic strangers/casual lovers/unfinished affairs/Always, always?). Later, while blaming her ex-lover, the speaker proclaims her own capacity to survive an uneasy relationship: "Cuando pienso/en las horas de tedio que me diste/oh, Venus Estresada/musito una plegaria: ¡Milagro, Milagro, sigo viva!" (17) (When I think about the hours of anguish that you gave me/Oh, Stressed out Venus!/I murmur a prayer: Miracle! It's a miracle that I'm alive).

Cárdenas' erotic discourse transforms and appropriates heterosexual cultural expressions by assimilating fragments of popular heterosexual love songs and imbuing them with lesbian meanings. Popular songs such as "Usted es la culpable" (You Are To Blame) and "María Cristina me quiere gobernar" (María Cristina Wants To Dominate Me) are part of the poetic lesbian text: "Ay, María Cristina qué me importa qué diga la gente/que soy tu gobernada en el amor" (50) (Oh, María Cristina, who cares if people say you dominate me). The meanings of these cultural expressions, placed within the context of a poetic lesbian love discourse, are thus subverted. Similarly, the author reframes observations about heterosexual behavior and places them in the context of lesbian relationships. Furthermore, Cárdenas proclaims the need to fight against stereotypical constructions and break with society's expectations of lesbians: "dejémonos crecer el pelo/como extensión viva dispuesta a la caricia,/evidencia de salud/señalamiento del día en que nos elegimos./(De paso haremos añicos el estereotipo)" (46) [let's let our hair grow/as a long invitation to caresses/witness to health/sign of the day we chose each other/(By the way, we'll smash stereotypes)].

This book by presenting a strong discourse against lesbians' stereotypes supposes a political act that claims and celebrates lesbianism as a possibility of life:

> Que no es
> antinatural, antisocial, antibiológico
> aceptan ya los que más saben
> de cuerpos y almas.
> Disfrutar este amor sin culpa
> es vivir en el siglo XXI:
> mujeres siempre en movimiento que se atreven
> a jugar a todo sin salirse de ellas mismas. (43)

> It is not
> anti-natural, antisocial, antibiological
> those who know bodies and souls most deeply
> now accept it.
> To live in the twenty-first century
> means to revel without guilt in this love
> women always on the move who dare
> to play any game without betraying themselves.

Cárdenas expands her view of lesbian love to integrate passion, spirituality, and love without contradictions or guilt:

> En ese amor del que te hablo
> no hay torturas ni contradicciones,
> no hay culpas ni agravios.
> Hablo
> del eterno paraíso de la salud emocional,
> de la inteligencia atávica de dos mujeres

capaces
en el verano de su vida-
de amar tan clara y apasionadamente
como dos niñas salvajes. (44)

In the love I am talking about
there are no tortures no contradictions,
no guilt no sorrow.
I am speaking of the eternal paradise of emotional
    health
of the atavistic intelligence of two women
capable
—in the springtime of life—
of loving clearly and passionately
as two wild girls.

Roffiel and Cárdenas, echoing Lorde's ideas, examine the question of loving and the power of the erotic. For the three of them, the erotic is a deep, enlightening force within women's lives, a source of creativity and knowledge.

*   *   *

NOTES

1 Ann Allen Shockley, "The Black Lesbian in American Literature: An Overview," *Home Girls: A Black Feminist Anthology*, Barbara Smith, ed. (New York: Kitchen Table: Women of Color Press, 1983), p. 83.

2 Audre Lorde, *Uses of the Erotic: The Erotic as Power* (Trumansburg, New York: Out and Out Books, 1978), p. 3-4.

3 Audre Lorde, *Sister Outsider* (New York: The Crossing Press, 1984).

4 Elena M. Martínez, "Entrevista con Rosamaría Roffiel," *Confluencia: Revista Hispánica de Cultura y Literatura*. Special Double Issue. Volumes 8-9, Numbers 1-2 (Spring 1993-Fall 1994): 179-180.

5 Luce Irigaray, *This Sex Which Is Not One*. Translated by Catherine Porter and Carolyn Burke (Ithaca, New York: Cornell University Press, 1985), p. 189.

6 Luce Irigaray, *Speculum of the Other Woman*. Translated by Gillian C. Gill (Ithaca, New York: Cornell University Press, 1985).

7 Hélène Vivienne Wenzel, "The Text as Body/Politics: An Appreciation of Monique Wittig's Writing in Context," *Feminist Studies* 7, No. 2 (Summer 1981), p. 268.

8 Hélène Cixous, "The Laugh of the Medusa." Translated by Keith Cohen and Paula Cohen, *Signs: A Journal of Women in Culture and Society* Vol. 1 (Summer 1976), Number 4, p. 889.

9 Hélène Vivienne Wenzel, "The Text as Body/Politics: An Appreciation of Monique Wittig's Writings in Context," *Feminist Studies* Vol. 7, Number 2 (Summer 1981): 264-287.

10 Octavio Paz, *The Labyrinth of Solitude*. Translated by Lysander Kemp (New York: Grove Press, 1961), p. 86.

11 See Francine Masiello, "Discurso de mujeres, lenguaje del poder: Reflexiones sobre la crítica feminista a mediados de la década del 80." *Hispamérica* 45 (1986): 53-60 and Francine Masiello, "Texto, ley y transgresión: especulación sobre la novela (feminista) de vanguardia." *Revista Iberoamericana* 132-133 (julio-diciembre 1985): 807-822.

12 David William Foster, "Review of Milagros Palma's *Bodas de cenizas*," *Chasqui* XXII, Número 2 (noviembre 1993): 160-161.

13 Rita Mae Brown, *Rubyfruit Jungle* (Plainfield, VT: Daughters, 1973).

14 Marguerite Fernández Olmos and Lizabeth Paravisini-Gebert, *Pleasure in the Word: Erotic Writing by Latin American Women* (Fredonia, New York: White Pine Press, 1993).

15 See Kate Millet, *Sexual Politics* (Garden City, New York: Doubleday and Company, 1970), pp. 47, 51, 62 and Jane M. Ussher, *Women's Madness: Misogyny or Mental Illness?* (Amherst: The University of Massachusetts Press, 1992), pp. 21-23.

16 Nel Noddings, *Women and Evil* (Berkeley: University of California Press, 1989), p. 37.

17 Audre Lorde, *Uses of the Erotic: The Erotic as Power* (Trumansburg, New York: Out and Out Books, 1978), p. 4.

CHAPTER IV

LESBIAN EROTICISM AND THE ACT OF WRITING: SYLVIA MOLLOY'S *CERTIFICATE OF ABSENCE*

I speak not with one voice
but with many.

Alejandra Pizarnik

The purpose of this chapter is to examine the relationship between lesbian eroticism and the act of writing in Sylvia Molloy's novel *En breve cárcel* (1981; translated as *Certificate of Absence*; 1989). This connection between lesbian eroticism and writing is brought to light in the text through the motif of Diana the huntress, a symbol of separation, rupture, and violence, all key elements of the novel.

Certificate of Absence tells the story of a lesbian who writes about her love affairs, dreams, and childhood. Through her writing, the woman analyzes her life as well as the process of writing fiction. The intertwining of her personal stories with reflections on the writing process allows for an interesting connection between tradition and singularity, and between writing and reading. By presenting a character dedicated to reading (interpreting) and writing about her lesbian love life, the novel supposes a rupture with and a separation from the traditional literary discourse.

While Molloy's novel indeed belongs to the literary traditions of the "nouveau roman" and the writings of the River Plate region, the lesbian themes articulated give the novel a space of its own within Latin American letters. Whereas the traditional literary discourse places heterosexual relationships at the center of human relational experiences, the novel privileges relationships among women. By writing, the woman claims lesbians' rights to articulate their lives as well as their history. However, most of the critics that have studied the novel have focused on its formal aspects, ignoring the novel's lesbianism. Perhaps this is due to the fact that in *Certificate* the lesbian identity of the protagonist-writer, as well as the identities of her lovers, is not problematized. Although in the novel the space of lesbian desire seems to be marginal—a small rented room—lesbians' existence, identities, and lives are at the center of the text.

The beginning of the novel is marked by the lesbian protagonist's arrival in a room. The interesting aspect of this room is that it is detached from emotional and social connections. Even though loneliness and emptiness are requirements for the protagonist's writing, writing and lesbian love and desire are inextricably intertwined. Writing emerges and is possible because of the absence of the woman's lover. Evoking and writing about her past love affairs becomes a passion and an obsession for the woman that provide the most erotic scenes in the novel.

The novel's erotic discourse, like that of Alabau's *Electra/Clitemnestra*, follows French notions of eroticism such as those proposed by Georges Bataille and those on lesbian eroticism presented by Monique Wittig in *The Lesbian Body*. Bataille and Wittig's notions on eroticism are different since the former proposes a view that is male-centered and heterosexist while the latter presents a lesbian perspective. However, Bataille and Wittig do coincide on two issues: first, that violence is an essential element of the erotic experience and, second, that it is textualized through the fragmentation of the body. For Bataille and Wittig, partners in the sexual act become unified, and the "I" and the "you" are interchangeable as a result of communication, the dissolution of the "I," and the discontinuance of space and time during the erotic experience. In *Certificate* Molloy underscores the notion of female bonding through the identification of the "I" and the "she." Furthermore, by relating the "I" and the "she" through violence and dissolution, Molloy keeps the discourse of love open, thus preventing the novel from falling victim to melodramatic views on love and female bonding. In the end, the conjunction of a passionate lesbian erotic discourse and a discourse on female centeredness defines the novel and gives it its singularity.

Eroticism and love in the novel are associated with passion, feelings of excitement, and overpowering emotions as well as with ambiguous feelings toward the loved one. The relevance of passion is stressed in the cover of the Spanish version (a painting by Michelangelo with the title "Woman Kneeling Down with the Instruments of Passion"). The various definitions of the word passion highlight the elements of violence and intensity present in the novel. Passion is defined as an intense and overpowering emotion; an eager outreaching of mind toward some special object or an ardent affection for someone; a fit of intense and furious anger, rage; any transport of excited feeling, and violent agitation.

The woman's need to write about her love life emerges because of the absence of love and the pain caused by her lover's abandonment. Writing is for the woman an exercise that has a dual and contradictory purpose. On the one hand, writing helps the protagonist recover her lost lover; on the other hand, it helps her to purge herself of the feelings she has for her ex-lover. The woman attempts to recall the feelings of the affair and at the same time to liberate herself from them. The double purpose of the act of writing in *Certificate* is textualized through the words "olvidar/fijar" (to forget/to shape):

> Comienza a escribir una historia que no la deja:
> querría olvidarla, querría fijarla. Quiere fijar la historia
> para vengarse, quiere vengar la historia para conjurarla
> tal como fue, para evocarla tal como la añora. (13)

> She begins to write a story that will not leave her
> alone. She would like to forget it; she would also like
> to give it shape, and, in shaping it, find revenge: for
> herself, for her story. She wants to exorcise that story
> as it was, in order to recover it as she would like to
> remember it. (3)

The words "forgetting" and "remembering" underline the ambiguity of the woman's feelings. "Forgetting" connotes abandonment and lack of feeling, while "remembering" connotes establishment, affirmation, and reassurance. However, the protagonist's desire to recover the story is not an attempt to recreate it in the way it was but rather as she now wants to remember it. Through the writing process the woman attempts to rewrite the history of her love life to give it meaning in the present. The desire to reshape a coherent story is motivated through the memories of various moments in her life, her dreams, as well as in her relationships with other women (her lovers, her sister, her mother, and her aunt).

Certificate not only emerges as a result of the rupture of a lesbian love relationship, but it also supposes a separation from a heterosexual literary tradition. The novel is based on a tension of several oppositional forces. This tension that characterizes the writing and the eroticism in the text is synthesized through the mythological figure of Diana the huntress.

In *Certificate*, as in Alabau's *Electra/Clitemnestra* and Umpierre's *The Margarita Poems*, female mythological figures are reread as symbols of lesbian culture. In one of the most singular dreams in the novel, the protagonist's father asks her to go to Ephesus to see Artemis, the goddess of fertility. However, the father's message, which is rather ambiguous, makes the protagonist unsure if she is being asked to go and worship or to destroy. The woman disobeys the imposition of the father altogether. Instead of going to Ephesus to see the goddess of fertility, the protagonist realizes she prefers Diana. The act of disobedience is necessary for the lesbian writer who takes her own path and detaches herself from what is established for her.

It is not accidental that the first part of *Certificate* ends with the dream of Artemis and the motif of fertility. The mythological figure of the huntress remains at the center of the novel (as the search for other women and the discourse of desire and violence have been at the core of the narration). The dream connects the literary and the lesbian erotic discourses by reaffirming the lesbian meanings of the text and destroying heterosexual alternatives. Thus, the first part of the novel symbolizes a journey in search of the significance that fecundity has for the woman. Procreativity is, in the case of the lesbian writer, not linked to her body and the institution of motherhood, but rather to her literary practice inspired by lesbian desire and love. The ungovernable huntress contrasts with the fixed, imposing image of fertility represented by Artemis:

> Ella prefiera otra Artemisa, otra Diana, la cazadora
> suelta, no inmovilizada por un pectoral fecundo, pero
> para esa figura no parece haber santuario estable. Sí
> la deleitan los pechos de esa otra Diana, pequeños y
> firmes, apenas perceptibles bajo la túnica con la que
> la visten sus celebrantes del siglo dieciséis en cuadros

> y estatuas. Disponible, armada de arco y flecha,
> seguida de lebreles, no se detiene; no la lastran los
> racimos de pechos, maternales y pétreos, de su
> contrafigura, la enorme figura de Efeso, cifra de la
> fecundidad. No, la otra Diana, la que ella prefiere—la
> Diana suelta—,no es fecunda. Reacia, desafía como
> cuerpo siempre deseable y siempre fuera de alcance:
> si hay algo de fecundo en ella es ese propio desafío,
> del que se alimenta. (78)

> She prefers another Artemis, another Diana—the
> free huntress, not weighed down by a breastplate of
> fertility–though no fixed sanctuary seems to have
> been built to her. Indeed, she delights in the small,
> firm breasts of that other Diana, barely visible
> beneath the tunic her sixteenth-century celebrants
> give her in their paintings and statues. Poised for
> action, armed with bow and arrow and attended by
> hounds, she is on the move: not burdened by the
> clustering stone breasts of her mothering
> counterfigure, the huge image at Ephesus, symbol of
> fertility. No, this other Diana, the one she prefers–the
> free Diana—is not fertile. Ungovernable, she
> tantalizes with her always desirable, always
> unreachable body: if there is something fertile about
> her it is the challenge itself, which nourishes her. (57)

Through the protagonist's preference for the violent and erotically charged goddess, the writer privileges lesbian existence and identifies violence with writing. Therefore, her passion for writing and the primacy of lesbian eroticism and lesbian meanings are brought forth through the novel's motif of Diana the huntress. Monique Wittig and Sande Zeig have pointed out the mythological figure's relevance for lesbian culture. In *Lesbian Peoples: Material for a Dictionary* they assert:

> [Diana the huntress] Most recent name of Artemis, the
> only known Amazon goddess to whom all the lesbian
> peoples remained attached after the time of the
> amazons, writing poems and celebrations in her name.

> Diana was represented as a goddess of the horned
> moon, hunting with bow and arrows. She was
> celebrated in Etruria during the beginning of the Iron
> Age as the one who calls to arms once again the
> amazons who, in that obscure time, had already begun
> to scatter. Each of those eager to rejoin the dispersed
> amazons consecrated her daughter to Diana.[1]

The protagonist's interest in Diana is based on the huntress' defiant character and multiplicity: "She would like to see herself in harmony, in a happy conjunction, with Diana, toward Diana, through *multiplicity and contradiction.*" (118)[2] Through the writer's identification with Diana, she breaks with impositions and expectations of gender roles since males have traditionally been associated with the ability to hunt and kill while females have been associated with the capacity to reproduce and nurture.[3] Her identification with the huntress underlines the woman's preference for mobility, change, action, and aggression instead of the passive role that has been assigned to women.

The mythological figure of Diana the huntress represents not only action and aggression but also lesbian sensuality and lesbians' rights to a sexual life. Lesbians' lives suppose a detachment from heterosexual norms of love, desire, and the established institutions of marriage and motherhood. Identified with what Diana represents, *Certificate*'s love discourse is characterized by violence, ambiguity, and elusiveness.

The lesbian protagonist of *Certificate* pursues violence because she sees that it allows her to strip herself of what is no longer a part of her and at the same time to keep what she has cast off. She writes with fury, in a state of passionate exaltation, guided by fear and anger. The protagonist's state of mind is one of restlessness and the need to write about her love affairs takes over her life. I was surprised to read in Gonzalo Navajas' article "Erotismo y modernidad en *En breve cárcel* de Sylvia Molloy" (Erotism and Modernity in Sylvia Molloy's *Certificate of Absence*) that "the novel's narrator has laboriously created a peaceful, private and clear cosmos, full of light, that contrasts with the dark appearance exterior to the self."[4] Navajas' affirmation is quite off target. *Certificate* presents a turbulent world of love in conjunction with notions of bonding among women. The novel's discourse breaks from conventional and ideal forms of loving as it presents loving with all its complexities and contradictions.

In *Certificate* lesbian love and desire have an ambiguous and mimetic nature that is elaborated through the abundance of love triangles. Molloy's strategy of introducing and privileging triangular relationships challenges and threatens the gendered system of binary oppositions. Triangles prevail throughout the woman writer's adulthood and childhood. While the writer examines her relationships with two lovers, Vera and Renata, the analysis of her relationships with them illuminates and leads to other triangular forms of love in the woman's childhood (the mother, the father, and the writer; the mother, the writer, and her sister Clara; the mother, Aunt Sara, and the writer). Triangular relationships are an important part of both the writer's consciousness and dreams. In the first dream of the novel the significance of triangles is established:

> Tres mujeres jóvenes, rubias, muy grandes, en un
> campo de pastos muy altos. Las mujeres irradian luz,
> la claridad de la escena es total y perfecta. Llevan
> túnicas blancas, cruzadas por una diagonal roja y
> bastarda, buscan el mar. Se dirigen a ella para que las
> oriente. La contrafigura se da dentro del mismo
> sueño. (21)

> Three tall blond young women, radiating light, stand
> in a field of high grass. The scene is dazzling and
> perfect. The women are wearing white tunics with a
> red diagonal stripe. They are looking for the sea and
> turn to her for directions. A counter-image appears in
> the same dream. (9)

As Magdalena García Pinto has noted in her article "La escritura de la pasión y la pasión de la escritura: *En breve cárcel*, de Sylvia Molloy," (The Writing of Passion and the Passion for Writing in Sylvia Molloy's *Certificate of Absence*) the motif of the triangle is also related to Diana since Hecate who was represented with three bodies or three heads was also known as Trivia or Diana of the Crossroads.[5]

Triangular love relationships are connected to jealousy, another motif of the novel's love discourse. The mentioning of the opera based on Shakespeare's *Othello* in chapter 3 (part I) reiterates the triangular structure and jealousy. The situation of Desdemona, Othello, and Roderigo is transformed in the novel into a lesbian triangle. Jealousy reinforces the triangular nature of the love discourse since it involves a third person toward whom envy is directed. It contains an element of love for someone as well as an element of fascination with the beloved's lover. Jealousy is here related to violence since it evokes the desire to take the loved one away from the relationship with someone else. When this attempt fails, there is a feeling of impotence, anger, irritation, and discomfort for not being able to obtain the desired object of love. Envy, jealousy, and rivalry are among the sources of resentment in the novel and provoke the writer to spy on and appropriate the lives of others.

Triangular relationships and feelings of jealousy offer the woman writer the necessary distance to analyze her love life and to reaffirm her desire to look at what is forbidden and secretive. Love triangles and jealousy prevent the woman from getting too close to a lover and reiterate the ambiguity of her feelings. The involvement with two women allows the protagonist to keep her emotions in perspective during the act of writing.

Writing in the novel emerges as a process of reading the woman's relationships with other women. The processes of writing and reading imply the appropriation of other women. The definition of reading given by Julia Kristeva has stressed the relationship between the act of reading and an act of aggressive appropriation: Reading was also to collect, to spy, to take from, to steal.[6]

The appropriation of others through the acts of writing and reading is connected to the novel's narcissism, the self-absorbed aspect of the writer who contemplates herself and her body through the exploration of her relationships with other women. Writing becomes the narcissistic tool for the protagonist that allows her to examine her life through others and through the use of a third-person narrator. The narcissism of such an act is something that Molloy has recognized. In an interview with Magdalena García Pinto she states:

> I've always been attracted to spying, which is what I
> did when I was a child; it's the idea of seeing the
> forbidden, the hidden, of coming upon what is
> strange. And the novel was a way of spying on
> myself, of spying on the material I'd tried to take out

of myself by using third person. Without doubt it's
very narcissistic, looking at yourself in third person.[7]

Narcissism becomes obvious in the significance that the gaze
and glance have in the novel. Gazes and glances are alluded to
through a series of references to "endless board games," a metaphor
for the woman's looking at herself and seeing herself through the
image of others. The conjunction and repetition of "ritos/espejos
enfrentados/infancia" (rituals/two facing mirrors/childhood) refer to
the narcissism of the woman writer as well as that of the exercise of
writing. Whereas references to mirrors create a doubleness, facing
mirrors create multiplicity. Mirrors, by bespeaking the motif of
sameness, are also a reference to the woman's lesbianism and her
love for someone like herself. The voyeurism of the writer and the
insistence upon the importance of the gaze reiterate the
protagonist's identification with other women (her lovers, her sister,
her aunt) and her self-examination through writing:

> Se mira en lo que escribe, en lo que acaba de escribir.
> Así leía: para distanciar, no para vivir mundos; la
> lectura era tan cerrada como su vida. En los libros
> veía representaciones, actitudes que luego imitaba en
> sus juegos con plena conciencia de la duplicación:
> ella era ella imitando. Cuando jugaba lo hacía
> siempre ante una mirada: la de su hermana. (29-30)

> She looks at herself in what she writes, in what she
> just wrote. That is how she used to read: to keep
> things at a distance, not to open up other worlds.
> Reading was as confining as life itself. In books she
> saw representations, attitudes she later imitated in
> her games, fully conscious of the doubling: in that
> mimicry she was herself. When she played, she
> always did so before a witness: her sister. (17)

In the novel the protagonist's narcissism is matched by that of
her ex-lovers Vera and Renata. The protagonist compares Vera with
Narcissus: "Tu reserva me atrajo y me halagó al principio, luego la
viví como desafío. Te veía ensimismada como un Narciso" (131) [At
first I was attracted and flattered by your reserve. Later I took it as a

challenge. You were wrapped up in yourself, like Narcissus (102)].
Even the name of that character is an allusion to the act of looking
or seeing [Ver/a: literally: to see someone]. A form of identification
between the protagonist with her ex-lovers takes place through the
act of looking. Elsewhere in the novel, the protagonist compares
herself with Renata: "Renata se mira: es Renata cuando se mira vivir"
(21) [Renata looks at herself; she is Renata when she watches herself
live. (10)]

Sexual and emotional identification among women is
textualized in the words "mask" and "body." The repetition of the
word "mask" in *Certificate* emphasizes the duplicity of the process of
writing as well as the integration of other women into the
protagonist's identity. The mask permits the writer a transformation,
offering her the possibility of being someone else. It supposes a
dissolution of the writer's identity and becomes a sign of total
liberation.[8] It allows the woman writer to annihilate the "I" and
reaffirm the dialogue between the "I" and the "she" (that is, the other
woman, the ex-lovers). In the text the narrator expresses the
functions of her mask: to help her go out of herself, to protect herself
from others. Moreover, the mask serves as a metaphor for the need
to insure the privacy of a lesbian amorous discourse in a repressive
society. By using masks the protagonist imitates Diana the huntress
who had many masks and names.

In addition to the narcissism that characterizes the love
discourse, the novel also presents another level of narcissism, the
narcissism of self-reflexive or metafictional works that reflect upon
their own process of writing. In her book *Narcissistic Narrative: The
Metafictional Paradox,* Linda Hutcheon establishes a parallel between
the act of Narcissus looking at himself in the waters and the process
of self-analysis that some literature inscribes in itself.[9] *Certificate,* as a
self-reflexive or metafictional novel, allows for the exploration of
fiction and the examination of literary problems. One of the most
interesting aspects of the narcissistic nature of the novel is the
parallelism that it establishes between writing, reading, and the
lesbian body, a prominent feature of the lesbian theme of the novel.

The metafictional quality of the novel emphasizes the
similarities between writing and reading. The acts of writing and
reading in the novel evoke many of the concerns and strategies used
by Borges and discussed by Molloy in *Signs of Borges* (Molloy has
stated in an interview that she wrote the novel while she was writing

her book on Borges).[10] The emphasis on the act of writing as synonymous with the reading act is related to the notion that a text is the result of confluences of voices and part of a literary tradition.[11] The lesbian writer, by connecting what is part of her life experience with that of her readings underscores the relationship between literature and life and erases the separation between them that traditionally has prevailed. The novel is characterized by its elusiveness and the narrator's insistence that the woman protagonist is not interested in writing realistic literature. She rejects the idea that the novel that she is writing could see reality as an object.

The connection between writing, reading, and the lesbian body may create the idea that Molloy is re-affirming the concept of "writing the body" as it has been postulated by French feminist writers such as Hélène Cixous and Luce Irigaray. However, Molloy's novel does not follow the postulates of "writing the body." Moreover Molloy, in an interview with Magdalena García Pinto, has defined writing as a violent act that is different from a physical and natural one:

> ...the act of writing is an act against nature, so I don't agree with some women writers who speak of the almost physical naturalness of the act of writing. For me, writing entails pulling out demons or ghosts that are extremely violent. I perceive myself as a very violent person, always critical of myself, always keeping myself under control, always like a pot that's about to boil over. That is, it's a question of taking off the lid and at the same time imposing the violence of the word on what emerges, channeling it through writing.[12]

Whereas the notion of "writing the body" is based on physiological difference and pleasure, the novel presents writing as an aggressive act toward the self; a form of challenge, an inquisitive act through which some form of knowledge can be obtained.

The notion of writing as an aggressive act is a feature that the novel shares with works of other women writers, Virginia Woolf and Joan Didion, among others. Woolf, in her essay "Professions for Women" states that women's writing begins with an act of aggression. For Woolf, women's writing begins with "killing the image of the angel of the house" and breaking with a cultural

tradition that has undermined women's experiences.[13] Joan Didion
has also pointed out that writing is an aggression because it is an
imposition on and an invasion of someone else's most private
space.[14] The invasion of the private space is part of a struggle to reach
a balance between the desire to reveal and then conceal knowledge,
the woman's desire to express herself and to protect herself:

> Ella también, ella que escribe, surge, como tantos
> dioses, de un juego de palabras y de lo que las
> palabras-pesadas como la matrona de Efeso,
> huidizas como la cazadora—muestran y esconden.
> Se ha escrito, a lo largo de este relato, sin
> nombrarse; se ha fabricado, producto de un
> adulterio entre ella y sus palabras, y—por fin—
> apenas empieza a conocerse. (150)

> Like so many gods, she, the writer, is the product of a
> play on words: words heavy as the matronly figure at
> Ephesus, or flighty like the huntress, at once secretive
> and revealing. She has written of herself, throughout
> this story, without giving herself a name. A product of
> the adultery between herself and her words, she has
> given herself being and is—finally—just beginning
> to know herself. (118-119)

Writing as a result of the woman's contradictory feelings and desires
to reveal and protect herself is related to the non-referential aspect
of the novel and the impossibility of representing reality in its
totality. The novel reiterates the idea that a text is not a cohesive
totality but rather the product of fragmentation. The fragmentation is
textualized in the novel's structure and language.

   Certificate's non-referential aspect is elaborated through the
use of language and the repetition of words, verbs, and structures
["Someone is leaving, someone has left, someone finds it hard to
leave..." (123)]. The text introduces a defamiliarization with language
as the author explores and exploits the different connotations of
words. The writer in the novel deals with opposites and oxymoronic
constructions to express what a referential language cannot. Thus
the writer privileges the indetermination and openness of language
and prevents the reduction of meanings in her story.

Reflecting continuously upon the process of writing, the woman employs an erotic language to speak about that very process that brings forth the connections between writing and her emotional and sexual life. A body vocabulary that is commonly used to speak about an erotic experience is used to articulate ideas on writing, particularly notions of non-referential literature. The words that the woman utilizes to define her writing help her to articulate the non-referential aspect of her text as well as to allude to the erotic ["Manoseo, toqueteo circunstancial" (20) [She reaches out, gropes at the edges of things (8-9)]. There is the impossibility of anchoring meanings to a language that belongs to the erotic. Later in the text the connection will become clearer as the woman writer defines her writing as "a product of the *adultery* between herself and her words..." (119). The word "adultery," implying secrecy and lying, underlines the non-referential aspect of the text that cannot be truthful to reality but rather present a different perspective from that of reality.

In conjunction with the problems that language poses for any writer, the novel presents the particularity of the problem of language for a lesbian writer. *Certificate*'s language, as a novel that articulates love affairs and break-ups, is characterized by ruptures. Through language the narrator highlights the woman's love failures as well as the problems she faces as a lesbian writer. The woman has to deal with the fact that language, as it has been constructed socially, does not codify lesbian experiences and consciousness. Traditionally lesbians have been forced to use a language of euphemism and encoding in which their lesbianism has been transformed into socially-acceptable forms.

In addition to a reflection on the use of language, the novel presents the literary problems of character representation. As in the use of language, the characters are presented not in totality but rather as fragmented and the result of contradictory ruptures. The novel goes against the notion of representation and the construction of characters is based on vagueness and ambiguity. The narrator, as many narrators in Borges' and Juan Carlos Onetti's works, cannot represent the characters in a referential way. In many episodes of *Certificate* the narrator highlights insignificant characteristics that are not that obvious while omitting others which are more relevant. The question of the construction of characters in non-referential literature is something that has special interest for Molloy. She has stated that her book on Borges, *Signs of Borges*, came out of her preoccupation with Borges' characters, and her discovery that Borges never composed characters but rather fragmented them. It was this aspect of Borges' work that got her interested in writing fiction.[15]

Molloy's strategy of not giving a name to the lesbian protagonist contributes to the ambiguity and vagueness of the text. It can also be read as a political comment on lesbians' invisibility. This strategy claims the lesbian condition as one of an outsider erasing her individuality. Nameless, the lesbian writer embodies an identity that challenges the traditional notion of identity as a cohesive and organized totality. The character constructed upon ambiguity and vagueness defies definite forms and prevents the text from establishing authoritarian modes of self-representation. This non-traditional form of representation as a response to authoritarian discourse has been studied by Francine Masiello in her essay "Feminist Literary Culture in the River Plate Region."[16] According to Masiello, Molloy's text, like other feminist texts, rejects the idea of an essential self as it has been constituted by official texts and ideology.[17]

The protagonist of *Certificate* is dedicated in body and soul to the exercise of writing and reading. And as mentioned above, the eroticism of the writing is emphasized through the narrator's continuous use of words such as satisfaction, pleasure, and delight:

> De aquella noche, como de ésta, sólo quedará una cáscara ritual de palabras, cierto *placer* de la sintaxis, cierta *demora* en los nexos, el *goce* de las innovaciones repetidas, la satisfacción de las junturas. Despertará exhausta y desmembrada, con la sensación de haber perdido para siempre su letra, pero hasta ese momento se atreve a hablar de armonía. (70)

> She remembers from that night, as she will from this one, only an empty ritual of words: a certain *pleasure* in syntax, a certain *lingering over* connectives, the *delight* in repeated invocations, the *satisfaction* of finding transitions. She will wake up exhausted and dismembered, with the sensation of having lost her word definitively. Until that moment, however, she dares speak of harmony. (50)

Writing as an erotic experience alienates the protagonist from her body which she sees only in terms of the function of writing and as a separate entity different from herself:

> ...buscarle cigarrillos, alcohol, algo de comer, comprarle un semanario de espectáculos a los que no lo llevará, hacerle limpiar la ropa, conseguirle remedios por si se le enferma, papel y tinta para cuando escriba. (71)

> She finds it cigarettes, alcohol, something to eat, a weekly entertainment guide it will disregard; she takes its clothes to the cleaners, gets it medicine when it is sick, paper and ink for it to write. (51)

In Molloy's novel, as in the works of Borges and the autobiography of Victoria Ocampo, reading and writing are privileged over living.[18] Presented as passionate erotic activities, writing and reading make the woman protagonist in *Certificate* forget her physical needs. One could say about Molloy's novel what Molloy has said about Ocampo's autobiography, that what the protagonist lived and what she read are complementary and often interchangeable categories.[19] The woman-writer does not take care of her body and what prevails is its abandonment. While eating, the woman reads about complicated recipes that do not have anything to do with the simplicity of her menu. By reading recipes the woman nurtures herself with the reading and not with the food. In addition, the practical and direct discourse of the recipes is in opposition to the language of the book the woman is writing.

Through the woman's alienation from her body, the experience of violence in the protagonist's life takes a prominent place. Violence adds an interesting and controversial dimension to the lesbian theme of the novel because it presents the complexity of the woman's feelings and relationships with others, thus preventing the novel from offering a simplistic perspective on female bonding. As a young girl the writer had a conflictive relationship with her younger sister Clara whose birth triggered jealousy and anger in her. The writer remembers many instances in which she felt pleasure in hurting her sister Clara. As an adult, the protagonist has not only felt pleasure in hurting but she has also allowed others to hurt her physically.

In *Certificate* the lesbian body and the lesbian text are identified through the experience of violence. The narrator emphasizes that the identification of bodily fragmentation with the text is due to violence. However, violence is not seen as something negative but rather as something positive:

> Hoy ha caído, junto con su letra, pero hoy también—
> como en el mar—hace pie. Ve que las palabras se
> levantan una vez más, como se levanta ella, agradece
> la letra ondulante que la enlaza, reconoce las
> cicatrices de un cuerpo que acaricia. Vuelven a
> romperse cuerpo y frase, pero no en la misma cicatriz:
> se abren de manera distinta, le ofrecen una nueva
> fisura que esta tarde acepta, en la que no ve una
> violencia mala, en la que sospecha un orden. (67)

> Today she falls to the ground, together with her words,
> but regains her footing: the words arise once more, as
> she herself rises. She is thankful for those undulating
> words that hold her again, caressing her body and
> recognizing her scars. Her body and her phrase will tear
> again, but not at the old scars: they will split open in a
> different way, revealing new fractures. She accepts this
> future violence as something not necessarily negative,
> as a sign, perhaps, of a secret order. (48)

The narrator's insistence on hands, skin, and voices throughout the text embodies the connection between the writing process and the erotic discourse of the novel. The writer underlines the significance that hands have for her writing and for her sexual life. The numerous references to hands (her own, her father's, and her lover's) all share fragmentation and physical violence. The hands hold a prominent position since with them the woman writes and obtains sexual pleasure as well as providing pleasure to her lovers:

> La mano que un día se acercó a Vera, la mano que ya
> no acaricia a Renata, ahora escribe rechazada, morosa
> e insegura: avanza para retroceder, enloquecer al no
> encontrar signos ni gestos, teme y no logra construir,
> practica una larguísima censura, escribe vacía. (108)

> The hand that reached for Vera one day, the hand that
> no longer caresses Renata, now writes. Rejected,
> listless, unsure of itself, it starts out, then stops,
> maddened at not finding either signs or gestures.
> Afraid, unable to shape words, it censors what it
> writes: it writes in a void. (82-83)

Like hands, skin is also central to the lesbian love theme of the novel and to the literary discourse. Here, like in Monique Wittig's *The Lesbian Body*, allusions to skinlessness and to the act of "peeling off" abound, as Kaminsky has noted. Peeling off in the novel is a metaphor for what the protagonist does through her writing, that is, going into herself in order to get to know her feelings. From a literary point of view the protagonist removes layers to search for authenticity, unmasking herself, as well as removing what is artificial from language. By doing this the woman writer reiterates Roland Barthes' idea that a text is like a tissue of multiple layers.

Voices function within the text as part of a literary system and are always related to other texts as well as to the notion that the lesbian's identity is defined in terms of her literary, sexual, and emotional relationships with other women. More specifically, voices in this novel, like in Cárdenas' *Cuaderno de amor y desamor*, Roffiel's *Amora*, and Umpierre's *The Margarita Poems*, privilege a female literary tradition. The woman writes within the context of a female tradition and through her writing attempts to rescue and privilege her relationships with other women. However, the female tradition that sustains the writer is not a written tradition but rather an oral one. The oral communication (or the lack of) among women in the text is seen through a fictional chain, represented in Sara's and Vera's stories that the protagonist cannot forget, that inspire the writer either to re-establish a connection that she had and lost or to invent connections through her writing.

Within the chorus of voices of a female tradition, the writer's Aunt Sara is vital. The fact that the woman's inspiration stems from her aunt is not accidental but rather significant since Sara is a single woman who did not accommodate to society's heterosexual expectations. Thus, the woman writer's desire to hear her single aunt's voice over her mother's voice which she cannot remember underscores her preference for a lifestyle that does not correspond to models of heterosexuality.

The appropriation of other female voices and their integration into the protagonist's own voice makes the reader think of the Borgesian notion of a text as a re-reading of previous texts, a mosaic of diverse influences. Molloy, in her essay on Victoria Ocampo, has noticed that in Ocampo the process of writing is synonymous with the appropriation of texts and voices of others.[20] By insisting upon the integration of voices, the novel reinforces the idea of intertextuality: the voices of others will become, as she writes them down, her own voice. This idea is in accord with what Molloy herself has stated in "Sentido de ausencias" (A Sense of Absence) about her writing being shaped and modified by reading texts of other writers.[21] Molloy has asserted that her fiction is made of the threads of all the writer's voices that come together in her own.[22]

Certificate, like Umpierre's *The Margarita Poems*, inscribes the woman's search for an expression that might articulate a lesbian discourse. While incapable of recognizing her own voice, the woman identifies herself through the voices of other women and through the voices of others looks for her own "intonation." This search poses many difficulties since what prevails is the absence of a lesbian tradition. However, that quest is essential for the woman's survival and she undertakes it as a challenge: "With a voice, with her own broken voice, she will have to link these fragments together if she is to live." (23)

The woman protagonist's search for her own "intonation" establishes a link between written and oral language. The stories of the protagonist's Aunt Sara as well as those of her ex-lover Vera bring a different discursive practice. In spite of the fact that the woman writer is inspired by her aunt and her lovers she looks for a written expression and not an oral communication. However, in the case of her Aunt Sara she would like to talk to her using the expressions her aunt used when she was a young girl. The use of special expressions that the protagonist and her aunt used to communicate reaffirms the existence of a common language and a special bonding between the protagonist and her aunt:

> Hoy querría unirse a la voz de Sara viva. No puede describir su propia voz, no puede oírse, sólo oye las palabras que anota. Ve el gráfico de una voz—la suya— ve la arquitectura que va estableciendo, siente el placer físico que le proporciona la palabra por un momento justa, luego reemplazable, pero ignora el tono. (37)

> Today she would like to lose herself in Sara's voice, as
> it was when she was alive. She cannot describe her
> own voice, cannot hear herself speak, only hears
> words as she jots them down. She sees the graph of a
> voice (her own voice), sees the structure it gradually
> builds, feels physical pleasure in finding the right
> word, even if it is right for only a moment and
> ultimately replaceable. She does not know, however,
> what tone her own voice has. (23)

Embodied in the stories that Sara used to tell the young girl
are illusions of exclusion and violence, features of the protagonist's
love life as well as of her literary practice. Implicit in Aunt Sara's
expression "the game of the birthing cat," a reference to a lack of
fabric when she was sewing, is aggression. In this game, as
explained by Sara to her niece, a row of children pushes and shoves
until the last child on the line loses place and becomes an outsider.
This outsider is identified as a newborn kitten, thus finishing the
game. Sara's comparison between this game of exclusion and
sewing is a clear allusion to the erotic discourse of the novel based
on lovers who are taken away by other women as well as to the
discourse of writing based on acts of aggression, appropriation, and
exclusion. The violence of writing is symbolically presented in Aunt
Sara's explanation of that expression. That is the meaning that Sara
gave when she was trying to make all the pieces of her pattern fit the
material with the "kitten not pushed out," that is, successful
containment.

Containment, limits, and boundaries are key elements of the
love discourse and of the process of writing since the writer
struggles to obtain balance through her writing and to avoid
melodramatism and sentimentality. Also, containment is pursued by
the writer in her rigorous search for a language and a literary voice
that will articulate her lesbian experiences. It is clear that what the
woman-protagonist does in her writing, Sara used to do, that is, to
make a pattern fit the material without going beyond the limits. The
woman-protagonist explores the limitations of language, text, and
the writing process as well as her detachment from domestic tasks
such as sewing.

Limits and boundaries become for the woman writer an
obsession, and she looks for them in her writing as a way to distance

herself from her love affairs. Actually, the act of writing is insured only because of the absence of the lover. Writing about her love affairs occurs while she waits for a lover, putting limitations and imposing some form of control over her writing. Identification with the other women and with the love story is achieved through a play of closeness and distance between herself and the story and, ultimately, with the reader who is also trapped in the threads of the narration.

The relationship of writing with limits and boundaries is also underlined in the novel by references to the protagonist's task as a translator. Suzanne Jill Levine describes the process of translation as "a balancing act that requires and attempts to push language beyond its limits while at the same time maintaining a common ground of dialogue between writer and reader, speaker and listener."[23] The reference to the woman being a translator serves to bring forth the connection between limits, exclusion, and exile. As discussed in chapter I of this book, the themes of exclusion and exile have particular interest in a lesbian novel since they are emblematic of lesbians' marginality in homophobic societies.

The lesbian's need to find her own space and to find her own definition as a woman and as a writer is shown by her obsession with finding an order for her story and at the same time with her fear of losing control in her writing. She is troubled by a continuous search for an itinerary to tell the story, and she gets anxious because she does not know where the story is going:

> Una clave, un orden para este relato. Sólo atina a ver capas, estratos, como en los segmentos de la corteza terrestre que proponen los manuales ilustrados. No: como las diversas capas de piel que cubren músculos y huesos, imbricadas, en desapacible contacto. Estremecimiento, erizamiento de la superficie: ¿quién no ha observado, de chico, la superficie interior de una costra arrancada y la correspondiente llaga rosada, sin temblar? En ese desgarramiento inquisidor se encuentran clave y orden de esta historia. (23)

> A key, an ordering principle for this story. She can see only layers, strata, as in the segments of the earth's crust shown in schoolbooks. No, more like the various layers of skin that cover muscles and bones,

overlapping, in unpleasant contact. Quivering, bristling surfaces. Who has not observed as a child, after pulling off a scab, the inner surface and the pink sore that goes with it—and looked at it without trembling? In that inquisitive act of destruction she finds the key and ordering principle for this story. (11-12)

The writer realizes that it is impossible to find order and that, while ambiguity prevails, she can see only fragments resulting from different forms of violence. Ambiguity appears in the woman's story and in her affective life. This prevents the novel from closing and limiting the meanings of the texts. Order and control are also related to the themes of passion and madness in the novel. The woman's literary practice and her erotic life are conditioned by her desire to go beyond her limits, to exceed herself and to impose control. Madness interested and awoke curiosity in the protagonist who, as a young girl, heard that her Uncle Arthur went mad. In her life as an adult, madness is related to the woman's fear of losing control and being ruled by her emotions and sexual desire. She tries to create balance between her contradictory feelings.

Contrary to the woman's search for order in her life and her desire to organize her life's anecdotes, what prevails in the novel is violence and fragmentation. In spite of the autobiographical features that *Certificate* presents, the novel is not an autobiography since autobiography implies the confirmation of a complete and coherent discourse within which disseminated parts have been submitted to a specific arrangement to create uniformity. As the woman asserts in the novel:

Autobiografías: qué placer seguir a un yo, atender a sus mínimos meandros, detenerse en el pequeño detalle que, una y otra vez, lo constituye. Qué placer recordar que alguien se cortó el pelo y dejó de comer queso... Estas líneas no componen, y nunca quisieron componer, una autobiografía: componen—querrían componer—una serie de violencias salteadas, que le tocaron a ella, que también han tocado a otros. (68)

What pleasure to recall that someone cut her hair and stopped eating cheese, what pleasure to recall

> that someone kept the shuttle from his mother's
> loom, useless to him, when it might have been useful
> to others. What she writes does not constitute, and
> will never constitute, an autobiography: rather, it tries
> to reproduce a disjointed series of acts of violence
> that befell her, that also befell others. (49)

Molloy, who has written a number of critical works on autobiography in Spanish America, plays with the autobiographical process when she presents a protagonist who writes about autobiography because she cannot outline the boundaries of her own life. The consciousness of the self and the examination of a life from a particular moment are features that *Certificate* shares with autobiography. The novel, like many lesbian texts, is characterized by the presentation of a confessional tone, that is, the need to reflect the inner world.

As a self-reflexive and metafictional novel, *Certificate* presents an examination of the autobiographical mode. The concern with autobiography as a genre in *Certificate* makes the reader think of Molloy's interest in autobiography as well as the elements that the protagonist's life shares with Molloy's. As the author has explained, the novel is a combination of autobiographical details as well as many things that are not autobiographical. Molloy stated in an interview with García Pinto that what is really autobiographical in the novel is that she found her voice and her language.[24]

Although Molloy's narration uses many of the elements of the autobiographical model, it uses the third rather than the first person. The use of the third-person pronoun creates an effect of ambiguity, and it also contributes to decentralizing the text and the subject. As Maurice Blanchot has pointed out, the use of the third person does not create a center but, on the contrary, prevents the work from having a center.[25] The use of the "she" instead of the "I" allows for the interchangeability of positions with the reader. In *Certificate*, however, there are several ruptures in the narration in which the "I" replaces the third person. In a rigorously written novel like *Certificate*, the confusion between the "I" and the "she" has to be intentional. It stresses the woman-writer's functional duplicity since she is formulating the discourse as well as being the subject of the discourse; she is both author and character; she is both a writer and reader. The employment of the "I" in a number of instances textualizes the seduction that a first-person narration offers to any writer and the narcissistic satisfaction involved in the act of representing oneself. Once again, the narrator is placed in an intermediary position, and she oscillates between her desire to express herself and to conceal her identity. What prevails is the impossibility of fixing meanings.

From the point of view of the erotic discourse, the interruption of the third-person narration and its replacement with the "I" supports the idea that the boundaries of the lesbian lovers' identities are fluid. What may be perceived as a lack of continuity reiterates the union of the subject and the object in both the act of writing as well as in the erotic experience. Therefore, what seems to be a lack of precision in the novel is a deliberate strategy which functions together with the novel's ambiguity and openness.

The ambiguity and openness that prevails throughout the novel is reinforced at the novel's end; with the story completed, the woman is going to read her manuscript. Once her story is completed, she leaves the room that protected her and was the site of her love affairs. The act of leaving the room and being placed outside without a destination is symbolic of the woman's loneliness and emptiness. By locating the woman in an airport, a place of transition (just as the room that she occupied was described as a place of transit and transitory loves), Molloy underscores the idea that any writing or any love affair may not last. Thus, the protagonist, like the elusive Diana, is condemned to restless travel. Identified with Diana the huntress, the lesbian writer always in pursuit, desires other women, and places herself outside the traditional coordinates of motherhood, domesticity, and heterosexuality. She proclaims her rights to pursue intellectual work and her erotic autonomy. The lesbian writer, like Molloy herself, forges through violence and rupture, a new tradition and space, breaking ground for a lesbian Latin American perspective.

*   *   *

NOTES

1 Monique Wittig and Sande Zeig, *Lesbian Peoples: Material for a Dictionary* (New York: Avon Press, 1979), p. 43.

2 Emphasis has been added.

3 Simone de Beauvoir, *The Second Sex* (New York: Alfred Knopf, 1953), p. 58.

4 Gonzalo Navajas, "Erotismo y modernidad en *En breve cárcel* de Sylvia Molloy," *Revista de Estudios Hispánicos* Vol. 22, número 2 (May 1988), p. 101.

5 Magdalena García Pinto, "La escritura de la pasión y la pasión de la escritura: *En breve cárcel*, de Sylvia Molloy." *Revista Iberoamericana* 132-133 (July-December 1985): 688.

6 Julia Kristeva, *Semiótica* (España: Editorial Fundamentos, 1981), p. 236.

7 Magdalena García Pinto, *Women Writers of Latin America: Intimate Stories* (Austin: University of Texas Press, 1991), p. 134.

8 Julia Kristeva, *El texto de la novela* (Barcelona: Editorial Lumen, 1981), p. 233.

9 Linda Hutcheon, *Narcissistic Narrative. The Metafictional Paradox* (New York: Methuen, 1984).

10 Magdalena García Pinto, *Women Writers of Latin America. Intimate Stories* (Austin: University of Texas Press, 1991), p. 136.

11 Jorge Luis Borges, "Kafka y sus precursores," *Obras Completas* (Buenos Aires: Emecé, 1974), p. 710.

12 Magdalena García Pinto, Op. Cit., p. 135.

13 Virginia Woolf, "Profesiones para la mujer," *Las mujeres y la literatura*. Selección y prólogo de Michèle Barrett. Traducción de Andrés Bosch (Barcelona: Editorial Lumen, 1979), p. 70.

14 Susan Braudy, "A Day in the Life of Joan Didion," *Ms. Magazine* 5 (February 1977), p. 109.

15 Magdalena García Pinto, Op. Cit., p. 132.

16 Francine Masiello, "Feminist Literary Culture in the River Plate Region," *Chasqui* XXI (May 1992), pp. 39-48.

17 Ibid., p. 41.

18 Sylvia Molloy, *Las letras de Borges* (Buenos Aires: Editorial Sudamericana, 1979), p. 64.

19 Sylvia Molloy, *At Face Value: Autobiographical Writing in Spanish America* (Cambridge: Cambridge University Press, 1991), p. 58.

20 Ibid., p. 73.

21 Sylvia Molloy, "Sentido de ausencias," *Revista Iberoamericana* LI, números 132-133 (julio-diciembre 1985), p. 487.

22 Magdalena García Pinto, Op. Cit., p. 136.

23 Suzanne Jill Levine, *The Subversive Scribe: Translating Latin American Fiction* (Saint Paul, Minnesota: Graywolf Press, 1991), p. 4.

24 Magdalena García Pinto, Op. Cit., p. 133.

25 Maurice Blanchot, "The Narrative Voice," *The Gaze of Orpheus and Other Literary Essays*. Translated by Lydia Davis (Barrytown, New York: Station Hill Press, 1981), p. 135.

CHAPTER V

SEXUAL AND POLITICAL AFFIRMATION IN LUZ MARÍA UMPIERRE'S *THE MARGARITA POEMS* AND *...Y OTRAS DESGRACIAS. AND OTHER MISFORTUNES...*

> To survive the Borderlands
> You must live sin *fronteras*
> be a crossroads.
>
> *Borderlands/La Frontera.*
> Gloria Anzaldúa

Latina writing describes the literary production of Latin American women in the United States. This type of literature experienced a growth during the 1980's when Chicanas began to develop their own literature committed to the concerns of their status as a racial and social minority. Thus, this literature emerged from the preoccupations of marginality of Latinas as an ethnic group in the United States.

However, the literary production of lesbian Latinas in the United States reflects the consciousness of a more complex form of marginality within the social concerns of Latina writers. In conjunction with their racial, cultural, and social status as a minority in the United States, these women explore an awareness of a different sexual orientation that has been silenced by the Anglo as well as the emerging Latino literary canons in this country. Claiming differences from the Anglo-lesbian movement that focuses mainly on the issue of sexuality, self-identified lesbian Latina writers are interested in exploring the connections between the specificity of their sexual identities and social and racial issues. It is thus not surprising that many of the Latinas whose works present lesbian issues, themes or lesbian sensibilities have also been involved in lesbian activism. Most visible among these women is the Puerto Rican writer and critic Luz María Umpierre.

While identifying herself as a lesbian and as a woman of color, Umpierre shares the concerns of Chicanas Gloria Anzaldúa and Cherríe Moraga as well as of African American writers, particularly Audre Lorde and Cheryl Clarke. For these women the fight against homophobia has to be connected with their positioning as women of color. In the essays of *This Bridge Called My Back: Writings By Radical Women of Color* (1981), Latinas and African American authors emphasize the importance of recognizing that the fight for women's equality and women's rights to sexuality has to be understood in the context of other political struggles against patriarchy and the power structures of a male-dominated society.[1]

Umpierre's poetry collections *En el país de las maravillas* (In Wonderland; 1982), *...Y otras desgracias. And Other Misfortunes...* (1985), and *The Margarita Poems* (1987) are highly political texts that include her criticism of Puerto Rico's colonial status as well as an open representation of lesbianism. The latter theme is a political act because it defies the structures of a patriarchal society.

The purpose of this chapter is to examine the lesbian themes and issues in Umpierre's works. As in the works of Anzaldúa, Moraga, and other Latinas, the lesbian themes and issues are represented alongside other socio-political issues. These themes are specifically tied to a criticism of Puerto Rico's colonial situation and of the stereotypes of Puerto Ricans in the United States. I will focus my attention on the poetry collection entitled *The Margarita Poems* (1987), which is Umpierre's lesbian manifesto. This book consists of nine poems ("Immanence," "Transcendence," "No Hatchet Job," "The Statue," "Only the Hand That Stirs Knows What's in the Pot," "Título: En que trata de lo que es y no hay mah ná,'" "Madre," "Ceremonia Secreta" and "The Mar/Garita Poem") that deal with social and cultural issues, linking both the personal and the political as the writer has asserted in an interview that I had with her in 1991.[2]

This collection of poetry is marked by Umpierre's experiences as an immigrant in the United States and by the discrimination and racism that she has suffered as a Puerto Rican. In this book, like in her previous collections of poetry, Umpierre presents the theme of the immigrant who lives within two cultures: the Puerto Rican and the Anglo American.

While this chapter primarily concentrates on *The Margarita Poems*, I will also make references to other poems found in Umpierre's *...Y otras desgracias. And Other Misfortunes...*, a collection that questions gender and socio-political issues, as well as initiates a process of encoding lesbian motifs that will later be developed more openly in *The Margarita Poems*. The strategy of encoding lesbian themes can be found in poems such as "In Response," "Clímax," "Cuento sin Hadas,""Transference,""The Astronaut,""Lista de supermercado,"and"Cruising."

In *The Margarita Poems* political struggle and lesbian identity are unified. The nine poems of this collection articulate clearly the lesbian speaker's search for her ex-lover (Margarita). The order of the poems ("Immanence," "Transcendence," "No Hatchet Job," "The Statue," "Only the Hand That Stirs Knows What's in the Pot," "Título: En que trata de lo que es y no hay mah ná,'" "Madre," "Ceremonia Secreta," and "The Mar/Garita Poem") traces the development of that search. As Umpierre states in her introduction:

> There is a reason for the order in which the poems
> appear. If you find that reason, you must be very close
> to finding your Self, your Margarita. And if you find
> her while pounding through these lines, the best that
> you can do is fall in love and call Julia forth. (3)

The motif of the speaker's search for Margarita and the desire to engage the female reader in that search is linked to the theme of female connectedness. That theme, central to the book, appears at different levels: literary, emotional, and sexual. The connection is first made explicit in the dedication and the poet's introduction. Secondly, it is seen in the quotes, allusions, and references to women writers that abound in the book. The dedication and the references to women writers reflect a spectrum of diverse literary expressions: Latin American, Latino, African American, and Anglo American. This poetry collection is a lesbian text not because it is centered on emotional and literary connections among women but rather because the book proclaims the sexual nature of lesbians' relationships. Moreover, the poet stresses that the theme of lesbian love and lesbian sexuality is essential to the process of writing. Writing thus emerges intertwined with lesbian love and sexuality.

The significance of women writers in Umpierre's work is stressed in the dedication and the introduction to the book. The dedication "for Margaret and Julia" is, as the poet states in the introduction, for several women (Margaret Randall, Julia Alvarez, and Julia de Burgos) as well as for a former lover named Margarita. By choosing names of women writers and that of a former lover, the poet recognizes the union of different spheres of her life: the literary, the emotional, and the sexual. Such an affirmation acknowledges the integration of aspects that, traditionally, have been considered separate. By uniting female literary mentors and lovers, the poet ratifies the link between her writing and her emotional and sexual life.

Among several women writers mentioned in the collection, Umpierre emphasizes the significance of and the identification with the Puerto Rican poet Julia de Burgos. Moreover, she claims de Burgos as her literary precursor. Julia de Burgos (1914-1958), well-known Puerto Rican poet, is the author of *Poema en veinte surcos* (Poem in Twenty Furrows; 1938), *Canción de la verdad sencilla* (Song of the Simple Truth; 1939) and *El mar y tú* (The Sea and You; 1954). Like Umpierre, de Burgos lived in the United States for part of her life. Umpierre's poetry shares with de Burgos' the prominent role of emotions and love as a constant passion. In conjunction with the theme of love, there appears the struggle against social conventionalism and the political militancy against the colonial status of Puerto Rico. At the personal level, Julia de Burgos and Luz María Umpierre share a historical context: the lack of opportunities for women. Moreover, these two poets have suffered racial and social prejudices as Puerto Ricans living in the United States. However, as a self-identified lesbian writer, Umpierre confronts a different form of marginality than that suffered by de Burgos. As a lesbian writer in the United States, Umpierre is divided not only between two different cultures, the Anglo American and the Puerto Rican, but also between the heterosexual and the lesbian.

Therefore, while claiming de Burgos as a literary predecessor and sharing views with her, Umpierre's relationship to de Burgos is a complex one. On the one hand, Umpierre states the significance and the influence of de Burgos on her work. On the other hand, she highlights her "anxiety of mothering" and the need to detach herself from de Burgos and from other literary figures to establish her own lesbian literary voice. *The Margarita Poems* precisely textualizes the speaker's journey to communicate with, understand, and paradoxically, to free herself from Julia de Burgos, as Carlos Rodríguez Matos has pointed out in the introduction to the book.[3]

The notion of writing as a way to communicate with, understand, and liberate herself from the influence of other women writers is clearly explored in two poems of *The Margarita Poems* ("Título: En que trata de lo que es y no hay mah ná'" (Title: Where she deals with what it is and there is nothing else) and "The Mar/Garita Poem") and the first poem of *...Y otras desgracias. And Other Misfortunes....* "Título: En que trata de lo que es y no hay mah ná'" establishes a dialogue with other women writers and a process of redefinition of both poetical forms and female subjects. The poem presents a communication between Chicana writer Ana Castillo and one of the first Latin American feminists Sor Juana Inés de la Cruz. Thus, this poem is a mediator between two women writers, Juana Inés and Ana Castillo, as well as two historical periods, the seventeenth and the twentieth centuries. The allusion to Juana Inés relates the Mexican nun's struggle against the political power of the Catholic church to Umpierre's search for truth and equality for women in a contemporary society very much still controlled by patriarchal values.

The poem, which has the form of a memo from Juana de Asbaje to Ana Castillo, proposes a revision of notions of poetical forms as well as concepts of women. Through the framework of the memo, Umpierre emphasizes the need to redefine the formal concept of poetry to include more direct messages. In this poem, the speaker proposes the redefinition of the concept of women as "margaritas" instead of "roses":

> To: Ana Castillo
> From: Juana de Asbaje
> Re: Newly defined concepts
>
> Women are not roses;
> they are *all* margaritas.
>   (sic) circa 17th. century. (27)

Margarita, a central motif of this poetry collection, is related to the spirit of rebellion that permeates the book and to the political lesbian voice. However, Margarita is, as the author indicates in the introduction, many things:

> an intoxicating drink, a flower back home in Puerto
> Rico, the title of a traditional "danza" that was a

favorite of my mother and the name of a woman I
love. Margarita is all of these and none. Margarita is
my muse, Margarita is my poetry, Margarita is my
imaginary lover, Margarita is my Self. (1)

By identifying Margarita with diverse things (a Puerto Rican *danza*
her mother liked, her lover, her muse, and her Self), the poet
reiterates the conciliation of many aspects of her life, her Puerto
Rican heritage, the emotional, and the sexual.

In "The Mar/Garita Poem," the last poem of the collection and
the one that gives its title to the book, the speaker again stresses that
she has borrowed the voices of other female poets: Julia de Burgos,
the Chilean writer Marjorie Agosín, Marge Piercy, and Juana de
Asbaje. The emphasis on other women writers reinforces the poet's
desire to inscribe herself within a female tradition. Her text is thus
an intertextual space in which the voices of other women writers can
be heard:

> mujeres sabias
> que me prestan
> sus letras, sus alfabetos,
> vómitos, vómitos caen en el papel,
> y vamos hilando,
> hilvanando, conectando las piezas
> de este rompecabezas eterno,
> piezas dispersas. (37)

> Wise women
> who lend me
> their words, their alphabets,
> Vomit, vomit falls on the paper
> and we weave
> and we weave
> joining pieces
> of this eternal puzzle,
> scattered pieces.

Female tradition and intertextuality create here the idea of
women's community and provide for their empowerment. Linked
with a female literary tradition and a political strategy is the idea that

women's writing must articulate a common and collective story instead of an individual one.

Writing, as a collective work of women writers and as a political strategy to bond with other women, is stressed in the use of the first person plural "we." The use of "we" is significant in "The Mar/Garita Poem," "Ceremonia Secreta," and "No Hatchet Job." The poet employs this pronoun to stress the building of alliances with other authors, readers, and women in general. For the female reader, the use of "we" makes her feel included and a participant in the writing process. The idea of the female reader's participation and the creation of writing that can express female views and their cultural and racial identities is emphasized throughout the collection:

> Debemos generar
> nuestras metáforas
> para poder hilar,
> hilar en fino,
> hilar, hilar, hilar
> al mundo,
> unir, unir, crear brocado
> el tapiz
> que salve a nuestras musas. (34-35)

> We must generate
> our own metaphors
> to be able to weave
> a fine weave,
> to weave, to weave, to weave the world,
> to connect, to connect, to brocade
> the tapestry
> that will save our muses.

Moreover, the collaboration with other women is seen as a necessary act to win two struggles which, according to the speaker, are united. One is the struggle for women's equality and the other, the liberation of Puerto Rico from its colonial status. Through the alliance with other women writers, the speaker gains the necessary strength:

> Julia de Burgos,
> Marjorie Agosín,

Marge Piercy
me han prestado sus palabras,
y la mar ha llegado a mi puerta
ya hoy
mi isla ya tiene su mar
y su lenguaje. (39)

Julia de Burgos,
Marjorie Agosín,
Marge Piercy
they have lent me their words,
and the sea has come to my door
today
my island has its sea
and its language.

The connection with other women writers is elaborated through the metaphor of writing as weaving. Not only weaving but also other traditionally feminine activities like cooking become metaphors for the act of writing. With this association, the poet is subverting a tradition of submission and powerlessness and transforming it into a tool of women's autonomy.

Writing as an intertextual weaving process is clear in "In Response." In this poem, the first of ...*Y otras desgracias. And Other Misfortunes...*, Umpierre establishes a direct dialogue with Sandra María Esteves' poem "María Christina." Sandra María Esteves, a Puerto Rican-Dominican poet, is the author of *Yerba Buena* (1980) and *Tropical Rains: A Bilingual Downpour* (1984).[4] For Esteves, as well as for Umpierre, de Burgos has also been an inspiration as is obvious in the title of one of Esteves' poems, "A Julia y a mí" (For Julia and for myself). However, Umpierre's literary relationship to Esteves is conflictive as the title itself, "In Response," indicates.

In Esteves' "María Christina," the speaker celebrates her Puerto Rican heritage and takes pride in following the traditional roles established for women. Throughout the poem, the female speaker emphasizes the heterosexual option of bonding with men and taking care of them as a mother or a wife. The heterosexual connection is expressed in the use of the possessive pronoun "our" when speaking about men and in the use of the word "negra":

"My Name is María Christina"

My name is Maria Christina
I am a Puerto Rican woman born in el barrio

Our men...they call me negra because they love me
and in turn I teach them to be strong

I respect their ways
inherited from our proud ancestors
I do not tease them with eye catching clothes
I do not sleep with their brothers and cousins
although I've been told that this is a liberal society
I do not poison their bellies with instant chemical food
our table holds food from earth and sun

My name is Maria Christina
I speak two languages broken into each other
but my heart speaks the language of people
born in oppression

I do not complain about cooking for my family
because abuela taught me that woman is the
master of fire
I do not complain about nursing my children
because I determine the direction of their values

I am the mother of a new age of warriors
I am the child of a race of slaves
I teach my children how to respect their bodies
so they will not o.d. under the stairway's shadow of
shame
I teach my children to read and develop their minds
so they will understand the reality of oppression
I teach them with discipline...and love
so they will become strong and full of life

My eyes reflect the pain
of that which has shamelessly raped me
but my soul reflects the strength of my culture

My name is Maria Christina
I am a Puerto Rican woman born in el barrio
Our men...they call me negra because they love me
and in turn I teach them to be strong.[5]

Esteves' poem shares with Umpierre's and de Burgos' poetry the protest against oppression and racial discrimination. However, while Esteves' poem offers a heterosexual perspective of solidarity with and support of Latino men, Umpierre's "In Response," an intertext of Esteves' poem, is a proclamation against gender roles and male-oriented ideology. Umpierre transforms Esteves' verses and challenges the traditional ideological content of her poem.

Umpierre's speaker begins by defining herself as a Puerto Rican woman in terms opposed to those used in Esteves' poem. In the first two stanzas, the speaker affirms what she is not (My name is not María Cristina/I am a Puerto Rican woman born in another barrio). In the third and fourth stanzas, the speaker affirms what she is through a negative identification with the men of her culture. This definition of the self does not occur through loving relationships with men. The speaker proclaims that she does not have a husband or a loving father, that she has her own perspectives and does not rely on those of men. Whereas Esteves' verse, "Our men call me negra," implies a loving relationship with men (because of the affective connotation of the word "negra" in Puerto Rican vocabulary), Umpierre's verse ("Our men call me pushie") indicates the tension and animosity that prevails between the female speaker and the men of her culture.

In "In Response," the speaker's affirmation of the self occurs through what she does for herself and not for others or through others. While rebelling against culturally assigned labels and gendered positions, the speaker states her "puertorriqueñismo." She asserts her Puerto Rican heritage but differently from Esteves' speaker because she stresses her disagreement with social impositions and sexist cultural values. Because Umpierre resists and opposes the Anglo and Latino male-oriented societies, the reader witnesses the speaker's quest to achieve self-definition as a woman. Umpierre's speaker detaches herself from the domestic roles that have been assigned to her by the culture, and she assumes the role of an independent and aggressive woman who does not conform to the accepted, culturally constructed image for women and the conventional forms of female power. By rejecting the institution of motherhood, she breaks with the traditional vehicle of social power for women.[6] The speaker attains her strength by questioning authority, speaking for herself, and rebelling against restrictions imposed on women's sexuality. Through Umpierre's poem, the female self is re-constructed and emphasis on "I," in a series of anaphores, adds strength to the speaker's political voice:

"In Response"

My name is not María Cristina
I am a Puerto Rican woman born in another barrio.
Our men...they call me pushie
for I speak without a forked tongue
and I do fix the leaks in all faucets.

I don't accept their ways,
shed down from macho-men ancestors.
I sleep around whenever it is possible;
no permission needed from dearest marido
or kissing loving papa.
I need not poison anyone's belly but my own;
no cooking mama here;
I cook but in a different form.

My name is not María Cristina.
I speak, I think,
I express myself in any voice,
in any tone, in any language that conveys
my house within.
The only way to fight oppression is through
resistance:

I do complain
I will complain
I do revise,
I don't conceal,
I will reveal,
I will revise.

I am not the mother of rapist warriors,
I am the child that was molested.
I teach my students to question all authority,
to have no fears, no nail biting in class,
no falling in love with the teacher.

My eyes reflect myself,
the strengths that I am trying to attain,
the passions of a woman who at 35 is 70.
My soul reflects my past,
my soul deflects the future.

My name is not María Cristina.
I am a Puerto Rican woman born in another barrio.
Our men...they call me bitchie
for I speak without a twisted tongue
and I do fix all leaks in my faucets.
(...*Y otras desgracias. And Other Misfortunes...* 1)

As in "In Response," in "Cuento sin Hadas" (Tale without Fairies) from ...*Y otras desgracias. And Other Misfortunes...*, Umpierre continues to re-read and to challenge a sexist tradition. The poem "Cuento sin Hadas" is the deconstruction of myths that are commonly presented in fairy tales. Two of these myths have centered around women's passivity and the exaltation of women's beauty and emotional life.

Whereas fairy tales are characterized by creating an idealized and harmonious world with a happy ending which overlooks the complexity of life and ideological tensions, "Cuento sin Hadas" questions the constructions of gender roles and social conventions.[7] In addition, the poem attacks the conventions of marriage and undermines the supposed harmony of the married couple. Umpierre caricaturizes the life of husband and wife and presents how the rigidity of social structures limits their lives and transforms them into "paper dolls." In this transformation, Umpierre challenges the image of passivity in women by transforming the (female) doll into someone who pisses and speaks, while the (male) doll remains passive:

La muñeca que ríe, la muñeca que espanta.
La muñeca que mea, la muñeca que habla.

La que camina y se mueve, la de la ropita enana.
El muñeco de cartón, el que se recorta de la página.
El muñeco que no ríe, el muñeco que no habla.
(...*Y otras desgracias. And Other Misfortunes...* 45)

The female doll that laughs, the doll that scares.
The doll that pisses, the doll that speaks.
The one who can walk and move, the one in
    dwarf clothes.
The cardboard male doll, the one cut from a page.
The male doll that does not laugh, that does not
    speak.

Criticism of gender roles is also present in "The Astronaut," another poem of *...Y otras desgracias. And Other Misfortunes...* However, in this poem Umpierre specifically criticizes women who accommodate themselves to gender roles in a peculiar way that involves simultaneously yielding to the mainstream pressure and taking on the aspect of enforcing male authority. The title, "The Astronaut," and the last line of the poem, "the man in the moon who is a lady," allude to the theme of female "tokenism" that the poem presents. Women are made to believe that they are insiders while in fact they are merely responding to patriarchal needs. Female tokens refer to women who place themselves outside society's expectations and culture by achieving positions that have been traditionally denied to women. As defined by Adrienne Rich in her essay "What Does a Woman Need to Know?," the token woman is someone "who is encouraged to see herself as different from most other women, as exceptionally talented and deserving, and to separate herself from the wider female condition; and she is perceived by 'ordinary' women as separate also, perhaps even stronger than themselves."[8]

In this poem, Umpierre criticizes the false power granted to a few women on the condition that they use it to maintain the status quo as well as the women who accommodate themselves to the establishment:

You have seen her!
Haunted.
With her taut braids,
her liturgical expression,

trepidating in her elevated shoes,
hermetically tightening her thighs–
the fear of expression is too cumbersome.

....

Yes, we have seen her!
And her actions bequest honor,
and she loathes the word sister
and she is never to be seen
in pink or lavender.
She is a sell out.
She is a locker.
She is a clam.
A woman who no longer answers to her gender.
A patriarchal tool,
a matriarchal break-up,
Someone in need of transcendental etude;
the man in the moon who is a lady
(...*Y otras desgracias. And Other Misfortunes...* 5)

Rewriting and transforming traditional values is central to Umpierre's works. For her, writing is a rebellious act. Writing is a way of surviving in a society that discriminates against her because she is a woman, a Puerto Rican, and a lesbian. Umpierre has encountered problems publishing her works because of their lesbian content and because she "is not the typical Puerto Rican woman writer that some critics and publishers would like to see."[9]

As part of Umpierre's speaker's search for a redefinition of her literary voice and her perspective as a woman in a sexist society, the speaker of ...*Y otras desgracias. And Other Misfortunes...* and *The Margarita Poems* re-appropriates and challenges the cultural meanings assigned to certain spaces within the house. In ...*Y otras desgracias. And Other Misfortunes...*, there are frequent allusions to the space of the kitchen and the act of cooking as is indicated in the titles "La receta" (The Recipe), "Fortune Cookies," and "Cocinando" (Cooking). In "La receta" (The Recipe), Umpierre attacks the American idea of the melting pot. She sees the melting pot as an American fantasy that supposes the destruction of identity instead of equality for everyone. In this poem the domestic task of cooking adopts a different meaning: to cook ("cocinar") is a synonym for destroying her cultural identity and for making her fit into the patterns of middle-class, white American culture.

Interestingly, the verb "to cook" adopts a diverse political voice in one of the poems of *The Margarita Poems*. In "Only the Hand That Stirs Knows What's in the Pot," cooking is transformed and associated with lesbian sexual pleasure:

> Some old, from the island, you know,
> some new, made in sexual passion
> for the most recent of lovers,
> none borrowed,
> many blue. (25)
>
> ....
>
> fermentation in my gray cells,
> fool's parsley from my breasts,
> savory aromas from my loins,
> all for the guests in my banquets. (25)

As mentioned above, the process of writing as redefining and challenging traditional norms is problematic for the writer. The conflict between the woman writer, especially the lesbian writer, and society is elaborated in Umpierre's poem "Immanence." Here, the speaker's creative impulses are in conflict with society's rules. The confrontation between the poet and society is reiterated in the structure of the poem and the poem clearly indicates the opposition between the poet's voice ("I") and that of society ("we"). Throughout the poem, the poet reproduces society's assertion in an ironical way. The verbs "domesticated," "saved," "cured," "reduced," "found" textualize society's desire to change the speaker, "cure her lesbianism," and transform her into a conventional woman:

> "We have domesticated this unruly woman."
>
> "We have saved, we have cured this vulnerable woman."
>
> "We have finally reduced this superior woman."
>
> "We have found you this cadaverous woman."
> (*The Margarita Poems* 21)

Despite society's desire to transform the woman into someone acceptable, the speaker proclaims her survival and her liberation from society's impositions. The two last lines articulate the speaker's strength and her capacity to succeed in expressing herself, both as a writer and as a woman, thus manifesting herself against society's will. Here, the poet, through the use of capital letters, stresses the words *writer* and *woman*:

> Eternally she breathes
> one line after next,
> unrestrained, unshielded
> willfully
> WRITER
> WOMAN

> (*The Margarita Poems* 22)

The theme of liberation from society's constraints, which becomes a clear manifesto of the poet's lesbian sexual identity, is central to *The Margarita Poems*. The poet makes a strong statement of her lesbianism and the oppression that she suffers in a society that does not accept lesbians. Therefore, Umpierre's writing about her sexual orientation and her love for Margarita is a form of rebellion against the establishment as well as a form of political empowerment:

> These poems are a product of love and obsession, of pain and lust. They were all written between 1985 and 1986 with a sense of love and urgency. The loss centered itself on the fact that some women whom I love more than my Self were no longer in my life. The urgency was dual. First of all, I needed to say, to speak, "lo que nunca pasó por mis labios," that which I had not uttered, and which was being used as a tool in my oppression by others, murmured behind closed doors, brought up as an issue to deny me my rights by those enemies who read my poetry too well. What I needed to verbalize is the fact that I am, among many other things, a Lesbian. Second, I wanted to communicate in some viable form with some One who came to represent all women to me. (*The Margarita Poems* 1)

In *The Margarita Poems* political empowerment comes through "the process of coming out," that is, the articulation of the poet's love for women and the awareness of its social implications. Emerging from love and the poet's need to state her lesbian identity, *The Margarita Poems* offers the reader a highly charged lesbian erotic discourse which revises and reframes the heterosexual literary tradition.

In the poem "Madre" (Mother), Umpierre, like Magaly Alabau in her poetry collection *Electra/Clitemnestra* (1986) and Alma Villanueva in her poem "Mother, May I?," explores the conflictive aspect of biological and sexual bonding with the mother.[10] In "Madre," the speaker elaborates the quest for her mother, which is to be understood in this poem in a literal as well as in a metaphorical way. For the lesbian speaker here is a biological mother as well as a literary role model. Throughout the poem, the speaker searches for a relationship that never existed because of the physical and the emotional absence of the mother. The mother-daughter relationship is presented through images of what is missing, what is absent or negative and the speaker presents the emotional and physical effects of the absence of the mother in her life:

> *No* bebí de tu leche,
> *no* tuve en mis labios
> tus cómodos pezones,
> *no* sentí tu amargura.
>
> En tiempos de antaño
> *padecí* de anorexia
> por no tener tu elixir. (28)
>
> I *did not* drink your milk
> *did not* hold in my lips
> your comfortable nipples
> *did not* feel your bitterness
>
> In the old days
> I *suffered* from anorexia
> lacking your elixir.[11]

As a result of the mother's absence, the speaker looks for a special physical and emotional bonding with other women:

Más tarde, con la sabiduría,
me vino el ansia de caminar
por cuerpos en busca
de tus zumos. (28)

Later with my wisdom
came the desire to walk
through other bodies
in search of your juices.

Therefore, motherhood and lesbian eroticism are connected in
this poem, like in Magaly Alabau's collection of poetry
Electra/Clitemnestra (1986). However, contrary to what Alabau does
in *Electra/Clitemnestra*, Umpierre conciliates the traditional motherly
nurturing role with the lesbian erotic discourse. The poet connects
the body of the mother with the female lovers' bodies in which the
speaker looks for her mother and her own self.

Linking the nurturing role of the mother and lesbian eroticism
is brought forth through words which emphasize the sexual aspect
of the speaker's relationship with the mother. Words like "milk,"
"nipples," "elixir," "juices," "lips," "mouth," and "sweat" are used to
describe the speaker's relationship with the mother as well as with
lovers. The speaker uses metaphors like "monte de Venus," (mount of
Venus) and metaphors of natural life: "petals," "flower," "caves,"
"crevices," to refer to female genitals. There is an abundance of verbs
that are either related to the sexual or are used as metaphors for the
sexual: "to lick," "to swallow," "to suck," "to taste," "to drink," "to
chew," "to relish," "to go up," "to go down," and "to touch."

The poem presents three different moments in the
relationship between mother and daughter. These moments are
indicated through the use of "en tiempos de antaño" (old days) "más
tarde" (later) and "finalmente" (finally). In this search there is a
progression through several stages until the speaker finds her
"mother within herself." The speaker finds her mother through the
discovery of her lesbian sexual identity. Whereas the entire poem
speaks of a search and the absence of the mother, it concludes with
the speaker's recognition that she has found her mother in her own
blood and her own body. Thus, the speaker stresses her capacity to
nurture herself:

> Y heme aquí hoy, madre,
> intoxicada en jugos de Margarita,
> feliz, al fin, de conocerte
> y saborearte en este líquido rojo
> que escapa por mi piel. (29)

> And here I am, mother,
> intoxicated with Margarita's juices
> Happy, finally, to get to know you
> and taste you in this red liquid
> seeping from my skin.

In "Madre," as well as in many poems of *The Margarita Poems*, the reader witnesses the exploration of the relationship between the "I" and the "you," that is, between the speaker and another woman. Before *The Margarita Poems*, Umpierre elaborated the lesbian theme through the relationship of the "I" and the "you" in "Transference" and "Clímax" from *...Y otras desgracias. And Other Misfortunes....*

In *The Margarita Poems*, the "I" and the "you" are constantly identified. Through this identification between the "I" and the "you," the mother and the daughter, the mother and the female lover, and the sister and the lover, Umpierre underscores the lesbian theme of the text. In contrast to the identification between the "I" and the "you" (both female subjects) is the opposition between the female "I" and society. That opposition speaks of the conflict that lesbians encounter in non-accepting societies.

In "Immanence," the repetition of certain words ("To cross"/"Julia"/"desire") synthesizes and reaffirms the lesbian character of the poem and the special connection between the speaker's "I" and the evoked "you." This poem articulates the process of bringing Julia and Margarita back. Here, the evoked women (Julia and Margarita) represent both the lesbian lover, the poet's muse, and the speaker's lesbian self. Thus, the invocation of Julia is synonymous with the invocation and the reaffirmation of the speaker's lesbian self.

The lover and the lesbian self represent a spirit of rebellious freedom and strength in "Immanence." The idea of freedom is reiterated through the references to mythological female characters, particularly the Amazons. Through these allusions, the speaker stresses the desire to find a family of women within which she can place herself. The Amazons, female warriors of Greek legend who fought as allies of the Trojans, have been commonly used by women writers as a metaphor for female culture and especially as a symbol of lesbian lives. In Umpierre's poetry, like in Monique Wittig's *Les Guérillères* (1968) and in Albalucía Angel's *Las andariegas* (Wandering Women; 1984), the Amazons are a metaphor for a female-centered culture. Moreover, the Amazons speak of an ideal of freedom implied in lesbian eroticism and sexual desire as an alternative to heterosexist society:

> my narrow body
> covered with pictures
> of women I adore or I desire,
> armies of Amazons
> that I invoke
> in this transubstantiation
> or arousal
> that will bring my Julia forth. (16)

Through the repetition of the words "crossing," "traversing" and "transferring," the speaker states the power of her lesbian desire:

> I am crossing
> the MAD river in Ohio,
> looking for Julia
> who is carrying me away
> in this desire. (16)

All the images of "Immanence" articulate the speaker's desire for freedom. That freedom is achieved through the reaffirmation of the speaker's sexual identity as well as through the poetic inspiration. The conjunction of sexuality and poetic inspiration is expressed through the verb "to come":

> Come, Julia, come
> come unrestrained,
> wild woman,
> hilarious Julia,
> come Julia come forth
> to march the streets

at winter time,
to walk my body,
to proclaim
over the radio waves
the coming of the lustful
kingdom,
in sexual lubrication
and arousal
over my Margarita,
my yellow margarita,
my brilliant daisy. (17)

Julia, the muse, the lover, and the lesbian self is a symbol of sexual and poetical freedom.

Whereas in "Immanence" the speaker evokes Julia as her lover and her muse, in "Ceremonia Secreta" (Secret Ceremony) she looks for Margarita, the lost lover, whom she will bring back through a secret ceremony. The repetition of the question: "¿Dónde está Margarita?" (Where is Margarita?) emphasizes the absence of the lover and the speaker's desire to find her.

In this poem, the speaker makes the reader (here, "you") a participant in the process of rescuing her ex-lover. The "you" is not the lover, but rather, the reader who will also be part of the process of finding the speaker's lover:

Tú, luz que lees,
¿estás ya lista a alumbrar en el rescate?
Haz la señal,
vira la página que aquí termina
y que comience la ceremonia secreta. (32)

You, light who reads this poem,
are you ready to shine on the rescue?
Give the signal,
turn the page that stops here
and let the secret ceremony begin.

"Madre," "Immanence," and "Ceremonia Secreta" make explicit various aspects of the theme of emotional and sexual relationships between women. This theme was also present in

Umpierre's earlier collections of poetry, in particular in "Transference" and "Clímax," two of the poems from Umpierre's collection ...*Y otras desgracias. And Other Misfortunes....*

In "Transference" and "Clímax," like in *The Margarita Poems*, the poet elaborates the lesbian theme through the relationship between the "I" and the "you." "Transference" begins with the speaker's invitation to a woman to explore their sexuality and their emotional connection:

> Probemos ensartarnos
> tú y yo
> placentas en la boca
> y el fino cordonsillo
> umbilical, elástico
> que se extiende
> Entre Nous (55)

> Let's try
> you and I, to string
> placentas in our mouths
> and the slender umbilical cord
> that stretches
> Entre Nous

In this poem, the poet expresses different aspects of women's relationships. Those relationships are of biological or sexual and emotional nature as is expressed in the connotations of the words "sister," "mother," and "female lover." The semantic exploration takes place at the same time that the women explore their sexuality. The speaker highlights different moments of the women's sexual encounter while they try to define the nature of their bonding. "Sister," "mommy," "amante" (lover), "amada" (beloved), and "hija" (daughter) are the names that the two women lovers use for each other while having sex.

Intertwined with the theme of lesbian love and desire is the theme of artistic creativity in "Clímax," presented through the tension and animosity between the two women. The speakers named Isadora and Giselle, an allusion to the ballet dancer and a character she played, are antagonists in a dispute. The "I" and the "you" are seen as opposites. One woman represents science and the other one represents the arts. However, the antagonism and tension between the women are functions of their sexual attraction. The title, "Clímax," refers to the moment of highest tension of the lovers' battle as well as the culmination of their sexual relationship.

The connections between lesbian love, desire, and creativity that appear in "Clímax" from *...Y otras desgracias. And Other Misfortunes...* predominates in *The Margarita Poems*. In this book, like in Audre Lorde's, Nancy Cárdenas,' and Rosamaría Roffiel's writings, sexuality is associated with women's creative power. In "In Cycles," Umpierre's introduction to *The Margarita Poems*, she quotes from a fragment of Audre Lorde's *Sister/Outsider*. What is quoted from Lorde reiterates the connection between creativity and sexuality, thus conciliating both aspects of the speaker's life:

> I find I am constantly being encouraged to pluck out
> some one aspect of myself and present this as a
> meaningful whole, eclipsing or denying the other
> parts of self. But this is a destructive and fragmenting
> way to live. My fullest concentration of energy is
> available to me only when I integrate all the parts of
> who I am, openly, allowing power from particular
> sources of my living to flow back and forth freely
> through all my different selves, without the
> restrictions of externally imposed definition. Only
> then can I bring myself and my energies as a whole
> to the service of those struggles which I embrace as
> part of my living. (1)

As mentioned above, a key feature of the integration of lesbian identity and sexuality and the poet's creativity is the proclamation of freedom. In *The Margarita Poems* freedom is identified with madness. However, madness is re-appropriated and redefined as a sign of strength, unruliness, and the poet's strategy for survival in a repressive society. Madness is part of the struggle for liberation, as Roger Platizky has stated in the introduction to the book:

> In this collection, however, insanity is seen as a
> liberating force (both socially and artistically) since it
> is the ostensibly sane society that would like to

domesticate and dehumanize women by putting a
"tick and flea collar" around their necks ("No Hatchet
Job"). To protect herself from having her creative
"unruliness" destroyed and to experience her deepest,
socially-forbidden feelings as a woman, the speaker
invokes Julia, who in her transubstantiated lust, will
help in the mythic quest to liberate the "glorious
daisy," Margarita, from the social miasma to which
she has subjected herself. (13)

The theme of madness is central to "Transcendence" and
"No Hatchet Job." In "Transcendence," madness represents breaking
with and confronting the establishment's ways. The voice of the
lesbian writer antagonizes society's rulings. "Transcendence"
articulates lesbian desire and presents Julia as the muse and
inspirational force for the speaker, who emphasizes the process of
emancipation that she goes through. That process is indicated
through the use of verbs conveying non-conformity: "soltar" (to
unleash), "despeinarme" (to ruffle my own hair), "desgreñarme" (to
dishevel myself), "abandonar" (to abandon), "declararme" (to declare
myself), "no bañarme" (not to bathe). Here, the speaker presents
herself as a madwoman who, breaking with canons of conduct,
returns to "unleash Julia" inside of herself.

The theme of madness in this poem is also related to the
marginality that lesbians suffer in homophobic societies and the
ways in which they are judged by others because of their sexual
orientation:

> for those who'll call me
> sinful, insane and senseless,
> a prostitute, a whore,
> a lesbian, a dyke
> because I'll fall,
> I'll drop,
> I'll catapult
> my Self
> into this frantic
> excitement for your
> SEX (16)

The use of capital letters lends greater visibility to key words (Mad, Self, and Sex) of the lesbian discourse. They show the intertwining of the speaker's self and her sexual identity, thus reiterating the political empowerment that takes place through the recognition of her sexual orientation.

"Transcendence" and "No Hatchet Job" are connected because there is a stanza from "Transcendence" that is repeated in English in "No Hatchet Job" thus underscoring the poet's biculturalism. The repetition of that stanza lends strength to the political discourse and emphasizes the significance of madness in Umpierre's poetry while working as a gesture of self-affirmation.

In "No Hatchet Job," madness is identified with the speaker's rebellion against people's desire to domesticate her and their willingness to make her fit into socially accepted patterns:

> Algunos querrían ponerme
> al cuello una cadena y pasearme
> como a una perra callejera.
> Otros querrían llamarme
> una mujer loca. (19)

> Some people want
> to put a chain around my neck
> make me walk behind like a bitch.
> Others would rather call me
> crazy woman.

Another feature of Umpierre's poetry which is linked to the lesbian theme is experimentation with the linguistic code and a preoccupation with finding a language that may be more inclusive for lesbians, that is, a language that may articulate the specificity of lesbian desire and lesbian identities.

The concern with language has been a common theme in women's literature because language is attached to a legacy of oppression and a tradition of women's silencing. Language has played an important role in maintaining and perpetuating existing social structures that undermine women's experiences.

The linguistic code in Umpierre's works reflects the tendency among Latino writers in the United States to mix both Spanish and English. Umpierre, like other Puerto Rican writers in New York, among them, Tato Laviera, Pedro Pietri, and Sandra María Esteves, often uses Spanish and English simultaneously. Other Puerto Rican writers like Carmen Valle and Iván Silén only write in Spanish.

Through the use of a hybrid linguistic code, Umpierre's poetry expresses the duality she experiences as a Puerto Rican in the United States as well as her duality as a lesbian writer who lives between two cultures, the heterosexual and the homosexual. Thus, Umpierre's language is a feature of the biculturalism of her works. By alternating Spanish and English and moving from one language to the other, the poet reinforces an effect of cultural duality. Most of the poems of *...Y otras desgracias. And Other Misfortunes...* are in English, while in *The Margarita Poems*, as is indicated in the titles of the poems ("Immanence," "No Hatchet Job," "The Statue," "Only the Hand that Stirs Knows What's in the Pot," "Título: En que trata," "Madre," "Ceremonia Secreta," "Transcendence" and "The Mar/Garita Poem"), the author employs both English and Spanish.

Moreover, in *The Margarita Poems* Umpierre achieves a perpetual interaction between Spanish and English and the result is an "interlingual" code, the term Juan Bruce-Novoa uses for mixing Spanish and English, referring specifically to the works of Chicano writers. In this way, he has established the difference between bilingual and interlingual. According to Bruce-Novoa, bilingual implies moving from one language to another, while "interlingual" implies the constant tension of the two at once.[12] The tension that emerges because of the use of two languages is intentional and is part of a political strategy. When asked about the use of English in her poetry collection *...Y otras desgracias. And Other Misfortunes...* Umpierre has stated:

> ...lo que pasa es que a mí me parece que he
> establecido de una manera personal cierta paz
> conmigo misma entre los dos idiomas. Entonces hay
> temas que yo no puedo tratar de escribirlos en
> español porque mi lector ideal es una persona
> norteamericana. Y hay otros poemas que necesito
> escribirlos en español porque ese lector ideal es una
> persona de habla hispana, o porque trata sobre algo
> norteamericano pero que no quiero que el lector
> norteamericano se entere. Es como un código que
> tengo de tratar de comunicar algo sin que esa

persona se entere de lo que estoy tratando de
comunicar. Lo que he hecho es sí es una separación,
porque la necesitaba, la necesitaba de una manera
personal—establecer esa separación para poder
entonces tratar de desarrollar ambos como una
persona bilingüe.[13]

...What happens is that I think I have in a personal
way established a certain peace within myself with
both languages. There are themes that I can't try to
write about in Spanish because my ideal reader is
North-American. There are other poems that I need
to write in Spanish because the ideal reader is a
Spanish-speaking person or because they're about
something that I don't want the North-American
reader to know. It is like a code in that I have to
communicate something without letting that person
know what I am trying to communicate. Yes, what I
have created is a separation, because I needed it, I
needed it in a personal way—to establish a
separation in order to then be able to develop both
languages as a bilingual person.

Throughout *The Margarita Poems* prevails the poet's need for finding
a new language to articulate her experiences as a woman, a Puerto
Rican living in the United States, and a lesbian who wants to express
her love for women.

Umpierre's project of finding a new language is similar to the
attempt of other Latina and lesbian writers. Whereas women
writers, in general, have argued the importance of finding a
language to communicate their perspectives, it has been central to
Latinas and lesbian writers. Cherríe Moraga and Gloria Anzaldúa
have emphasized the search for a language to express themselves.
Moraga, in her *Loving in the War Years: Lo que nunca pasó por sus
labios*, states the importance of this language to express that which
was never uttered. Anzaldúa, in her essay "Speaking in Tongues: A
Letter to Third World Women Writers," encourages women to
formulate a language that will liberate them.[14]

Other lesbian writers, like Monique Wittig and Adrienne Rich,
have stressed the need to articulate the specificity of their

experiences and to transform language. Wittig has stated that the modification of reality "cannot happen without a transformation of language as a whole."[15] Wittig, in her books *Les Guérillères* and *The Lesbian Body*, experiments with language as a way to challenge the heterosexual values and the restrictions that women suffer in general. Whereas in *Les Guérillères* Wittig uses "elles" as an attempt to universalize the feminine point of view, in *The Lesbian Body* she plays with je/tu (I/you) to make the language more inclusive for lesbian experiences. Wittig has stated on several occasions the need "to lesbianize the symbols, and lesbianize men and women."[16]

Umpierre's attempt to lesbianize language becomes clear in the poem that gives the collection its title, "The Mar/Garita Poem." In this poem, the poet presents the traditional silencing of women and the need to re-articulate through a female language her own expression. The poetic voice evokes the task of a female Orpheus who descends to the bottom of the sea to rescue a lost language and a lost tradition. It is an attempt to rescue the voices of other female poets who have deconstructed their experiences in a patriarchal society in which dogmatism and guilt prevail.

"The Mar/Garita Poem" establishes a dialogue with Adrienne Rich's poem "Diving into the Wreck."[17] In Umpierre's, like in Rich's poem, the speaker seems to search for a voice and a tradition that has been silenced, that "has been buried," "cemented in," "mummified," and "petrified." What the speaker searches for is a lesbian voice and a tradition that has been suppressed and denied to all lesbians. It is not that it did not exist but rather that it had been hidden from history.

Therefore, the speaker's task of disarticulating and decoding language is essential in "The Mar/Garita Poem." She must find a language that breaks with the contamination of patriarchal power and with socially constructed values. Here, the gesture to transform language is not only poetical but political. That transformation takes place through experimentation with the language, through deviations from conventions of language, and through the use of playful combinations of words.

The poet is transformed into a warrior who, as part of the process of liberation, attacks and destroys the establishment:

> Explosions in my poet's brain.
> Observant of the Muse's burial, of her language,

nightwatching for years to see her words emerge
to dismember the patriarch,
to destroy the colonizer's tools,
to crush the merchants of her pain,
undressing herself from dogmatic lies
and religious guilts. (34)[18]

However, that process of liberation cannot be achieved in isolation. The poet needs to take into account the voices of other women writers as well as the voices of female readers:

se necesitan
tus palabras,
Sí, las tuyas,
hermana que lees
este poema en prosa. (36)

your words are needed
your words,
yes, yours,
sister, who reads
this prose-poem.

Other women's voices and alliances are required to gain political power.

As noted above in the discussion of "Immanence," in "The Mar/Garita Poem" the allusions to female mythological figures work as a symbol of strength and female solidarity. Cassandra appears in this poem as a symbol of strength and female wisdom. Umpierre pays tribute to Cassandra and rescues her from Apollo's condemnation of never being taken seriously. Whereas in classical mythology Cassandra's warning that the Greeks would capture Troy went unheeded, in Umpierre's poem Cassandra is transformed into an ally, a prophet whose prophecies must be heard.

"The Mar/Garita Poem" is a political text because it promotes women's struggle for equality and is a declaration against Puerto Rico's colonial status. The title of the poem articulates the opposition between freedom and colonization. The words "mar" (sea) and "garita" (garret) synthesize that antagonism as it becomes obvious in the use of the slash. With the slash, the female lover's name has been transformed into two words. The first one, "sea," represents freedom, while the second, "garita" (garret), evokes the colonization of the island:

> Los dos símbolos isleños:
> el mar, mi mar, verdoso, azul,
> y la garita, el puente del vigía, del colonizador. (35)

> Two symbols of the island:
> the sea, my sea, greeny, blue,
> and the garret, the colonizer's lookout.

The "garret" is a symbol of Puerto Rico's colonization, as it is a privileged place from which both the sea and the land can be observed. The place of colonization is a challenge for the lesbian point of view and the lesbian consciousness that is developed throughout the collection.

"The Mar/Garita Poem," a synthesis of the collection's themes and perspectives, traces the trajectory of a search, the moment of discovery and, finally, it states the political liberation. At the end of this poem, the poet gives the date of 1985 as the year of her liberation. The poem is a return to the speaker's land after Puerto Rico's proclamation of freedom as well as the return of the lesbian speaker's self to her origins. Understood in both ways, the end of the collection asserts a new Genesis and the celebration of a new beginning. The ultimate message of this book is of empowerment. Its optimism and the solidarity that it claims is engaging. The reader feels that s/he has been part of the process of catharsis and emancipation that the poetic voice has proclaimed throughout the collection.

*   *   *

NOTES

1 *This Bridge Called My Back: Writings by Radical Women of Color*, eds. Cherríe Moraga and Gloria Anzaldúa (New York: Kitchen Table: Women of Color Press, 1981).

2 Elena M. Martínez, "An Interview with Luz María Umpierre." *Christopher Street*, Vol. 14, No. 7 (October 1991): 9-10.

3 Carlos Rodríguez Matos, "Por el río a la mar, todo por Margarita," *The Margarita Poems* (Bloomington, Indiana: Third Woman Press, 1987), p. 9.

4 Sandra María Esteves, *Yerba Buena. Dibujos y Poemas* (New York: Greenfield Review Press, 1980) and *Tropical Rains: A Bilingual Downpour: Poems* (Bronx, New York: African Caribbean Poetry Theater, 1984).

5 Efraín Barradas and Rafael Rodríguez, *Herejes y mitificadores: Muestra de poesía puertorriqueña en los Estados Unidos* (San Juan, Puerto Rico: Ediciones Huracán, 1980), pp. 112-114.

6 Audre Lorde, "The Master's Tools Will Never Dismantle The Master's House," *This Bridge Called My Back: Writings by Radical Women of Color*, eds. Cherríe Moraga and Gloria Anzaldúa (New York: Kitchen Table: Women of Color Press, 1981), p. 99.

7 Teresa San Pedro, "La esperpéntica realidad del cuento tradicional en el poema 'Cuento sin hadas' de Luz María Umpierre." *The Americas Review*, Vol. 19, no. 1 (Spring 1991), p. 92.

8 Adrienne Rich, "What Does a Woman Need to Know?," *Blood, Bread, and Poetry: Selected Prose 1979-1985* (New York and London: W.W. Norton and Company, 1986), pp. 1-10.

9 Elena M. Martínez, Op. Cit., p. 9-10.

10 Alma Villanueva, *Mother, May I?* (Pittsburgh, PA: Motheroot Publications, 1978).

11 Emphasis has been added.

12 Juan Bruce-Novoa, "The Other Silence: Tino Villanueva," *Modern Chicano Writers: A Collection of Critical Essays*, eds. Joseph Sommers and Tomás Ybarra-Frausto (Englewood Cliffs, New Jersey: Prentice-Hall, 1979), p. 133.

13 "Luz María Umpierre-Poeta Puertorriqueña." Interviewed by Mireya Pérez-Erdelyi, *Chasqui* 3 (November 1987), p. 65.

14 *This Bridge Called My Back: Writings by Radical Women of Color*, Op. Cit., pp. 165-174.

15. Monique Wittig, "The Mark of Gender," *Feminist Issues* Vol. 5, Number 2 (Fall 1985), p. 6.

16 Ibid., p. 11.

17 Adrienne Rich, "Diving into the Wreck," *Diving into the Wreck; Poems 1971-1972* (New York: Norton and Company, Inc., 1973), pp. 22-24.

18 Emphasis has been added.

BIBLIOGRAPHY

Primary Sources:

Alabau, Magaly. *Electra/Clitemnestra*. Concepción, Chile: Libros del Maitén, 1986.

_____. *La extremaunción diaria*. Barcelona: Ediciones Rondas, 1986.

_____. *Hermana*. Madrid: Editorial Betania, 1989.

_____. *Hemos llegado a Ilión*. Madrid: Editorial Betania, 1991.

_____. *Hermana/Sister*. Bilingual Edition. Translated by Anne Twitty. Madrid: Editorial Betania, 1992.

_____. *Liebe*. Bilingual Edition. Translated by Anne Twitty. Miami, Florida: La Torre de Papel, 1993.

_____. *Ras*. Brooklyn, New York: Ediciones Medusa, 1987.

Angel, Albalucía. *Las andariegas*. Barcelona: Biblioteca del Fénice, 1984.

Bellessi, Diana. *Eroica*. Buenos Aires: Ediciones Ultimo Reino/Libros de Tierra Firme, 1988.

_____. *El jardín*. Buenos Aires: Bajo la Luna Nueva, 1992.

Cárdenas, Nancy. *Cuaderno de amor y desamor*. Unpublished.

Levi Calderón, Sara. *Dos mujeres*. Mexico City: Editorial Diana, 1990. Translated by Gina Kaufer as *The Two Mujeres*. San Francisco: Aunt Lute Books, 1991.

Mistral, Gabriela. *Poesías de Gabriela Mistral*. Mexico City: Editores Mexicanos Unidos, 1983.

Molloy, Sylvia. *En breve cárcel*. Barcelona: Editorial Seix Barral, 1981. Translated by Daniel Balderston with the author as *Certificate of Absence*. Austin: Texas University Press, 1989.

Peri-Rossi, Cristina. *Evohé: Poemas Eróticos*. Montevideo: Girón editorial, 1971.

_____. *Lingüística general: Poemas*. Valencia: Editorial Prometeo, 1979.

_____. *Diáspora.* Barcelona: Lumen, 1976.

_____."El exilio son los otros." *Las voces distantes: antología de los creadores uruguayos de la diáspora,* edited by Alvaro Barros-Lémez. Montevideo: Monte Sexto, 1985, p. 257.

Pizarnik, Alejandra. *La condesa sangrienta.* Buenos Aires: Aquaris, 1971. Translated and edited by Alberto Manguel, *Other Fires: Short Fiction by Latin American Women.* New York: Clarkson N. Potter, 1986.

Roffé, Mercedes. *Cámara baja.* Buenos Aires: Ediciones Ultimo Reino, 1987.

_____. *La noche y las palabras* (forthcoming). Translated by Kathryn Kopple as Words and Nights.

Roffé, Reina. *Monte de Venus.* Buenos Aires: Ediciones Corregidor, 1976.

Roffiel, Rosamaría. *Amora.* Mexico City: Editorial Planeta Mexicana, 1989.

_____. *Corramos libres ahora.* Mexico City: Femsol 1986; revised edition 1994.

Umpierre, Luz María. *Una puertorriqueña en Penna* (A Puerto Rican in Penna). San Juan: Masters, 1979.

_____. *...Y otras desgracias. And Other Misfortunes....* Bloomington, Indiana: Third Woman Press, 1985.

_____. *The Margarita Poems.* Bloomington, Indiana: Third Woman Press, 1987.

_____. *En el país de las maravillas* (In Wonderland) 2nd edition, Berkeley: New Earth Publications, 1990.

_____. *For Christine: Poems and One Letter.* Chapel Hill, North Carolina: Professional Press, 1995.

Secondary Sources:

Acevedo, Zelmar. *Homosexualidad: Hacia la destrucción de los mitos.* Buenos Aires: Ediciones del Ser, 1985.

Alvarez Bravo, Armando."El tono confesional recorre la poesía de Magali Alabau." *El Nuevo Herald* (Sept. 10, 1989): 5D.

Amat, Nuria."La erótica del lenguaje en Alejandra Pizarnik y Monique Wittig." *Nueva Estafeta* 12 (1979): 47-54.

Argüelles, Lourdes, and Ruby Rich."Homosexuality, Homophobia, and Revolution: Notes toward an Understanding of the Cuban Lesbian and Gay Male Experience." *Signs: A Journal of Women in Culture and Society* 9.4 (1984): 683-699.

Armstrong, Nancy, and Leonard Tennenhouse, eds. *The Ideology of Conduct: Essays on Literature and the History of Sexuality.* New York: Methuen, 1987.

Avellaneda, Andrés. *Censura, autoritarismo y cultura: Argentina, 1960-1983.* Buenos Aires: Centro Editor de América Latina, 1986.

Bachelard, Gaston. *The Poetics of Space.* Translated by María Jolas. Boston: Beacon Press, 1969.

Bankier, Joanna, et al. eds. *The Other Voice: Twentieth Century Women's Poetry in Translation.* New York: Norton, 1976.

Bataille, Georges. *Erotism: Death and Sensuality.* Translated by Mary Dalwood. San Francisco: City Lights Books, 1986.

Beaver, Harold."Homosexual Signs (In Memory of Roland Barthes)." *Critical Inquiry* 8 (1981): 99-119.

Benjamin, Jessica."The Bonds of Love: Rational Violence and Erotic Domination." *Feminist Studies* 6, no. 1 (Spring 1980): 144-173.

Bergmann, Emilie L, and Paul Julian Smith. *¿Entiendes? Queer Readings, Hispanic Writings.* Durham, North Carolina: Duke University Press, 1995.

Blanchot, Maurice."The Narrative Voice," *The Gaze of Orpheus.* Translated by Lydia Davis. Barrytown, New York: Station Hill Press, 1981.

Borges, Jorge Luis. *A Universal History of Infamy.* Translated by Norman Thomas di Giovanni. New York: E.P. Dutton and Co., 1972.

Braudy, Susan."A Day in the Life of Joan Didion." *Ms. Magazine* 5 (February 1977): 68, 109.

Bronski, Michael. *Culture Clash: The Making of Gay Sensibility.* Boston: South End Press, 1984.

Brown, Rita Mae. *Rubyfruit Jungle.* Plainfield, VT: Daughters, 1973.

Bruce-Novoa, Juan. "Homosexuality and the Chicano Novel." *Confluencia: Revista Hispánica de Cultura y Literatura* 2.I (1986): 69-77.

_____. "The Other Silence: Tino Villanueva," *Modern Chicano Writers: A Collection of Critical Essays,* eds. Joseph Sommers and Tomás Ybarra-Frausto. New Jersey: Prentice Hall, 1979, pp. 133-140.

Bulkin, Elly. "Racism and Writing: Some Implications for White Lesbian Critics." *Sinister Wisdom* 13 (Spring 1980): 3-22.

Bunch, Charlotte. "Lesbians in Revolt," *Lesbianism and the Women's Movement,* eds. Nancy Myron and Charlotte Bunch. Baltimore: Diana Press, 1975.

Butler, Judith. *Gender Trouble: Feminism and the Subversion of Identity.* New York: Routledge, 1990.

Califia, Pat. *Public Sex: The Culture of Radical Sex.* Pittsburgh, Pennsylvania: Cleis Press Inc., 1994.

Carrathers, Mary J. "The Re-Vision of the Muse: Adrienne Rich, Audre Lorde, Judy Grahn and Olga Broumas." *The Hudson Review* XXXVI, Number 2 (Summer 1983): 294-295.

Castellanos, Rosario. *Mujer que sabe latín.* Mexico City: Fondo de Cultura Económica, 1984; first edition 1973.

Castro-Klarén, Sara, Sylvia Molloy, and Beatriz Sarlo, eds. *Women's Writing in Latin America: An Anthology.* Boulder, Colorado: Westview, 1991.

Chesebro, James W., ed. *Gayspeak: Gay Male and Lesbian Communication.* New York: Pilgrim Press, 1981.

Chesler, Phyllis. *Women and Madness.* Garden City, New York: Doubleday, 1972.

Cixous, Hélène. "The Laugh of the Medusa." *Signs: A Journal of Women in Culture and Society* 1.4 (Summer 1976): 875-893. Translated by Keith Cohen and Paula Cohen.

Cohen, Ed. "Foucauldian Necrologies: 'Gay' Politics? Politically Gay?" *Textual Practices* 2.1 (1988): 87-101.

Connexions: An International Women's Quarterly. Lesbian Activism. Special Issue 29 (1989).

Correas de Zapata, Celia, and Lygia Johnson, eds. *Detrás de la reja: Antología crítica de narradoras latinoamericanas del siglo XX.* Caracas: Monte Avila, 1980.

Cortázar, Julio. "América Latina: exilio y literatura." *Cuadernos Americanos* No. 6 (November-December 1984): 7-14.

Daly, Mary. *Gyn/Ecology, the Metaethics of Radical Feminism.* Boston: Beacon Press, 1978.

Damon, Gene, and Lee Stuart. *The Lesbian in Literature: A Bibliography.* Reno, Nevada: The Ladder, 1967.

de Beauvoir, Simone. *The Second Sex.* Translated and edited by H.M. Parshley. New York: Alfred A. Knopf, 1953.

de la tierra, tatiana. "Argentina: Lesbian Visibility." *Ms. Magazine* 1 (May-June 1991): 16.

de Lauretis, Teresa. "Eccentric Subjects: Feminist Theory and Historical Consciousness." *Feminist Studies* 16, 1 (Spring 1990): 115-150.

_____. *The Practice of Love: Lesbian Sexuality and Perverse Desire.* Bloomington, Indiana: Indiana University Press, 1994.

de Quevedo, Francisco. *Poems to Lisi.* Edited by D. Gareth Walters. Exeter, England: University of Exeter, 1988.

Deredita, John F. "Desde la diáspora: entrevista con Cristina Peri-Rossi." *Texto Crítico* 9 (1978): 131-142.

Duberman, Martin, Martha Vicinus, and George Chauncey, Jr., eds. *Hidden from History: Reclaiming the Gay and Lesbian Past.* New York: New American Library, 1989.

Dynes, Wayne. *Homolexis: A Historical and Cultural Lexicon of Homosexuality.* New York: Gay Academic Union, 1985.

Esteves, Sandra María. *Yerba Buena: Dibujos y Poemas.* New York: Greenfield Review Press, 1980.

_____. *Tropical Rains: A Bilingual Downpour: Poems.* Bronx, New York: African Caribbean Poetry Theater, 1984.

Faderman, Lillian. *Surpassing the Love of Men: Romantic Friendship and Love between Women from the Renaissance to the Present.* New York: William Morrow, 1981.

_____."Who Hid Lesbian History?" *Lesbian Studies: Present and Future*, Margaret Cruikshank. Old Westbury, New York: The Feminist Press, 1982, pp. 115-121.

_____. *Chloe Plus Olivia: An Anthology of Lesbian Literature from the Seventeenth Century to the Present*. New York: Viking Penguin, 1994.

Farwell, Marilyn R. "Definition of the Lesbian Literary Imagination." *Signs: A Journal of Women in Culture and Society* 14, 1 (Autumn 1988): 100-118.

Ferguson, Ann. "Is There a Lesbian Culture?" *Lesbian Philosophies and Cultures*, ed. Jeffner Allen. Albany: State University of New York Press, 1990, pp. 63-88.

_____."Patriarchy, Sexual Identity, and the Sexual Revolution." *Signs: A Journal of Women in Culture and Society* 7, no. 1 (Autumn 1981): 159-172.

Fernández Olmos, Marguerite, and Lizabeth Paravisini-Gebert, eds. *Pleasure in the Word: Erotic Writing by Latin American Women*. Fredonia, New York: White Press, 1993.

Ferré, Rosario. *The Youngest Doll*. Lincoln, Nebraska: University of Nebraska Press, 1991.

Ferreira-Pinto, Cristina. "*En breve cárcel*: escribiendo el camino del sujeto." *Letras Femeninas* (Fall 1989): 75-82.

Filer, Malva. "Autorrescate e invención en *Las andariegas*, de Albalucía Angel." *Revista Iberoamericana* LI, Números 132-133 (julio-diciembre 1985): 649-655.

Fisher, D., ed. *The Third Woman: Minority Women Writers of the United States*. Boston: Houghton Mifflin, 1980, pp. 418-426.

Foster, David William. "The Monstruos in Two Argentine Novels." *Americas* 24, 2 (1972): 33-36.

_____. *Alternate Voices in the Contemporary Latin American Narrative*. Columbia, Missouri: University of Missouri Press, 1985.

_____."The Manipulation of the Horizons of Reader Expectations in Two Examples of Argentine Lesbian Writing: Discourse Power and Alternate Sexuality." In *Spanish and Portuguese Distinguished Series: Selected Texts*. Boulder: University of Colorado, Department of Spanish and Portuguese; Society of Spanish and Spanish American Studies, 1989, pp. 117-127.

_____. Review of *Amora*. *Chasqui* XIX, Número 2 (Noviembre 1990): 119-122.

_____. *Gay and Lesbian Themes in Latin American Writing*. Austin: University of Texas Press, 1991.

_____. Review of Milagros Palma's *Bodas de cenizas*. *Chasqui* XXII, Número 2 (noviembre 1993): 160-161.

_____. ,ed. *Latin American Writers on Gay and Lesbian Themes: A Bio-Critical Sourcebook*. Westport, Connecticut: Greenwood Press, 1994.

Foucault, Michel. *The History of Sexuality. Volume I: An Introduction*. Translated from the French by Robert Hurley. New York: Vintage Books/Random House, 1980.

_____. *Politics, Philosophy, Culture: Interviews and Other Writings 1977-1984*. Translated by Alan Sheridan and others, edited with an introduction by Lawrence D. Kritzman. New York: Routledge, 1988.

Franco, Jean."Apuntes sobre la crítica feminista y la literatura hispanoamericana."*Hispamérica* 45 (1986): 31-43.

Freud, Sigmund. *Beyond the Pleasure Principle*. Translated by C.J.M. Hubback. London: The Hogarth Press, 1948, c. 1922.

Friday, Nancy. *My Mother/My Self: The Daughter's Search for Identity*. New York: Delacorte Press, 1977.

Fuss, Diana. *Inside/Outside: Lesbian Theories/Gay Theories*. New York and London: Routledge, 1991.

García Pinto, Magdalena."La escritura de la pasión y la pasión de la escritura: *En breve cárcel*, de Sylvia Molloy."*Revista Iberoamericana* LI (julio-diciembre 1985): 687-696.

_____. *Women Writers of Latin America: Intimate Stories*. Austin: University of Texas Press, 1991.

García Ramos, Reinaldo."Sobre dos libros de Magali Alabau."*Linden Lane Magazine* 6, 1 (1987): 19.

Gascón-Vera, Elena."El naufragio del deseo: Esther Tusquets y Sylvia Molloy."*Plaza: Revista de Literatura* 11 (Autumn 1986): 20-24.

Gavalda, Antonio C. *Diccionario mitológico*. Segunda edición. Barcelona: Editorial Sintes, 1962.

Gilbert, Sandra, and Susan Gubar. *The Madwoman in the Attic: The Woman Writer and the Nineteenth-Century Literary Imagination.* New Haven and London: Yale University Press, 1984.

Graves, Robert. *Greek Myths.* New York: Doubleday, 1981.

Graziano, Frank, ed. *Alejandra Pizarnik: A Profile.* Durango, Colorado: Logbridge-Rhodes, 1987.

Greenberg, David F. *The Construction of Homosexuality.* Chicago: University of Chicago Press, 1988.

Gubar, Susan. "Mother, Maiden, and the Marriage of Death: Women Writers and an Ancient Myth." *Women's Studies* 6 (1979): 301-315.

Guibert, Rita. *Seven Voices; Seven Latin American Writers Talk to Rita Guibert.* Translated by Frances Partridge. New York: Alfred A. Knopf, 1973.

Hernández, Ana María. "Las máscaras en el espejo: Conversación con Magaly Alabau." *Brújula/Compass* 7-8 (Winter 1990): 14-15.

Hernández, Librada. Reseña a *Hermana. Revista Iberoamericana* LVI, 152-53 (julio-diciembre 1990): 1384-1386.

_____. "Marginalidad y escritura femenina: una poeta cubana en Nueva York." *Revista Hispánica Moderna* 45, no. 2 (December 1992): 287-297.

_____. Prologue to *Hermana/Sister.* Madrid: Editorial Betania, 1992.

Hobsbawm, E.J. *Culture, Ideology and Politics.* Boston: Routledge and Kegan Paul, 1982.

"Homosexuality in Cuba: A Threat to Public Morality?" *Connexions: An International Women's Quarterly* 2 (1981): 18-19.

Horno-Delgado, Asunción, et al. *Breaking Boundaries: Latina Writing and Critical Readings.* Amherst, Massachusetts: University of Massachusetts Press, 1989.

Howes, Robert. "The Literature of Outsiders: The Literature of the Gay Community in Latin America." *Latin American Masses and Minorities: Their Images and Realities,* edited by Dan C. Hazen, I: 288-304, 580-591. Madison: SALALM Secretariat, Memorial Library, University of Wisconsin, 1985.

Hozven, Roberto. "*En breve cárcel*: fe de erratas." *Discurso Literario: Revista de Temas Hispánicos* 5, no. 1 (Autumn 1987): 121-138.

Hutcheon, Linda. *Narcissistic Narrative: The Metafictional Paradox.* New York: Methuen, 1984.

Irigaray, Luce. "When Our Lips Speak Together." Translated by Carolyn Burke. *Signs: A Journal of Women in Culture and Society* 6, no. 1 (Autumn 1980): 69-79.

_____. *This Sex Which Is Not One.* Translated by Catherine Porter and Carolyn Burke. Ithaca, New York: Cornell University Press, 1985.

_____. *Speculum of the Other Woman.* Translated by Gillian C. Gill. Ithaca, New York: Cornell University Press, 1985.

Jones, Rosalind. "Writing the Body: Toward an Understanding of L'Ecriture Féminine." *Feminist Criticism: Essays on Women, Literature and Theory*, ed. Elaine Showalter. New York: Pantheon Books, 1985.

Kaminsky, Amy. *Reading the Body Politic: Feminist Criticism and Latin American Women Writers.* Minneapolis: University of Minnesota Press, 1993.

Keating, AnnLouise. "Hablando (hacia) el silencio: U.S. Latina Lesbian Writing." *Brújula/Compass.* Special Issue on Latina Lesbian Writing in the United States. Forthcoming.

Kellogg, Stuart. "Introduction: The Uses of Homosexuality in Literature." *Journal of Homosexuality* 8, 3-4 (1983): 1-12.

_____. ,ed. *Literary Visions of Homosexuality.* New York: Haworth Press, 1983.

Kennard, Jean E. "Ourself Behind Ourself: A Theory for Lesbian Readers," *Gender and Reading: Essays on Readers, Texts and Contexts*, ed. Elizabeth A. Flynn and Patrocinio P. Schweickart. Baltimore: Johns Hopkins University Press, 1986, pp. 63-80.

Kitzinger, Celia. *The Social Construction of Lesbianism.* London: Sage Publications, 1987.

Kristeva, Julia. *Semiótica.* Madrid: Editorial Fundamentos, 1981.

Lázaro, Felipe. *Poetas cubanas en Nueva York: Antología breve/Cuban Women Poets in New York. A Brief Anthology.* Madrid: Betania, 1991.

Leduc, Violette. *La Bâtarde.* Paris: Gallimard, 1964.

Levine, Suzanne Jill. *The Subversive Scribe: Translating Latin American Fiction.* Saint Paul, Minnesota: Graywolf Press, 1991.

Leyland, Winston, ed. *My Deep Dark Pain Is Love: A Collection of Latin American Gay Fiction.* Translated from Spanish and Portuguese by E.A. Lacey. San Francisco: Gay Sunshine Press, 1983.

Lindstrom, Naomi. *Women's Voice in Latin American Literature.* Washington D.C.: Three Continents Press, 1989.

Lorde, Audre. *Uses of the Erotic: The Erotic as Power.* Trumansburg, New York: Out and Out Books, 1978.

_____. *Zami: A New Spelling of My Name.* Freedom, California: The Crossing Press, 1982.

_____. *Sister Outsider: Essays and Speeches.* Trumansburg, New York: The Crossing Press, 1984.

Martínez, Elena M. "*En breve cárcel*: la escritura/lectura del (de lo) otro en los textos de Onetti y Molloy." *Revista Iberoamericana* LVI, número 151 (abril-junio 1990): 523-532.

_____. "An Interview with Luz María Umpierre." *Christopher Street* 14, No. 7 (Fall 1991): 9-10.

_____. "El constante vacío de la memoria. Conversación con Magali Alabau." *Brújula/Compass* 14 (Summer 1992): 6.

_____. Review of *Amora* by Rosamaría Roffiel and *Dos mujeres* by Sara Levi Calderón. *Letras Femeninas* XVIII, Nums. 1-2 (Spring/Fall 1992): 175-179.

_____. "Two Poetry Books of Magaly Alabau." *Confluencia: Revista Hispánica de Cultura y Literatura* 8, Number 1 (Fall 1992): 155-158.

_____. "Entrevista con Rosamaría Roffiel." *Confluencia: Revista Hispánica de Cultura y Literatura* 8-9, Nos. 1-2 (Spring 1993-Fall 1994): 179-180.

_____. "Interview with Magaly Alabau." Latina Lesbian Writers in the United States. Special Issue. *Brújula/Compass*. Forthcoming.

Masiello, Francine. "Discurso de mujeres, lenguaje del poder: Reflexiones sobre la crítica feminista a mediados de la década del 80." *Hispamérica* 45 (1986): 53-60.

_____. "*En breve cárcel*: La producción del sujeto." *Hispamérica* 41 (1985): 103-112.

_____. "Texto, ley y transgresión: Especulación sobre la novela (feminista) de vanguardia." *Revista Iberoamericana* LI, números 132-133 (julio-diciembre 1985): 807-822.

_____."Feminist Literary Culture in the River Plate Region." *Chasqui* XXI (May 1992): 39-48.

Meyer, Doris, and Marguerite Fernández Olmos. *Contemporary Women Authors of Latin America: New Translations.* New York: Brooklyn College Press, 1983.

Miller, Nancy K., ed. *The Poetics of Gender.* New York: Columbia University Press, 1986.

Millet, Kate. *Sexual Politics.* Garden City, New York: Doubleday and Company, 1970.

Molloy, Sylvia. "Sentido de ausencias." *Revista Iberoamericana* LI, números 132-133 (julio-diciembre 1985): 483-488.

_____. *At Face Value: Autobiographical Writing in Spanish America.* Cambridge: Cambridge University Press, 1991.

_____. *Las letras de Borges.* Buenos Aires: Editorial Sudamericana, 1979. *Signs of Borges.* Translated and adapted by Oscar Montero in collaboration with the author. Durham: Duke University Press, 1994.

Montero, Oscar. Reseña a *En breve cárcel. Revista Iberoamericana* XLIX, Nos. 123-124 (abril-septiembre 1983): 666-669.

_____."*En breve cárcel*: la Diana, la violencia y la mujer que escribe." *La sartén por el mango: Encuentro de escritoras latinoamericanas*, eds. Patricia Elena González and Eliana Ortega. Río Piedras, Puerto Rico: Ediciones Huracán, 1984, pp. 111-118.

Moraga, Cherríe. *Loving in the War Years: Lo que nunca pasó por sus labios.* Boston: South End Press, 1983.

_____. ,and Gloria Anzaldúa, eds. *This Bridge Called My Back: Writings by Radical Women of Color.* New York: Kitchen Table: Women of Color Press, 1981.

Muñoz, Elías Miguel. *Desde esta orilla: Poesía cubana del exilio.* Madrid: Editorial Betania, 1988.

Navajas, Gonzalo. "Erotismo y modernidad en *En breve cárcel* de Sylvia Molloy." *Revista de Estudios Hispánicos* 22, número 2 (mayo 1988): 95-105.

Nin, Anäis. "Eroticism in Women," *In Favor of the Sensitive Man and Other Essays*. New York: Harcourt Brace Jovanovich, 1976, pp. 3-11.

Noddings, Nel. *Women and Evil*. Berkeley: University of California Press, 1989.

Ostriker, Alicia. "The Thieves of Language: Women Poets and Revisionist Mythmaking," *The New Feminist Criticism: Essays on Women, Literature and Theory*. Edited by Elaine Showalter. New York: Pantheon Books, 1985, pp. 314-338.

Ostrovsky, Erika. *A Constant Journey: The Fiction of Monique Wittig*. Carbondale: Southern Illinois University Press, 1991.

Paz, Octavio. *The Labyrinth of Solitude*. Translated by Lysander Kemp. New York: Grove Press, 1961.

_____. *Sor Juana Inés de la Cruz o las trampas de la fe*. Mexico City: Fondo de Cultura Económica, 1982. Translated by Margaret Sayers Peden as *Sor Juana; or the Traps of Faith*. Cambridge, Massachusetts: Harvard University Press, 1988.

Pérez, Alberto Julián. "*En breve cárcel*: lo narrado y la narración." *Inti: Revista de Literatura Hispánica* 39 (primavera 1994): 121-133.

Pertusa, Inmaculada. "Revolución e identidad en los poemas lesbianos de Cristina Peri-Rossi." *Monographic Review: Revista Monográfica* 7 (1991): 236-250.

Picón Garfield, Evelyn. *Women's Voices from Latin America: Interviews with Six Contemporary Authors*. Detroit: Wayne State University Press, 1985.

Plummer, Kenneth. *The Making of the Modern Homosexual*. Totowa, New Jersey: Barnes and Noble Books, 1981.

Purkiss, Diane. "Women's Rewriting of Myths," *The Feminist Companion to Mythology*, ed. Carolyne Larrington. New York: Harper and Collins, 1992, pp. 441-457.

Ragazzoni, Susana. "La escritura como identidad: una entrevista con Cristina Peri-Rossi." *Studi di Letteratura-Ispano-Americana* 15-16 (1983): 227-241.

Ramos, Juanita, ed. *Compañeras: Antología lesbiana latina*. New York: Latin Lesbian History Project, 1984.

Rich, Adrienne. *Diving into the Wreck; Poems 1971-1972*. New York: Norton and Company, Inc., 1973.

_____. *The Dream of a Common Language: Poems 1974-1979*. New York: W.W. Norton and Co., 1978.

_____. *On Lies, Secrets and Silences: Selected Prose 1966-1978*. New York: W.W. Norton, 1979.

_____. *Blood, Bread and Poetry: Selected Prose 1979-1985*. New York: W.W. Norton and Company, 1986.

_____. *Of Woman Born: Motherhood as Experience and Institution*. New York: W. W. Norton and Company, 1986.

Rogers, Robert. *A Psychoanalytic Study of the Double in Literature*. Detroit: Wayne State University Press, 1970, pp. 126-137.

Salgado, María. "Women Poets of the Cuban Diaspora: Exile and the Self." *The Americas Review* 18, Números 3-4 (Fall-Winter 1990): 227-234.

San Pedro, Teresa. "La esperpéntica realidad del cuento tradicional en el poema 'Cuento sin hadas' de Luz María Umpierre." *The Americas Review* 19, 1 (Spring 1991): 92-100.

Schaefer-Rodríguez, Claudia. "The Power of Subversive Imagination: Homosexual Utopian Discourse in Contemporary Mexican Literature." *Latin American Literary Review* 33 (1989): 29-41.

Schwartz, Kessel. "Homosexuality as a Theme in Representative Contemporary Spanish American Novels." *Kentucky Romance Quarterly* 22 (1975): 247-257.

Schwarz, Judith. "Researching Lesbian History." *Sinister Wisdom* 5 (Winter 1978): 55-59.

Seidel, Michael. *Exile and Narrative Imagination*. New Haven and London: Yale University Press, 1986.

Shaw, Donald. "Notes on the Presentation of Sexuality in the Modern Spanish-American Novel." *Bulletin of Hispanic Studies* 59 (1982): 275-282.

Shockley, Ann Allen. "The Black Lesbian in American Literature: An Overview," *Home Girls: A Black Feminist Anthology*, edited by Barbara Smith. New York: Kitchen Table: Women of Color Press, 1983, pp. 83-93.

Showalter, Elaine. *The Female Malady*. London: Virago, 1987.

Silén, Iván. *Los paraguas amarillos: Los poetas latinos en Nueva York*. Hanover, New Hampshire: Ediciones del Norte and Bilingual Press, 1983.

Smith, Barbara, and Beverly Smith. "I Am Not Meant To Be Alone and Without You Who Understand: Letters from Black Feminists 1972-1978." *Conditions* 4.2, no. 1 (Winter 1979): 62-77.

Smith-Rosenberg, Caroll. "The Female World of Love and Ritual: Relations between Women in Nineteenth-Century America." *Signs: A Journal of Women in Culture and Society* 1, no. 1 (Autumn 1975): 1-29.

Soble, Alan, ed. *The Philosophy of Sex: Contemporary Readings*. Totowa, New Jersey: Rowman and Littlefield, 1981.

Spraggs, Gillian. "Exiled to Home: The Poetry of Sylvia Townsend Warner and Valentine Ackland." *Lesbian and Gay Writing*. Edited by Mark Lilly, Philadelphia: Temple University Press, 1990, pp. 109-125.

Stanley, Julia Penelope, et al. "The Transformation of Silence into Language and Action." *Sinister Wisdom* 6 (Summer 1978): 4-29.

Stimpson, Catherine R. "Zero Degree Deviancy: The Lesbian Novel in English," *Where the Meanings Are: Feminism and Cultural Spaces*. New York: Methuen, 1988, pp. 97-110.

Suleiman, Susan Rubin, ed. *The Female Body in Western Culture: Contemporary Perspectives*. Cambridge, Massachussets: Harvard University Press, 1986.

Tuttle, Lisa. *Encyclopedia of Feminism*. London: Longman Group Limited, 1986.

Umpierre, Luz María. *Nuevas aproximaciones críticas a la poesía puertorriqueña contemporánea*. Río Piedras, Puerto Rico: Editorial Cultural, 1983.

_____. "Incitaciones lesbianas en 'Milagros, Calle Mercurio' de Carmen Lugo Filippi." *Revista Iberoamericana* LIX, Números 162-163 (enero-junio 1993): 309-316.

Ussher, Jane M. *Women's Madness: Misogyny or Mental Illness?* Amherst, Massachusetts: The University of Massachusetts Press, 1991.

Vázquez Díaz, René. *La era imaginaria.* Barcelona: Montesinos, 1987.

Villanueva, Alma. "Mother, May I? "Pittsburgh, Pennsylvania: Motheroot Publications, 1978.

"Voices of Three Cuban Women Poets in Exile." *El Gato Tuerto: Gaceta de Arte y Literatura* 12 (Spring 1990): 1-2.

Walker, Barbara. *The Woman's Encyclopedia of Myths and Secrets.* San Francisco: Harper and Row, 1983.

Washington, Ida H., and Carol E. Washington Tobol. "Kriemhild and Clytemnestra—Sisters in Crime or Independent Women?," *The Lost Tradition: Mothers and Daughters in Literature.* Cathy N. Davidson and E.M. Broner, eds. New York: Frederick Ungar, 1980, pp. 15-21.

Webster's Third New International Dictionary of the English Language. Springfield, Massachusetts: Merriam-Webster, 1986.

Wenzel, Hélène Vivienne. "The Text as Body/Politics: An Appreciation of Monique Wittig's Writings in Context." *Feminist Studies* 7, No. 2 (Summer 1981): 264-287.

Wittig, Monique. *The Lesbian Body.* Translated by David Le Vay. Boston: Beacon Press, 1975.

_____. "The Straight Mind." *Feminist Issues* 1, no. 1 (Summer 1980): 103-112.

_____. "The Mark of Gender." *Feminist Issues* 5, no. 2 (Fall 1985): 3-12.

_____. *Les Guérillères.* Translated by David Le Vay. New York: Viking Press, 1971.

_____., and Sande Zeig. *Lesbian Peoples: Material for a Dictionary.* New York: Avon Press, 1979.

Yarbro-Bejarano, Yvonne. "Chicana Literature from a Chicana Feminist Perspective," *Chicana Creativity and Criticism: Charting New Frontiers in American Literature,* ed. Helena María Viramontes. Houston, Texas: Arte Público Press, 1988, pp. 139-145.

Zeitz, Eileen."Tres escritores uruguayos en el exilio: Cristina Peri-
Rossi: el desafío de la alegoría; Eduardo Galeano: El oficio de la
revelación desafiante; Saúl Ibargoyen Islas: El nosotros allá."*Chasqui*
IX, no. 1 (November 1979): 79-101.

Zimmerman, Bonnie."What Has Never Been: An Overview of
Lesbian Feminist Criticism."*Feminist Studies* 7, 3 (1981): 451-475.

INDEX